====== Learning to Listen ======

This book is printed on recycled paper.

Learning to Listen

Positive Approaches and People with Difficult Behaviour

by

Herbert Lovett, Ph.D.
Clinical Psychologist
Boston

Jessica Kingsley *Publishers* London • Bristol, Pennsylvania

First published in the United States of America in 1996 by
Paul H. Brookes Publishing Co., Inc.
Post Office Box 10624
Baltimore, Maryland 21285-0624
USA

First published in the United Kingdom in 1996 by
Jessica Kingsley Publishers
116 Pentonville Road
London N1 9JB
ENGLAND

Typeset by Brushwood Graphics, Inc., Baltimore, Maryland.
Manufactured in the United States of America by
The Maple Press Co., York, Pennsylvania.

The cases described in this book are based on the author's actual
experiences. Names have been changed and identifying details have been
altered to protect confidentiality. Though none of it has been created
ex nihilo, much of the dialogue here has been re-created from memory,
with whatever fallibility that implies.

British Library Cataloguing in Publication Data

Lovett, Herbert.
Learning to listen: positive approaches and people with difficult
behaviour
1. Mentally handicapped—Care   2. Mentally handicapped—
Behaviour modification
I. Title.
362.3'8

ISBN 1853023744

Contents

About the Author

Herbert Lovett, Ph.D., is a clinical psychologist in private practice in Boston, Massachusetts, and a program coordinator with the Institute on Disability, University of New Hampshire. He has worked throughout the Northern Hemisphere to promote inclusive supports in and equal access to education, work, housing, and human rights. He is the author of *Cognitive Counseling and Persons with Special Needs* (1985) and a past president of the Autism National Committee.

Foreword

*You've got to have something to eat and
a little love in your life before you can
hold still for anybody's sermon on how to
behave.*   *Billie Holiday*

I first met Herb Lovett in 1989. A friend had heard him
speak in another state and—knowing that we in Pennsylvania
were looking for a better way to help people with difficult
behavior—suggested that I ask him to speak at some upcom-
ing conferences. Herb agreed and was the sole presenter at
four 1-day workshops entitled "Positive Approaches for People with Difficult Behavior" conducted across the state.

A lot of different people came to these workshops: managers, psychologists, direct services workers, licensing inspec-
tors, and training directors—more than 600 people, in fact.

Herb Lovett, Ph.D., was not what they were expecting.
He wore wrinkled corduroy slacks, a sport shirt without a tie,
and sneakers. His manner was very casual and open, and he
was funny; that is, he had a sense of humor. He sat on a stool
holding a microphone and spoke all day without notes. Dr.
Lovett presented his listeners with a point of view and ideas
even more unexpected than he was.

In 1989 most of us, at least most of us in Pennsylvania, were
approaching people who exhibited difficult and dangerous
behaviors with a "control and correct" strategy. We'd get control of a behavior that we didn't like with any means available,
including physical and chemical restraint. Then we'd get the
person to do what we wanted by using reward and punishment techniques. But there are limits to these methods and
some of us were realizing them. The people with disabilities

living under this "control and correct" methodology were never happy. They rarely truly changed their behavior and, when the control was gone, usually reverted to the familiar difficult behaviors we were hoping we'd changed, which caused us to increase our efforts to gain control, often with more drastic and sometimes even dangerous methods.

Herb Lovett wanted to introduce a new way of thinking to those working in Pennsylvania's service system, to foster an openness to doing things differently, and to present the truth in a way that others could see and accept—a dangerous job. Not everyone wants to see the truth; history is full of examples of what can happen to those who speak it. Here, the truth was we'd been hurting some people instead of helping them. In fact, we'd been hurting them in the name of helping them. We didn't have to keep doing things the same way. There was another way, but we would first have to change the way we were thinking and behaving.

Participants in these workshops found understanding. Herb confessed to having been caught in the same senseless cycles of control with people he was trying to help as were his listeners. He described the pain of many people with difficult behavior in a way that allowed participants to again feel empathy—a critical, indispensable, and, in fact, very human reaction that is often corrected out of us.

Herb also gave participants good information, sound psychological theories, and new clinical insights. He discussed with them the importance of communication, relationships, sexuality, and the desire to be somebody in this world—aspects of life that are crucial to everyone, including people with disabilities.

And people responded to Herb's truth as we'd hoped they would—the way people can when they are spoken to with respect and humility. (Herb actually admitted to making "respectful guesses" when trying to figure out how to help some people.) They responded to being recognized for their efforts and good intentions and identified with the stories of botched helping strategies.

Participants were liberated to feel compassion, to follow their instincts to help, and to search for meaningful answers to why people exhibit certain behavior. Many said, "We've always known this" and "This is what we always wanted to do." They were relieved to learn that what came to them naturally was not only acceptable but, in fact, essential to helping people. Herb led his listeners to find truth and knowledge within themselves first, which then allowed them to open up to new ideas.

Herb Lovett stayed in Pennsylvania much longer than 4 days. He stayed with us as we moved from accepting new concepts to changing our behavior. He returned to help specific individuals and those supporting them by facilitating Individual Service Designs. (These planning sessions get those involved to see the world from the eyes of the person with the challenging behavior and consequently lead to a plan that truly supports and helps the person.) One of Herb's greatest contributions has been to give encouragement and recognition. He's helped those in Pennsylvania who are supporting people with challenging behavior to realize that they are making an enormous difference; and that is empowering knowledge.

In this book, Dr. Lovett has captured what he did in person in Pennsylvania and expanded upon it. He presents truth in a way that allows the reader to see it, while fully developing the background information, exploring similarities with other social movements, and telling stories in their entirety.

His approach is educational: He leads us to the truth. He provides the social, historical, therapeutic, and political contexts for behavior, thus giving us an understanding of the meaning of behavior. We begin to see irrational behavior as rational, the unproductive as productive, and the nonfunctional as functional.

Perhaps Herb's most effective teaching tool is holding his own behavior up to the light. No one reading this book will fail to identify with at least one of the episodes Herb describes. His gentle exposure of the harm being done in the name of treatment allows us to face the truth without debilitating embarrassment and shame; therefore, we are able to learn from what we read.

The contents are amazing: an exhaustive listing of ways to control people with disabilities. Although books have been written on each method, here they are presented as actions we commit against people who are our peers. Herb simultaneously holds us in the paradigms of treatment and control and real life. By doing so, he helps us come to the realization that these paradigms are incompatible and that placing people with disabilities in one and ourselves in another simply makes no sense.

It all seems so simple: Treat people like you would like to be treated. But it's not always that simple. When faced with frightening and dangerous behavior, it can be hard to remember what we know. When we're scared or under pressure to "fix" somebody, we can forget to ask, "If I were in this person's shoes, how would I feel? What would I need? How would I want to be treated?" This is why we need teachers and mentors—or good writers and their books—to constantly remind us of what we already know to be true and to suggest to us ways we can do better.

This is why I am so pleased about the publication of *Learning to Listen: Positive Approaches and People with Difficult Behavior*. Everyone can now benefit from the thinking of one of the pioneers in this movement of liberation from control and punishment. Anyone willing to take the time to read this wonderful book will have access to the best analysis and advice available on the topic of helping people with challenging behavior. But the value of Dr. Lovett's work is not limited to the field of developmental disabilities. I sincerely hope that those involved in programs for people with mental illness or substance abuse problems and even those who work with people who commit criminal offenses will have an opportunity to read this book.

Nancy R. Thaler
Deputy Secretary for Mental Retardation
Commonwealth of Pennsylvania

Preface

The working title for my first book was *Person to Person*, but my editor thought it needed more of an academic tone so it was published as *Cognitive Counseling and Persons with Special Needs*. At the time, this didn't bother me much. I thought the book would quietly disappear no matter what it was called. But, thanks to the kind support of virtual strangers, the book gained a wider readership and I was invited to talk about what I had written. Suddenly "cognitive counseling" seemed far too narrow for my purposes. But when people asked me what to call this way of thinking, I was somewhat at a loss. I had not developed a new technology, *per se*, but a way of thinking about behavior. And little of what I had articulated was any more modern than the Golden Rule. So it was hard to think of naming something as if I had invented it and owned the patent.

In 1988, I was invited to do a series of workshops in Pennsylvania and, when pressed to give these events a title, I suggested we just call them "positive approaches for people with difficult behavior." The idea was that positive approaches seemed too vague a phrase to suggest a technology but did imply the spirit of exploration, of working with—rather than on—people.

This has been a mixed blessing. The open-endedness helped people feel part of a process rather than tools in a program, but this way of speculating empathetically became reified as "Positive Approaches." New names and phrases always run the risk of becoming spiffy euphemisms for "business as usual."

I recently visited Jeanette, a woman living in an ICF/MR who likes to do needle-point and listen to classical music. She spoke in short phrases but understood both French and English. Unfortunately, as a child, she had done very badly indeed on an IQ test, which changed the course of her life. Fairly often, Jeanette got frustrated with the roommate assigned to her for the duration of their active treatment. Her roommate hallucinated and listened to country and western music played loudly. Jeanette sometimes got so upset that, for the first time in her 46 years, she started to slap her head and face quite violently.

Jeanette's sister, who was also her legal guardian, asked me to look at her records. I noticed a report that said, "Jeanette requires Positive Approaches in dealing with her self-injurious behavior to avoid injury." In a chain of logic that eluded me, the positive approaches were to praise Jeanette when she brushed her teeth. "Let Jeanette know that it is okay to do something instead of something else. In other words, reinforce Jeanette's choices so long as they are not detrimental to her health or the health of others. If Jeanette chooses not to brush her teeth, suggest a choice and ask her if this is okay. If she says 'yes' praise her for letting you know what she wanted to do. If the above Positive Approaches do not work, implement Crisis Management techniques"—crisis management techniques being agency-speak for physical restraint.

The crisis Jeanette needed managed was not her confusion about whether to brush her teeth, but that she was having her life stolen in the name of therapy.

Positive approaches are not about cheerfully reinforcing people to do what we expect them to do but about listening to their preferences and good reasons for what they are doing, no matter how difficult what they are doing might be. The term *positive approaches* is not a rhetorical flourish about preferring rewards to punishments but a way of life that moves from control to collaboration.

———

Nothing named can hope to remain the same. Since this is an attitude and a way of thinking, calling these generalities "positive approaches" has set them off on a path for which I can't be responsible. My hope is that the reader will take these things to heart and find a creative dialogue with this book rather than feel harangued or indicted by it. Still, I have been bemused to see how the word "positive" has suddenly developed magical powers of perceptual transformation. One author has written, "What used to be called behavior modification is now called positive behavioral programming for challenging behaviors." So far as I know, anyone can put a grass skirt on a cow, but it still won't hula.

In *Cognitive Counseling and Persons with Special Needs*, I wrote about how the simple principles of the behavioral technologies could be helpful and how they might fit in with ordinary life. In *Learning to Listen: Positive Approaches and People with Difficult Behavior*, those principles are examined in a more political context.

This has posed a difficult problem for me. On the one hand, it is easy for me to abhor the abuse of a powerful teaching technology to coerce people who are vulnerable. On the other, many of the people actively engaged in these controlling technologies either have no idea how hurtful this is or are decent people working in systems that don't allow them much freedom to do otherwise.

I have consulted, from time to time, in large institutions where all kinds of liberties have been lost to those who live in them. It really takes no particular courage or perspicacity to see how wrong and unnecessary these places are, but it has been difficult to express this view without diminishing the intentions of the people who work in them. The large majority of people in these places mean well and do the best they can, but their power to act is usually severely limited. As Ingmar Bergman wrote, "In hierarchies, all doors are closed."

I was once asked by a pre-vocational training center to help with Jerry, a man labeled autistic who was in constant, restless motion. He had been put on a simple program that rewarded him (with sugary snacks and drinks) for remaining seated while putting sales catalogues into plastic bags. When these small bribes didn't work, Alan was assigned to be with him at all times to prompt him to his task and, if Jerry tried to get out of his seat, to restrain him physically. This led to a great deal of apparently pre-vocational wrestling.

I asked Alan if Jerry wouldn't like a job where he could be out and about most of the day. Perhaps he could deliver these sales catalogues rather than package them. Alan, who spent every hour of every working day with Jerry, said that he, personally, thought that would be a great idea, but they could never get the staff to agree. Just as no one was paying much attention to what Jerry needed, Alan had apparently been left feeling that no one would listen to him either.

In writing this book, I have tried to be clear in analyzing abuse and suffering in the name of therapy. I have also tried to be clear that this analysis requires we listen to and respect not only the people we hope to support, but, as colleagues, one another. My argument is not so much with behavior modification, which as an intellectual construct is so slight as almost not to exist.[1] I am, however, moved by its abuses behind those closed hierarchical doors. Just as people with disabilities in controlling service structures are hurt, so, too, though to a lesser extent, the people hired to work in them are limited and put to hurtful work when what they would rather do is help.

Fortunately, several different trends are converging that might provide a remedy. The parent movement is being joined in its advocacy efforts by self-advocates, which brings to the conversation people who are speaking for themselves. Service providers, too, are slowly coming to the awareness that the people we serve are capable judges of what they need. More of us professionals are now working to support

---

[1]The informing syllogism of behavior modification is that reinforcers, defined as anything that increases behavior, increase behavior; and punishments, defined as anything that decreases behavior, decrease behavior. By manipulating rewards and punishments, behavior can be changed.

people in lives of their own choosing as the overall philosophy of the field moves from rehabilitation to accommodation. These developments are not about making our work perfect, so much as they are about making our work and our intentions more congruent.

No abstract ideal has much force outside of actual relationships. Few people would dispute the wisdom of the Golden Rule, but this concord breaks down when we actually try to use it. Living the Golden Rule requires us to be real ourselves and to have real neighbors to love as much as our actual selves. My relationship with the neighbors I know and the neighborhood I live in is complex. It's not always clear in every situation what loving them as myself would actually lead me to do. My commitment is not to a rigid code of behavior and I don't excuse all of my actions because I mean well; I do take responsibility as best I can for making what I do fit closely with what I say.

In general, I suspect preachers give the sermons they need to listen to; authors write the books they need to read. In specific, that seems to have been my fate. I have been moved to write about the need to listen empathetically and to trust the power of relationships from my own poor natural skills. This is not a matter of hypocrisy; it is, after all, the outermost border that defines the center. But insofar as I have learned to listen myself, it is because, in struggling to keep my own work and intentions one, I have been blessed with a wide and deep circle of friends. The way forward is not always direct or clear, and having trustworthy guides along the way has been invaluable. I don't have to name all the names. You know who you are.

In writing this book, I want to thank, specifically, Amanda Caine, Bruce Dake, Gunnar Dybwad, Susannah Joyce, Teresa Sotelo, and Jo Allard Krippenstapel, as always, for their critical readings of the various drafts.

I am humbled to be so generously praised by someone like Nancy Thaler, who has worked so diligently, bravely, and wisely as director of services in Pennsylvania to develop truly personal supports for people with disabilities in that Commonwealth.

And finally, I want to thank, for his constant understanding and love, Michael Dowling, *il miglior fabro*, without whom . . .

Herbert Lovett

Chapter 1

___

_____Learning to Listen_____

Recently, I was—as we human services workers often are— in a meeting about a person who was confusing and difficult to serve. Maureen spent the day talking constantly, sometimes screaming, and was, for her "service team," generally a nuisance. Also, as is often the case, people seemed to find her difficult and likable at the same time. "We have Maureen on a behavior program, but it's not working. Do you have any suggestions?" they asked.

I had never met Maureen so I was curious to learn a little more about her. People told me she was in her early 30s, she had lived most of her life with her mother, but she had become too frightening for her mom. When she got angry she would break things, and sometimes she would hit her mother. For a while she had lived with a boyfriend who had been violent and seriously abused her. Now she was living at a nearby developmental center where she was being given large dosages of antipsychotic and anticonvulsant medications that made her drowsy.

As people talked, I learned that Maureen did not want to do any of the piecework offered her every day, preferring instead to talk about her fantasy that two co-workers were having an affair. At times, she could become agitated and abusive for no apparent reason, screaming or hitting the people

1

around her. For a day's "good behavior"—not annoying or hurting people—she could earn enough points to "buy" two cans of caffeine-free diet soda. She could have only diet colas because the staff had decided she was overweight and shouldn't drink caffeine. The members of Maureen's team stopped talking at this point, obviously waiting for me to offer a—if not the—solution.

"If Maureen died tonight," I asked them, "who would care?" Someone said her mother probably would. "Anyone else?" I asked. The group thought about it and decided, "Not really." So this woman who has no home, whose one emotional relationship with someone other than her mother had been abusive, who makes about $5 a week, and who has no friends is difficult to be around. In the face of all this— by way of comfort and assistance—she is told that if she is "appropriate" she can earn two cans of diet cola a day. And then we get confused when she is *still* noisy, demanding, and "impossible."

I kept thinking about this conversation over the next several days. Like most interesting dialogues, this one was provocative as much for what had not been said as for what had. For example, when I asked people to tell me a little about Maureen, they had talked about the more human side of her life—her difficulties with her mother and her abusive boyfriend. It took me a while to notice the perilous gap between what we know and what we do. Knowing her plight as a homeless, poor, and battered woman would ordinarily move people to think in terms of getting her some emergency money, a reliable income, and a safe home. Instead, because of her labels as "mentally retarded" and "emotionally disturbed," she was seen as needing "treatment."

They might just as accurately have said, "This client is a left-handed 32-year-old Caucasian female, tending to obesity, with a history of grand mal seizures, borderline personality disorder, depression, and impaired intellectual functioning. She is currently a resident at the Dixon County Developmental Center where she is being treated with Haldol (a major tranquilizer) and Dilantin (an anticonvulsant). Her day is spent at a community vocational training program where she is delusional, withdrawn, and both verbally and physically aggressive." In fact, this probably is how Maureen had been described on her emergency admissions to psychiatric hospitals.

Clinicians worked hard to get that kind of precise and impersonal language because disease was once (and sometimes still is) somehow seen as the fault of the individual. A person with a seizure disorder was sometimes understood as symbolically fleeing problems. A child with almost any sort of difficulties was sometimes understood to be a punishment God had given the parents for their sins. Clinical, "objective" descriptions of people's conditions helped the scientific advance of medicine, but this early success tempted scientists and the general public to medicalize all human difficulties as if they were treatable diseases. Although Maureen could benefit from some specialized understanding of her seizure disorder, she did not need to live her entire life in an institution. The institution she lived in had been founded with the hopes that people would be "cured of their handicaps." We know now that this won't happen. Indeed, we now know institutions intensify disabilities rather than remove them.

Similarly, I did not try to "treat" her behavior as I was trained to do. At one time, I would probably have asked, "What was going on just before Maureen started to scream? What happened right after that? What do you think she was doing it for? Attention?" I would probably have written a program that required staff members to say to her every 20 minutes, "Maureen, you're doing fine. Keep up the good work!" My intention would have been to be positive and encouraging. In effect, my behavior would have been saying, "Maureen, all we can see about you is that you hit people or scream or tell lies. When you do that, we have a meeting to make you stop. When you don't do that, we smile and pretend that you ought to be as happy as we are."

Often, the more obvious the facts, the more difficult they are to recognize. I took a long time to realize that people labeled "retarded" had very different lives because of this label we psychologists had given them. "Those people," who might need help in ways large and small, almost always pay for the help they need with their freedom, their dignity, and a general loss of control over their own lives. By every ordinary consideration—income, housing, or relationships—we "human servants" have more power than the people we purport to serve. Indeed, the further removed people are from those who need help, the more powerful they tend to be. Administrators and consultants might go for weeks without even seeing a person with a disability, or, if they do meet, they do so in formal ways, such as in brief meetings or during standardized assessments, rather than in personal ways. Administrators and consultants often have more voice in the lives of service users than do the people who know them personally— the people who provide direct and daily assistance, for example. And often the newest staff person has considerably more influence than parents and involved friends. As a result, we have established services for *what* people are not, rather than for *who* they are.

This impersonal and deficit-based thinking hurts everyone it touches. Too often what we ask people considered retarded to do is boring and meaningless, and we expect them to live in poverty, chastity, and obedience. These activities (or inactivities) are often meaningless and boring for us as well. But when our day has ended, most of us get to drive in our own cars to our own homes. This is so ordinary—coming home from work—that we can hardly see that the ordinary itself is the invisible and, too often, impenetrable boundary between the lives of those who are "clients" and those who are "citizens."

It is always potentially dangerous when we act in ways that defy what we actually know, when our thoughts and actions are not congruent. Because of our history of medicalizing services and using the hospital as a model for people who are not sick, Maureen was seen primarily as a patient; her team had adopted the role of nurse, and the behavior specialist (whose idea her behavior program had been) was the doctor. Her behavior program—primitive as it was—was treating her behavior as a symptom that could be made to disappear with proper treatment. However, Maureen's team best understood her as a person, as a woman who had had a hard life. When asked to explain who they thought she was, they accurately described Maureen as an abused, estranged, and oppressed woman whose differences had led her to a life of poverty, uncertainty, and profound loneliness. Their confusion about her came because they had fallen into the gulf between the way they knew her as a *person* and the way they reacted to her as a *client*. On occasion, people working directly with her were friendly, but their actions were largely irrelevant to Maureen's most serious concerns. The behavior specialist, who knew Maureen only from passing her in the hall, had nothing whatever to say to these human problems.

This analysis of Maureen's situation could serve as a call for a spirited attack on behaviorists and behaviorism and on service systems and those who work in them, but that would radically misplace our limited time and energies. The problem is not behaviorism, but the way practitioners have chosen to apply it, nor is the problem service systems and service providers. After all—and before all—some people really need help to live. The problem lies in how we have chosen to view the people who need help and how we have acted on our subsequent good intentions. Our most pressing problem is that we have not listened carefully to those we would serve.

All technologies of control necessarily support a hierarchical vision of society—of leaders who know better than the led. The radical potential of a real community movement comes from the fact that no one can be wiser for a group than the group itself; no one can be better informed about individual wishes and needs than the individuals themselves. In this sense, for people with developmental disabilities, the community movement is visionary. By living with, working with, and respecting people who are "not in control," we can all learn an invaluable (and sometimes new) social skill—cooperation.

All over the world, the traditional hierarchy where one man controls the destiny of those beneath him is yielding to local autonomy. For some, this has granted the license to act violently on old grievances and hatreds, but for others, this has created an opportunity to learn how we can live cooperatively and listen to voices previously ignored. In the world of human services, more and more people are recognizing that professionals cannot ethically dictate to those who need assistance. Instead, we are learning to listen. For me, the excitement is not that people in positions of power are beginning to listen—they have always listened to advice, although usually from one another. Instead, the excitement comes from the voices now being heard. In working as a consultant in human services, I have noticed that more and more service providers are actively soliciting the opinions of the people who use their services, though often this is done in a symbolic, rather than a practical, way.

For the past 20 years, I have worked as a clinical psychologist for and with people with developmental disabilities whose behavior is considered difficult, troublesome, or dangerous. My initial training in this work was primarily in behavioral techniques to control the frequency or intensity of these disturbing events. Over time, I have gradually come to see that people whose behavior is difficult are not clients to be "fixed" so much as freedom fighters—the most vigorous critics of our attempts at service. Time and again, I have worked for people who have either told me directly or whose behavior has said: "These people who work for and around me are nice enough, but what they are doing is either irrelevant or detrimental to my wishes, my happiness, and even, at times, my survival."

My experience has been that extreme behavior often comes from not feeling listened to. Just as repressive organizational or political systems lead to aggression and revolution, the most profoundly disturbing behavior is often found in incompetent and unresponsive service systems.

Seeing people in a lateral rather than a hierarchical relationship opens us to the perspective that all disability is necessarily mutual. If people cannot communicate with words, then we cannot hear them. We might just as honestly describe a person's "learning disability" as our own "teaching disability." Traditionally, the words "handicap" and "disability" have been labels defined and applied by professionals. In a world dependent on authority, such a label has the power to oppress by stealing a person's individuality, and a collective stereotype replaces personal consideration. In a more mutually responsive world, labels would simply point out what people need and become a mandate for our help.[1]

The hierarchical, competitive culture in which most of us have grown up dismissed people with disabilities as "deficient" or "defective." In that world, an important question was: What is wrong with that person? Enormous effort—obviously—has gone into answering that question about people with disabilities. What we have slowly come to recognize is that this question, ultimately, can be applied to all of us. Inevitably, in such a culture there is something "wrong" with everyone, so if we really want a society for us all, we need to turn the question from "What is wrong with you so that you can't be a full member of society?" to ask instead, "How have we collectively built a society that keeps you out? What do you have to bring? What has your life taught you and what can we learn from you?"

This is heartwarming rhetoric and without some practical action that is all it ever will be. In working for people with difficult behavior, though, I have found that acting on the honest and creative answers to these kinds of questions can literally change the lives of everyone involved—the helpers and the helped.

The move from authoritarian and exclusive hierarchies to more lateral and inclusive communities represents a slow transformation in our ways of thinking about all people—not just those with disabilities. This new world asks of us a certain bravery as we adjust to its new ways of thinking. In such a culture, competition is a barrier to success, rather than its prerequisite, and cooperation is the hallmark of strength, rather than a sign of weakness. This spirit is moving in parallel ways in almost every area of human endeavor.

The resurging interest in Native American culture and traditional societies around the world is part of our hunger to

---

[1]Although slogans are important to raise consciousness quickly, they also strip ideas of their sustaining context. If I understand it correctly, "label jars not people," for me, misses the point: It is not the label that is the problem, it is its political use. The way forward from handicappism is not to pretend that disability does not matter but to focus on the ability that does. The way forward from anti-Semitism, by analogy, is not to say that a person's religion or heritage doesn't matter, but to say that Judaism and Jews do.

learn how we can live with one another and this planet in a way that respects the diversity of life and ensures its richness for the generations to come. This stands in direct opposition to the current dominant Western values that the earth is infinite, that it can be plundered endlessly, and that we can take all we want (and more) because the earth is ours. We are recognizing, perhaps belatedly, that the earth is not our possession but truly our mother. Mothers and children do not own one another, of course, but ideally they have a relationship where, in turn, each takes care of and loves the other.

In this context, the idea of a completely inclusive community as one in which everyone belongs is far more radical than it first appears. In the abstract, many people subscribe to the notion of an inclusive community whose criterion for belonging is that you have to be breathing. In practical fact, however, most of us draw lines somewhere. Typically, we justify our own specific boundaries by blaming those we would exclude. For example, among those who are breathing, I would exclude people who commit serial murders, even though my own reasons for excluding such people rest as much on my ignorance of how they might change as on an awareness of the danger they pose. I don't know how to include them in my own life safely. But if we did know how to help people never to act on their homicidal impulses, their presence would excite fewer passions because we would have confidence that we could safely move past the behavior and find the person.

For years, because we could not teach people, we labeled them "ineducable"; because we could not train people, we labeled them "untrainable."[2] Because we did not know how to listen to people's wishes and preferences and their worries and joys, we said, "Those people don't communicate, they don't think, they are indifferent to their environment, they don't feel pain as we do." Segregation always points to a defi-

---

[2]The difference between education and training struck me as largely semantic until I encountered the distinction made in the field of developmental disabilities, where the difference is based, apparently, on geography. Gunnar Dybwad has reminded me that in some states a person was educable with an IQ of above 50; in other states, it was 55. So a person could be significantly rehabilitated by moving over a state border (G. Dybwad, personal communication).

ciency in the wisdom and the capacity to love on the part of those who segregate. Unfortunately, when exclusionists are at work, the victims of their ignorance or indifference are made to feel what victims ordinarily feel: an irrational responsibility for their abuse, guilt for having "caused" their abuse, and shame simply for existing at all.

The work of creating an inclusive society appeals to many of us professionals. At the same time, people with disabilities have become increasingly vocal in pointing out that their status in society is a basic human right and, as such, is not contingent on rehabilitation or training. Taking this perspective seriously has wide implications for the way we professionals work. Instead of seeing ourselves primarily as trainers and managers, we might better see ourselves as facilitators helping people achieve their own goals. This is a simple observation, but a hard task.

For a long time, we have understood people labeled retarded as deficient and requiring energetic remediation. Recognizing that many people so labeled learn in unique ways led to the development of specialized teaching strategies. Somehow along the way we have forgotten what makes learning enjoyable for everyone, no matter what the technology or subject: First, everyone needs to know the benefit of learning what is being taught, and second, everyone enjoys learning better with teachers they like.

Instruction in both special education and rehabilitation services relies almost exclusively on behavioral principles that ignore or contradict these two rules. One of the great points of pride for behaviorism has been that the learner does not have to have any awareness of what is going on—the teaching takes place independent of the learner's wish to learn. In addition, the relationship between the teacher and the learner is considered irrelevant because behavioral programming is invariably seen as more powerful than the teacher. Indeed, I was taught that the operation of a "good" program is so clearly defined that anyone can implement it accurately. Mechanical efficiency has a justifiable appeal in a car, but it has far less value in the classroom. Even as children, most of us noticed the difference that a substitute for our regular teacher made in our school day. The personality of the teacher was so critical to our instruction that years later many people can remember far better how much they liked the teacher (or did not) rather than what was taught. I suspect that if asked to describe their best year in school, most people would choose the year they had a favorite teacher.

Specialized instruction for people with disabilities tends to instruct people in places that are irrelevant to the actual task. I know dozens of examples where the instruction has no apparent benefit for the instructed.[3] To take one example: Staff in a group home, two blocks from a grocery store, trained the residents "to shop" in the basement of the home by using play money to buy canned goods, which, once "bought," were then reshelved for the next round of instruction. Not surprisingly, the trainees were not particularly attentive or cooperative learners, and they did not make the connection between these odd make-believe transactions and the actual shopping they sometimes got to do in the local market. No one willingly accepts the imposition of being forced to learn just for the sake of learning so what pass for attempts to teach are justly resisted. When people fail to tolerate such misguided efforts, they are labeled as "uncooperative" or "untrainable." Our help, then, unwittingly becomes an instrument of oppression.

The goal of liberation movements is not rehabilitation but freedom. The work of liberation is not to train and shape the oppressed to be more accepting of or more acceptable to oppressing systems but to impart the vision, means, and power to contradict oppression and to disrupt and destroy the dynamics that support it. People with intellectual disabilities are in the early stages of a liberation movement—they are beginning to recognize that their lowly status in society is due not to their disabilities but to an unjust society. Until this awareness gains wider currency, however, most people—of all kinds—will see the status quo of oppression as "right." When people labeled retarded are seen as defective, it makes sense to assume that they cannot be included fully or valued

---

[3] I imagine readers saying, "But that is how I remember my own not-so-special education." There are long stretches in my own schooling where this type of learning occurred as well. So, if we know it doesn't work, why do we keep doing it?

equally in society. Custodial and paternalistic attitudes are seen as protecting the vulnerable rather than stifling untapped and unexpected abilities. One of the first struggles of any liberation movement is to gain an identity as an oppressed group and, at the same time, to confront the oppressors.[4] The problem is that, at the outset, a group's chief "protectors" and "allies" are often themselves oppressive.

It became a complicated struggle for everyone when women, for example, began to confront their protected status as a barrier to equal opportunity. What once seemed common courtesy came to be seen in another light as condescending. I was taught as a child to rise when a woman entered a room, to hold doors, to carry packages, and to offer my seat on the subway. The error of that upbringing was not in being considerate but in being considerate only to women. Courtesies make sense when offered graciously to anyone.

The group that women needed to confront first were their protector oppressors—men. The group that people with disabilities have had to confront first are their helpers— the professional community and those who fund services.

---

[4]There are, apparently, two steps necessary for an oppressed minority to become liberated. First, the minority must reclaim its identity—expressing that who they are can no longer be an occasion for shame or despair. As groups have begun the work of liberation, people have discovered the pride of being a woman, an African American, or a homosexual (or all of the above). Second, the majority has to recognize that labels are irrelevant to the rights and dignity of the people who bear them—hence, the struggle for a language that respects everyone alike and for practices that create opportunities for all people. As the liberation of people with disabilities begins, we can no longer talk about the "tragedy" of having a physical or mental disability any more than we can speak of the "tragedy" of having been born female. As a result, no one in good conscience or good consciousness will speak of people who "suffer" from Down syndrome or cerebral palsy any more than we speak about people who "suffer" from having been born anything except white, heterosexual, and male. Of course, people with Down syndrome or cerebral palsy suffer, but the pain connected directly to these conditions is chiefly caused by prejudice. As we grow away from these images of deficiency, we can no longer assume that people should necessarily be surrounded by a professional staff in protected environments selected by others as much as we should expect to meet people living lives that make sense to them in ways chosen by them. Our professional roles in such a world will be restored to their original premise of helping people to be who they want to be rather than in assessing who we think they are and getting them to accept our assessment as their reality.

Women have long understood that men have to change not only their behavior but their basic assumptions about what is fair. In the same way, service users are coming to expect that those who would help must fundamentally change their basic assumptions about what good support really is.

No liberation movement has ever required the people excluded to change. After a generation of struggle, the most recent wave of liberation movements—of women, African Americans, Latinos, and homosexuals—have all made some small progress, but women did not become men, African Americans did not become White, and Latinos did not abandon their culture nor homosexuals their sexuality. Progress has come from changes in the exclusionist attitudes of the mainstream culture. In this context—and the context of a liberation movement is critical to this point—it makes sense that, instead of trying to make people with intellectual handicaps act and appear "more normal," our energies would be better spent in learning to respect the existing skills of people and the choices they have already made as our first step toward a fully inclusive society.

Inclusion requires behavior changes, but we have consistently looked in the wrong places to achieve them. Inclusion requires behavior changes of the majority currently content with the status quo. When we professionals assume that people with behavioral differences have to change (and cannot really belong in society until they have changed), we run the risk of becoming the most dangerous kind of protector oppressors: people who not only keep others oppressed but also insist they are helping while they do it.[5]

---

[5]The business of being politically correct requires constantly shifting loyalties. For example, the concept of *age-appropriate* has an interesting history. We need to remember that this term began as an injunction upon people providing services but has gradually become a burden to be borne by the people with different abilities themselves. At first, in response to the misperception that people with learning disabilities were eternal children, people were reminded that their respectful friends regarded them as being their actual chronological age. This meant that for someone's 25th birthday—even if the person had been assessed as having a "mental age" of 2— one wouldn't presume to buy a plush toy. This has subsequently become a prohibition for the person, however. So an adult who likes trains or dolls is not "allowed" to have them. What began as a way of saying, "Let's make sure we don't insult a group of people who have been insulted enough," has become a practice that says: "Don't do what you want or be who you are. It embarrasses us."

The technologies for changing the behavior of people with disabilities are legion, and we often enlist families and direct service staff to implement these schemes. The next group we try to enlist is the general public, and we pursue this goal with late-night television spots, billboards, and pamphlets. Certainly, instructing others can be pleasant, but I have found it equally engaging to ask myself: How do I contribute to people's estrangement?

Even with the current flurry of educational and informing activity, I cannot think of a single time I was invited as a psychologist to join with other psychologists to consider how we might change our behavior or professional practices. This is not necessarily a matter of arrogance as I have never met a psychologist who claimed to know the truth about everything. We professionals often work in relative isolation and do not have enough opportunities to reflect on why, despite our best efforts, our work falls short of our intentions.

As a psychologist who has written his share of behavior plans for people, one trap I sometimes fell into was the idea that people need to be "made ready" for inclusion. I see now that I had it backward: Just as there are no special programs to prepare women to be citizens, we do not need to prepare a person with a disability to be included. Most of us live in a world where, in the most basic ways, we belong and would have to do something extreme to be sent away. Many people with differences are told from birth, "You do not belong. But, if you make an extreme effort, you might one day be allowed—in a limited way—to join in."

This, of course, can be oversimplified in ways I do not intend. I am specifically *not* saying that people with intellectual handicaps do not benefit from training, information, or instruction. The point is simply that people's sense of belonging, of being welcomed into ordinary society and having friendships, is the starting point and the context for learning and should *never* be abused as a contingency or a goal.

We will probably never achieve an inclusive society so long as we consider the struggle for inclusion as the proper work of the excluded. If our society is to include as many of us as we have the wisdom and love to embrace, inclusion really depends on everyone's understanding. When we attempt to bring people back from the brokenness of separation and

include them, we are forced to ask: What are our values—
what do we really believe is important? Obviously, for those
of us who grew up in a judgmental, hierarchical, and essentially exclusionary culture, our values will be forced to
change in ways we might not have anticipated.

I was once asked to demonstrate positive approaches at a
large professional training conference by listening and responding to stories about people who were difficult to serve.
The first person described was Robert. The staff of a group
"home" talked about how he had come to them from an institution, and on his first night he had become extremely destructive. Because of this violence, Robert had been immediately sent back. What exactly had happened? He had had a
reasonable evening, but when it was time to go to bed, he de-
stroyed his bedroom. I always assume that serious behavior
has serious meaning. It may not always be obvious to every
bystander, but most of us have good reasons for our behavior.
So, I wondered, why did going to bed have so much meaning
for Robert? My guess was that his anger was about something
bad that had happened in the past or that something was upsetting to him in the present. With whom did he sleep in the
institution, I asked.

People in institutions often sleep in the same room with
many others, most of whom they have nothing more in common with than their address. There may be partitions and
low dividing walls between the beds, but even then there are
often four beds in such an area. Although people are expected—contrary to all probability—to live asexually, they often form important relationships that are only rarely acknowledged in any sustaining way, if at all. Still, I was not
surprised when the people telling Robert's story knew exactly who his significant other had been. My suggestion was
that they begin to think of Robert's next living arrangement
not as a program but as his home. The best first step in this
planning would be to ask him if he wanted to live with his
friend. I made a small joke about how this would be an example of how, once again, doing the right thing would be cost-
effective because only one bed would have to be purchased.

The audience reaction to this mild observation was surprisingly vivid. Ostensibly, they were indignant to think that public money would be used to subsidize a sexual relationship. In retrospect, money was not the problem because Robert was already having this relationship in a publicly funded institution. The issue is partly the rights of any citizen to privacy, but the wider concern is Robert's right to choose his life as much as any of us choose ours. It hardly seems fair that the price for a decent and life-sustaining service should be his sexuality and most important emotional connection in the world. For these professionals, this man belonged in their community as long as he knew his place—the place where all oppressed people are supposed to stay, where they are invisible and can neither confront nor challenge a system that regards them as less than fully human.

The nature of oppression divides the oppressed from one another. Many of the people in this audience worked in poorly paid and highly demanding direct services jobs. Many of us working in human services ourselves do not command much respect and are the targets of various bigotries, and yet we fail to see how much our own difficulties have in common with those we would serve. By attempting to silence or hide Robert, these workers were colluding in their own oppression.

Institutions have disembodied people at every level. Institutions have separated citizens with disabilities from their communities, and institutional practices have further divorced people from their own bodies. Although people might have had preferences about when and how long they liked to sleep; when, what, and how much they liked to eat; what they liked to wear; and how they liked to look, none of these preferences was seen as worth attending to. Although not necessarily intentional, by ignoring individual differences and nuances, all the residents were seen to be the same idealized resident.

Given this group identity, it is not surprising that the literature of the institutional era referred to "the retarded," or "the retardate," as if such diverse people were one person. When we do not regard people as individuals, we are able to talk about them by freely replacing the individual with the collective, the same way people might talk about animals.

When people study animals, they might begin by referring to the elephant, but after living with and observing a particular herd, individual animals emerge with particular identities and nicknames. The tragedy is that people labeled retarded, just like every other living being, have always had unique personalities but these were just not seen through the opacity of the label.

People's bodies, in general, and their sexuality, in particular, often form the crucible in which the wide variety of individuals are reduced to a group (mis)identity or to stereotypes. Women, for example, still have to confront the curious division of themselves into "madonnas" (uncomplaining, passive, asexual nurturers) and "whores" (women possessed of a wild sexuality that exhausts and victimizes men). Neither role offers much room for reality.

These same unrealistic sexual stereotypes are commonly imposed on people with intellectual disabilities. Instead of being thought of as madonnas, they are seen as asexual "holy innocents"; instead of being thought of as whores, they are sometimes labeled as "children in adult bodies," capable of a dangerous and ungovernable sexuality.

One of the first tasks of a liberation movement is to reclaim individual identities from an oppressive stereotype. Whenever women have organized for their liberation, they have collectively used their individual experiences to define themselves independently of the stereotypes imposed by the male-dominant culture. Similarly, people with intellectual disabilities have begun to assert their rights to sexuality, to marriage, and to family as a matter of individual choice rather than accepting what others assume about them.

Stereotyping and sexuality can also inform us about the nature of institutions and community. The institution began as a place but became a set of values, while community began as a set of values that, for many people, has become a single place. The unreality and the "un-human-ness" of institutions were justified by the presumption that the people in them were less than real. As people with disabilities have become more vocal, they have claimed their right to full lives, which includes sexuality. Institutions began with the assumption that the people in them were asexual; and some institutions, recognizing that error, have wrestled with ways to reconcile that misperception with their operations. Many institutions have promulgated policies about opportunities for relationships and sexuality, often in the hope that this will make them more reasonable places in which to live. This is just another example of how institutions try to invent a world both parallel and superior to the real and ordinary one.

At the moment, the real and ordinary world of industrialized English-speaking countries is fairly confused on the topic of sexuality and who should be "allowed" to do what. Generally, though, citizens are subject to laws rather than policies and, even more generally, to the erratic enforcement of laws. A policy that would protect service users' rights to behave as they chose within the law would make sense, but here, as elsewhere, people with disabilities find their lives more strictly controlled than those of other citizens. One so-called community service had a policy that allowed people using their services to have sexual relationships, provided that the staff had determined that these relationships were "meaningful." This bit of naiveté revealed that these people might have moved into the community, but the ideology that governed them remained in the institution. As is too often the case in our work, the understandable need for a coherent set of values to govern services becomes an imposition on those who use them.

This issue can also be applied to just about every other aspect of service users' lives. Just as we expect people with disabilities to exist invisibly, even at the physical level, we also expect them to be invisible financially, except as the passive recipients of public welfare. Similarly, we do not expect people to take the initiative to speak for their rights as citizens or of their hopes as ordinary people. This failure to take seriously the most ordinary wishes and needs of people is sometimes masked by service agencies who want to "help." The help that is offered, though, is for an idealized or de-realized client rather than for a real person.

I doubt that Robert intended for his behavior to make him a test case. I suspect he was just asking for a home with the person with whom he most wanted to share his life. If that was indeed what his behavior was telling us, then having heard it, the most positive approach I can think of would be to provide that for him. Somehow, this idea that we should respond to people's requests still strikes some people as unnecessary or pointless.[6] If people labeled retarded were as stupid as they are stereotyped, then there might be little point in asking much less waiting for the answer. But experience has taught us that people labeled retarded are often well aware of who they are and what they need. It is surprising how smart people become once we find ways to understand what they really mean!

As we discovered our abilities to discern people's wishes and our capacities to respond to them, the rationale for the institution died. That institutions still exist shows how powerfully inertia protects people from the truth, not to mention how difficult it is for people to change their behavior. Unfortunately, some people have seen the growth of community services as "deinstitutionalization," which is not a positive framework in which to develop services. Deinstitutionalization too frequently has meant little institutions in the form of group homes. Too many service providers still think that by making institutions smaller, they are necessarily better and that by putting these little institutions into ordinary neighborhoods, they are somehow transmogrified into community programs.

Community has become a word greatly worked in recent years. In retrospect, I see how, for many people, community was a goal rather than a way of life. When group homes were still a new and optimistic idea for people to live in the community, "the community" often organized in angry protest. I used to dismiss these protesters as bigots and think that we should use every force of law to override their concerns. Today, if such a facility were proposed for my neighborhood, I would probably protest it myself, although for different reasons than these people. I don't see what uniquely qualifies people with disabilities to live with five (or, depending on the

---

[6]Generally, I have found people want fairly ordinary things—a home, something meaningful and agreeable to do with their waking hours, and someone to love and be loved by. Inevitably, some people want things that are impossible or dangerous, but that is implicit in the human condition.

funding source, almost any number of) relative strangers whose only common bond is an IQ score. However, if half a dozen people with disabilities decided to pool their resources and chose to live in my neighborhood, I would welcome them—communities can often benefit from greater diversity.

It's hard to see how arbitrarily assigning people to any living arrangement could ever bring them much happiness. Indeed, as we have learned, group homes, which once seemed like a good idea, merely continue the history of isolation and stigma. Had I been more thoughtful about what community really means, I would have listened more carefully to those ordinary people in their anger. I have yet to hear of an organized protest when people with disabilities live in their own homes or in arrangements of their own choosing. I have known people labeled retarded to be both charming and difficult as neighbors, but those are the kinds of people living in my neighborhood already.

Service systems that have attempted to develop responsive community services have succeeded better than those that have attempted to deinstitutionalize. This is not surprising given that the focus of their energy has the word institution built into it. No one lives in a "de-institution." Sometimes ideas are made clearer by explaining what they are not, but the strongest definitions usually rest on what they are. Some of the technologies developed to respond to difficult behavior have been characterized as "nonaversive," a description I would decline for any work I have done. I object to giving too much emphasis to aversives and, besides, saying something is nonaversive does not really tell what it *is*.[7] This may seem too fine a point, but casual language reveals our deeper intentions. The nonaversive literature has been, for the most part, about technologies of positive reinforcement to change behavior. When I imagine myself receiving some of these nonaversive services, I would not trust to my happiness. Difficult behavior expresses needs that are often more ordinary and direct than a sim-

---

[7]George Orwell (1950): "One can cure oneself of the *not un-* formation by memorizing this sentence: *A not unblack dog was chasing a not unsmall rabbit across a not ungreen field*" (p. 99). As with most rules of thumb in rhetoric this is not an absolute, and in ordinary conversation it is not indefensible.

plistic cry for a behavior plan. "Positive reinforcement" technologies are perfectly capable of being controlling, demeaning, and, hardest of all to see, irrelevant and frustrating to people's real needs and wishes.

I have spent some time trying to figure out an etiquette of talking about people's difficult behavior. When I first started working, I was surprised by the unquestioned assumption that people would not be included in meetings about them, a tradition based on the institution's basic belief that people were too incompetent to understand or to contribute meaningfully to the meetings or to their own lives. I started insisting that people attend meetings about them in hopes that their presence would help break down these stereotypes and break up the tradition of exclusion.

Some people who use services, however, had decided meetings were held only to design punishments for them so they did not want to come. I also know people who get anxious when they are aware that others are going to discuss them. Although I feel more comfortable talking about people's lives with them there, I can also respect how difficult that might be to sit through. There have also been times when people very much want to come to a staff discussion, but I knew the staff were so angry and resentful that what they needed most was to talk their frustration out. Because this kind of meeting is primarily to help the staff, I find it sensible to respect their needs as well. Happily, the people who use services often see the wisdom of giving staff time to work things out. Eventually, I came to recognize that specific situations vary widely and that no one set of practices is always helpful. An underlying attitude of accommodation, though, can be consistent. The most immediate goal, for me, is to get the person in crisis some relief. This typically requires that all the people involved are comfortable enough to speak freely, that I listen carefully, and that I honor what I hear.

Generally, I have found that inviting people to meetings is helpful. Sometimes people insist that if people cannot speak, they cannot contribute. My experience has been that ability has nothing to do with a person's contribution. Some people who do not speak with words can change the atmosphere of a meeting simply with their presence. Other people, of course, do speak and can add a great deal with their observations.

I facilitated a planning session for Michael—a man who had been difficult to serve because of his unpredictable and violent behavior. For 2 full days he sat while his family, some family friends, and a host of complete strangers made guesses about him and his life. Every now and again, Michael would make a comment. At first, these comments seemed off the mark and random to me because they seemed unconnected to what I thought was happening. My experience has been that people's words do not always express what they really mean, that sometimes words are like a nervous gesture that reveals anxiety more than anything else. It was easy to guess that Michael might be nervous when people were trying to figure out how to help him with every aspect of his life. Just because we had good intentions was no guarantee we would come up with good ideas.

The turning point in my awareness came when Michael said, "That doesn't make sense!" And it was true: What we were doing was really confused and needed to be reconsidered. When he started saying, "That's it!" it was easier to recognize the importance of what we were talking about. Michael's comments were, like everyone else's, sometimes more to the point than other times, but once we started *really* listening to him, we realized how accurate his comments were. By the end of the 2 days, some of the group had organized an informal circle of support with the common understanding that Michael could and should be the circle's voice. This was quite a shift from the beginning when people were thinking of him as a "behavior problem" rather than as a guiding spirit.

One of the first steps in any positive approach almost always involves starting with ourselves. If we are serious about changing other people's behavior, we should look at our own as well. Michael hadn't really changed a great deal in 2 days but the group around him had.

I also spent a day designing a service[8] for Steven, a 16-year-old with autism whose behavior was considered too difficult to allow him ever to live outside a "special" institution. The staff on his unit insisted that Steven should not come to this meeting because he would only become upset and disruptive and could not possibly sit through the entire day. They told me Steven had almost no attention span and that he did not speak.

My thought was that no one was going to sit the entire day. Naturally, we would take breaks as a group, and I try to make meetings relaxed enough that people who need to stand up and stretch can do so without feeling disruptive. So I persuaded them that Steven should start the day with us, hear the plan for the day, and if he needed to leave he could do so at any time without feeling he had somehow failed. And, like anyone else who might take a break, he should feel welcome if and when he decided to rejoin the group.

So when we began, I explained to Steven that we would be going back over his life, that the day would be focused on talking about him, that this might be painful to hear, and that he should, like anyone else, feel free to take a break when he needed to. He gave no indication that I could see that he had heard me. Just as people had predicted, at the beginning he was restless and noisy, and someone left with him for a while. When he came back, people were talking about his childhood, but I asked them to add an extra piece. When they said that he had been placed in another foster home at age 3, I asked everyone present to guess what it would be like to experience that. I asked people to give adult language to a 3-year-old's feelings at having lost his birth family and a foster family, and being confronted with a new family yet again: *If you were Steven, how would you feel?* People came up with some insightful and deeply felt guesses: *I would feel I was bad. I would wonder why I was being punished. I would think no one loved me.*

As people were talking, their tones changed. Instead of the staccato, just-the-facts way we had been looking at his life, people took longer to speak up. Some people were consider-

---

[8]There are several "person-centered planning" strategies in use. These are summarized in *Finding a Way Toward Everyday Lives: The Contribution of Person-Centered Planning* (O'Brien & Lovett, 1993).

ing their own experiences as children as they thought about Steven's life. The room got quieter. Steven stopped pacing and sat quietly. By the end of the meeting, when people were talking about how a person this estranged and systematically rejected needed personal experiences of love and acceptance, Steven had curled up with his head in someone's lap, calm and intent.

It seemed to me that Steven had done two things. First, he had demonstrated to people how long he could attend to things when things were worth attending to. Second, he had served as a barometer for the group. When we began, people were pessimistic and unfocused. They were sure that "he couldn't . . . he will never. . . ." Their predictions were not as specific as they were negative. But as they became more aware of Steven as a person, they looked more at who he was rather than what he was not. By the end of the day, they were clear about what he needed and what they could do to help him get it. Having experienced so much rejection, we wondered if he would want to live with a family. Not every teenager claims to need one, but we thought Steven did. He needed to have his abilities respected so that he could start looking for work. As the group's optimism and sense of purpose increased, Steven steadily became calmer. Just as he had listened to the heart of people's discussion, they were beginning to learn they could listen to the hidden heart of his behavior.

Although Steven did not use words to communicate, the group began to realize that their behavior interacted in a dialogue with his. Just as they wanted him to be more responsible about his actions, they recognized that they needed to be more responsible about their own. When people of good will sat down and tried to translate his life and everyday behavior into ordinary words and into an experience seen from *his* perspective, not just from their own, they were able to listen more carefully to Steven.

When a person cannot sit, we say from our vantage point, "He is hyperactive." If we translate this into Steven's language, the same behavior might be saying, "I am bored." If people hit us, we can dismiss them by saying, "These are violent clients." We could just as easily be more respectful and say, "We have not paid attention to the fact that for most of your life you have had your every basic need and wish frustrated." This is not to say that Steven's difficult behavior was suddenly transformed; however, the way people understood it was. Rather than seeing him as a problem, they began to understand that all of them—Steven and the staff—were engaged in a painful dialogue of misunderstanding. Instead of trying to change Steven, the staff wondered how they could change to be more responsive. And rather than trying to change the staff, they wondered how they could change the nature of the service: This institution cannot be a family, so how can we use our abilities to find a family for him and help this family support him as a person?

As it turned out, the institution that invited me to consult with them about Steven sent me a polite letter saying they had found the process "very helpful." I later was told that the administrators (who had not been present) found the recommendations of our planning day "unrealistic," "preposterous," and "a waste of money." Because they could not see past their own perspectives of Steven and people like him, they could not really see him. They could not see that they had defined realistic only in negative and oppressive ways. These same people also explained that they were the only ones in the state who truly understood people with autism and that theirs was the most advanced service available. As far as I know, Steven is still in a "basic skills program," living with a dozen other teenagers with disabilities in this "special school." I, obviously, am no longer welcome there; yet, the administrators are more likely to invite me to come back in before they ever give Steven a way to get out.

It would be simple to blame these administrators for their lack of vision and their resistance to change. Had I been more astute, I would have discerned that in any strongly authoritarian organization, the people with power must be consulted—and included—first. Sometimes, I naively trust that if something beneficial makes sense and can be achieved in a practical way, then it will inevitably happen. It doesn't always. In retrospect, I should have thought to include the director. Having met him, if just to shake hands, it would have been unfair to characterize his motives in vetoing the plans the group had for Steven, and besides, it teaches me nothing to blame and dismiss him. Just as this institution kept Steven locked up physically, I have also seen directors of institutions so locked up intellectually that they cannot understand a life for people, and perhaps not even for themselves, except in institutional terms. As Nirje (personal communication, 1991) said, institutions ultimately make everyone stupid. They impair the people who live in them. They stunt those who work in them, and they stupefy those who fund them.

We are slowly recognizing the need for people with disabilities to connect in socially ordinary ways. We have been less astute, I think, in recognizing that we also need to allow people to reconnect with themselves, with their own sense of accomplishment and dignity. At the moment, we are not doing this very well, especially for people with difficult behavior.

Intentionally or not, we have too often subjugated people who use services to professional rule. Ironically, services whose stated mission is "to promote independence in the community" typically make both communities and individuals passive and dependent upon professional judgment. In our zeal to provide help, we have managed to give some people the reputation of being helpless.

I first met Betty because Ed, her primary support worker, was worried about her depression. Betty had become apathetic and started to need help doing things she had been able, until recently, to do on her own. When I met her, she struck me as a shy person who had found being "helpless" a useful, if not necessary, social strategy. She had been sharing a home with a couple who were younger than she, and for many little reasons (rather than one big one) she was not happy living with them. Whenever she particularly wished she did not live with them, she had ways of making them wish they did not live with her. After a while, they decided not to.

We talked about how she was happy to leave them but hurt by the rejection. Fortunately, Betty and Ed got along very well and talking with them was more like spending time with two friends than it was a "clinical case consultation."

Seeing that Betty's life was becoming isolated and boring, Ed helped Betty find an apartment, get a job, and join Weight Watchers. This did not, of course, just happen; it took some months, but these changes occurred largely because of Ed's gifts of love and invention and Betty's strength to trust and grow.

Betty seemed less depressed. Perhaps it was because she had changed her perception of herself from an "overweight client" to a woman who could make her own decisions about her body. When we went to lunch, she would take a distinct pleasure in choosing a lo-cal special rather than the cheeseburger and fries she used to order. And like other people in the Weight Watchers program, she had some weeks of losing weight and some of gaining. She started seeing herself as having things in common with ordinary people. Unfortunately, like other ordinary people, Betty got laid off from her job.

By coincidence (if there really is such a thing), the agency serving Betty needed someone to help Jack, an 11-year-old boy with autism. Jack's parents needed someone to stay with him after school until they got home from work, but they had a hard time keeping people because he could get so upset that he would scratch and bite and generally make people want to leave. Betty needed a job, and this agency had the good sense to hire her to work for him. As it turned out, Betty stayed longer than anyone previously. The arrangement ended only because Jack's family moved out of state.

I was curious to learn how Betty had managed with a child who might well have been on various strict programs of behavior control. Betty said, "When I first met him, he didn't know me. It's really hard to really judge someone if they don't know the person. Jackie didn't know me so it was really hard—he kept punching me. It was like every day he punched me. I used to have a staff person there. Now I don't have anybody."

"When he was punching you, why did you think he was doing it?" I asked.

"I think he did it because he didn't know me, and I think he did it because he wanted to see if he could get away with it. And as Jackie and I grew together, Jackie didn't punch me and Jackie hung his coat up. Every Friday, we would go out for ice cream and he would love that and that was his treat from me."

"When he was hitting you, what did you do?" I asked.

"Nothing, I didn't do anything," Betty answered.

"You'd just stand there?" I asked.

"I just took his hands and I took him and held him like this [hugging] and that's all you could do until he stopped," she replied.

"What did you say to him?" I asked.

"I'd say, 'Jackie, stop now,' and he'd stop. And he hung up his coat and he did everything I asked him. As months went down, Jackie did not hit me. Jackie began to love me more. When Mr. Nealon said I no longer worked there any more Jackie didn't like that. Jackie started to cry. And Jackie asked, 'Can Betty come with us?' I said to Jackie, I said, 'No, your mother is going to be with you, and it will be best for all three of you.'" Betty then told me she didn't go to visit Jack much because it would be too hard on her to say good-bye again.

I think the agency working with Betty provided a real community service. The staff got excited for Betty about these changes in her life. Ordinary people tend to celebrate one another as individuals; institutional organizations tend to celebrate themselves. I get newsletters from various organizations calling themselves community programs that enthusiastically describe the agency's accomplishments. For example: Our agency has received the biggest increase in funding of any in the state! Or, the agency provided 68 clients a vacation in Florida. This type of news is not as compelling as learning that Rich, who used to be hidden at home, is happy to be working more hours at his job or that Karen, who used to live in a state school, is now sharing an apartment with a friend and that the arrangement is going well.

Institutional thinking, wherever it is done, often focuses on what people cannot do or what they need to learn. The communities I want to be a part of celebrate the gifts people already have and delight in mutual learning. In Rhode Island, a group of like-minded service workers meets regularly to consider how they can support people in ways that help them feel supported. Recognizing that many people who use services are lonely and unconnected, they have made an effort to link people with common interests. These introductions have led to relationships that are more like friendships than those with volunteers unilaterally "helping." This group has had celebrations where people show slides and videos or picture and storyboards of how their lives have changed with one another. What struck me about the group was the way the people talked about one another, about what they had done for one another, and about what each had learned from the other. This language cut across the grain generally found in such relationships. Instead of talking like charitable volunteers, people talked as friends.

Institutions, in whatever guises we find them, speak *for* people. This gives some pause when we reflect that advocacy means, from its Latin root, to call on behalf of someone, to speak for someone else. In a world of hierarchical oppression, advocacy is the best, and perhaps only, way for oppressed people to be heard. Inclusive communities, however, allow us all a voice to speak for ourselves. In a real community, everyone who speaks is listened to. Obviously, not everyone agrees with or takes seriously everyone else all the time, but one is listened to and the merits of what one has to say get assessed. Self-advocacy groups—People First, Personnes d'Abord, and Speaking for Ourselves—might once have been dismissed as little social clubs for the impaired, but more and more, people are learning from these groups that the members are brave and strong and have something valuable to offer.

Being needed is a genuinely important status. When we are needed, we belong and we have a reason to speak up; and when people are needed, that is when we most often find the ways to listen to them.

All of which brings me back to Maureen, the woman whose behavior program caused me so much concern at the beginning of this chapter. After hearing that this woman was being subjected to a "positive reinforcement program" where she could earn diet sodas for "good behavior," I wrote to the program director. I explained that this meeting had convinced me that not only had I accomplished nothing, I had no hopes of ever making myself clear. I quit. To my surprise, the director called back and said that he had been unaware of this situation and promised to change things.

So many large community services are really just institutions broken up and scattered around. No amount of good will, regulation, or monitoring can ever make either a large institution or its smaller community analogs a home. I often despair that these so-called community services will never change as they work under the misperception they are just fine as they are.

On the other hand, as a psychologist who believes people really can change individually, I have to believe people in these organizations can change the way they think and act collectively, too. If they are working to change, then I need to act on my faith in the power of listening and responding. So, we agreed I could help them organize the people who use their service into an autonomous group. I don't know how this will work out, but I will keep working with them so long as I have a little hope they will change. If I expect an agency to serve people with disabilities respectfully and wholeheartedly, then I will hold myself to the same standard in my work for them. There have been other occasions, though, when services have been incapable of doing anything other than changing their rhetoric and simply saying they were doing person-centered planning or supported living or nurturing self-advocacy and I have made the difficult decision to give up on them. There comes a point where it is better to leave than be co-opted into a destructive and dysfunctional organization.

I would like to have written: Today Maureen is living in an apartment with a friend who helps her with her money and meals and with keeping the apartment tidy, she's joined a local group of women at the church, she volunteers at the shelter for battered women, she has a part-time job at the supermarket, last Christmas she had her parents over for dinner, and she's been seeing Fred who seems to like her, too. I know women whose lives were difficult in many of the ways Maureen's has been and their lives have worked out as I just described. But these stories of individual success are clearly in the minority of people receiving services. Although

Maureen's life could turn out to be more satisfying for her and for those nearest to her, it hasn't yet, and I think in some ways she embodies the struggle of many people with disabilities and not just those with difficult behaviors. Many of us have a clear vision—and firsthand experience—of how people with disabilities can live in ordinary places and contribute significantly to the wider lives of our communities. Meanwhile, most people with disabilities are living with services that, in effect, keep them homeless and poor, lonely and ignored, and, worst of all, powerless to change any of it. The real work before us lies in putting that to an end.

Fundamentally, the most helpful thing I have found is to listen to what people have to say. By now, I suppose it's obvious that by listening, I mean the act of attending carefully to what is said as well as to what is meant, to regard actions as communication, and, most profoundly, to possess the spirit of taking other people seriously.

Our confusion and uncertainty about "difficult behavior" have been a barrier to full inclusion. Even when we believe in everyone's right to full presence and full participation, some people have behaviors that are difficult, antisocial, or dangerous. This book is about the positive ways we can respond to help people change through what I believe is necessarily a mutual process. I have examined some of the practices and traditions we professionals have developed in order to see which of these help and which hinder people with difficult behavior. This book is about how we can learn to listen and how we can listen to learn.

I hope this point is obvious: There is no such thing as a value-free way of working with others. The challenge is to keep ourselves honest and to consider what values we actually use in our work, not just what values we say we have. One of the sad and painful ironies of psychology in the field of developmental disabilities is that we psychologists have judged (and often hurt) people on the basis of their observed behavior. We, however, have excused and even congratulated one another on the basis of our intentions.

Chapter 2

The Politics of
——Labeling Behavior——

The president of a chapter of Personnes d'Abord, a self-advocacy movement in Québec, explained over lunch, "We do not like labels. We just want to be seen as people."

This issue of what to be called is a central concern in all liberation movements and is not a trivial matter of semantics. The dangers of labeling are, at heart, political dangers, and we cannot have positive approaches to people without taking seriously the economic and political contexts in which they live. People who use services are, overwhelmingly, poor and politically powerless. Just as there can be no value-free therapy, there really cannot be a diagnostic system or descriptive terminology free of political import. When we fail to consider these wider political realities of people with disabilities, we ultimately fail to support people in their lives.

I asked the president of this group about this political problem of language, "People who have been labeled often need help to do some of the things they themselves want to do. It's wrong to reduce people to a diagnostic label, but how are we to talk about people in a way that respects both their dignity and their needs?"

She thought for a moment and said, "That is a very interesting question and I don't have an answer."[1]

So far, none of us does. I do not like the idea of people being identified in ways that are dismissive or rude, but there is no way to describe someone that doesn't invoke a series of impressions, prejudices, biases, and opinions—although not necessarily completely negative ones.

A person goes downtown, orders lunch, is served, and leaves. "So what?" one might ask. Well, suppose the person is a man. That doesn't add much. He's African American. This still probably does not add much for most people. It is 1962 and he is in Greensboro, North Carolina. The drama of this simple event takes shape purely from its political context.

Similarly, if this sequence were about a Caucasian woman, you might not take much notice until you learn the woman had never before been downtown alone; she had never before ordered her own lunch and paid for it with money she had earned. Again, the story suddenly changes from an unremarkable event to a personal landmark.

When we fail to take a person's differences into account, we lose the context to understand that person in a realistic way. However, there is danger in making every small step an occasion of artificial enthusiasm ("Good sitting!!"), and trivializing people. Yet, if learning some ordinary task has been the result of great personal effort, we need to make sure we celebrate these gains with the people who accomplished them..The first danger leads us to infantilize people with disabilities; the second leads us to be too blasé about their personal growth.

So, in some ways, knowing a person's labels is a reasonable and potentially helpful piece of information. For example, audiences frequently respond to speeches by self-

---

[1]In June 1993, 1,300 delegates from 32 countries met at the Third International Self-Advocacy Conference, in Toronto, Canada. Delegates frequently spoke about words such as mental retardation being unacceptable, even in a people-first format, such as "a person with mental retardation." Many delegates said they preferred to be known as "disabled people." "People-first" language is the standard that North American self-advocates have set for respectful terminology. I use this term in this book, although in Europe (and increasingly in North America) disability rights activists have adopted "disabled person" as a respectful descriptor.

advocates with a standing ovation. Many of the speeches are, in fact, exceptional no matter who gives them, but there is the ever-present awareness that typically this speaker did not go to general schools, never led the class in pledging allegiance to the flag, never had a chance to speak as a candidate for student council, never performed in a school assembly, and yet has been able to speak, often without notes, in a way that is both well-organized and compelling. Our applause for these speeches takes the individual's history into account as much as the finished product.

The Canadian Association for the Mentally Retarded and the (Canadian) National Institute on Mental Retardation both changed their names, respectively, to the Canadian Association for Community Living and the G. Allan Roeher Institute. A number of people correctly pointed out that these changes would obscure the organization's purposes, but the impetus for this change came from the self-advocacy group People First. This group said that the word retarded was offensive so that any organization on behalf of people with disabilities would naturally respond to their concern. Without an awareness of the political context, the significance of these name changes is lost.

Liberation movements justifiably pay attention to terminology because language is not just empty symbolism. African Americans were once known, apparently without any particular malice intended, as "niggers." It's hard for me even to write that word because it ultimately devolved into such a hateful whiplash of a word. But I have friends who use the word with one another with complete affection. They are African Americans, and they took the word back. Some lesbians have reclaimed "dyke," and the protest group Queer Nation has stolen "queer" from the hate-mongers. People with physical disabilities sometimes use "crips" as a collective name for themselves.[2]

---

[2]To draw an analogy between people with disabilities and groups to whom the term oppression has been applied is by no means new. In the literature of disability, a number of studies comment, but do no more than comment, on the similarity between interactions between people with and without disabilities and those between African Americans and Caucasians that are encountered in the studies of race relations. Barker, for example, remarked as long ago as 1948 that: "The physically disabled person is in a

Schaef (1985) and Van der Klift and Kunc (1994) developed progressive stages of awareness around difference. Schaef wrote: "Many of the problems we have in communicating with one another have to do with the fact that people speak from different levels of truth and are often unaware of the other levels" (p. 152).

Using as an example people's awareness of "gayness," Schaef suggested four separate levels of truth; looking at difference more generically, Van der Klift and Kunc saw a similar progression.

Schaef's observations about progressive stages of awareness seem just as relevant to disability as to any other difference such as race, gender, or as seen in her analysis of homophobia:

1. Awareness and familiarity generally determined one's "level." Hence,
2. It was difficult, if not impossible, to go from a "higher" level to a lower one.
3. Vehemence diminishes with awareness. A person with little information will be both more intense and insecure than a person with more information.
4. Each new level of awareness almost always moves in a direction opposite the previous one. This means growth in awareness can appear as inconsistency.
5. . . . each level of truth bears a strong behavioral resemblance to the one two behind it or two ahead of it. They are quite different attitudinally, though. (pp. 156–157)

Table 1 provides a comparison of the levels of awareness formulated by Schaef and by Van der Klift and Kunc and applies these to language and policies about disability.

Most people in human services work from Schaef's Level 3 liberal phase, whereby they carefully avoid language that draws negative attention to difference. We use people-first language and generally work to show how all people are more alike than otherwise. Snow (1992), for example, referred to disability as "giftedness"; others refer to people as

position not unlike the Negro, the Jew, and other underprivileged racial and religious minorities" (Barker, 1948, p. 31); but Handel in 1960 observed that this report "sounded as though we were considering a problem of race relations instead of disability" (Handel, 1960, p. 363).

Table 1. Levels of awareness and their application to policy and language about disability

Schaef (1985)	Van der Klift and Kunc (1994)	Policy applications and language about disability
Level 1. *Ostrich phase*: People are unaware of gayness and lack even a vocabulary for it.		People with disabilities are hidden away or "allowed to die."
Level 2. *Homophobic phase*: People have little information about gay people and are defensive and hostile. They use terms such as dyke, faggot, and queer in derogatory ways.	1. *Marginalization*: Social policy supports removal and segregation.	People with disabilities are known to exist, but "there should be special places for them" such as institutions, special education, group homes, day activity centers, workshops, and Special Olympics. Retardates The mentally retarded
Level 3. *Liberal phase*: People develop enlightened attitudes, have recognized homophobia, and work to use language that will not offend. Dyke and faggot do not appear in their conversations.	2. *Reform*: Differences among people are minimalized, and commonalities emphasized. Services focus on rehabilitation with the goal of assimilation. 3. *Tolerance*: Resignation and benevolence characterize this phase.	People's lives should look like yours or mine. Activities should always look and be ordinary and age appropriate (social role valorization, normalization). People-first language: people with disabilities People with disabilities are just like you and me. But I don't think of you as disabled (as a compliment).
Level 4. *Full awareness*: Aware of the previous three levels, people have worked	4. *Value of diversity*: Recognition of equal worth; em-	People with disabilities have different support needs and their own perspectives on

(continued)

Table 1. *(continued)*

Schaef (1985)	Van der Klift and Kunc (1994)	Policy applications and language about disability
through their homo-phobia. Especially if they are gay them-selves, they might af-fectionately say, "You old dyke," or "You old faggot." The terms have taken on an endear-ing and affectionate tone and are a nat-ural part of their lan-guage. (p. 155)	phasis on the mu-tual benefit that comes from cele-brating diversity.	how these should be met. Different is not better or worse; it is different. People live where and with whom they want and work at jobs they choose. "Crip" "But I don't think of you as disabled" is heard as an insult (cf., "played like a White man"; "she thinks like a man").

Note: Abberley (1992) says, "Evaluative connotations are cognitively, as well as effec-tively, contained in terms which themselves imply deficiency, in contrast to 'woman' and 'Black.' This is not to suggest that perceptions can be changed by changing words but to point to the deeply entrenched rejection of 'impairment' as a viable form of life and to the 'common-sense,' 'natural,' and unconscious nature of ideologies and impair-ment, disability and handicap. The rejection of the authenticity of impaired life forms is exhibited both in the obvious form of what Dartington et al. (1981) call the 'less than whole person' view and its inverse, the 'really normal' ideology, which finds its expres-sion in everyday life in the exceptionalism of 'but I don't think of you as disabled,' denying a key aspect of a disabled person's identity in what is intended as a compliment. Compare this phrase to 'played like a White man' and 'she thinks like a man'" (p. 235).

"differently abled." These assimilationist impulses fit with the melting pot metaphor that once dominated both American culture's response to ethnic diversity and the professional ideology of "normalizing" the lives of labeled people.[3]

But writing as a self-described disabled person, Abberley (1992) claimed:

---

[3]The melting pot was almost plausible as a metaphor for the integra-tion of the relatively similar northern European cultures into one Ameri-can *über-kultur*, but our definition of American now has to include literally people from everywhere in the world, not just Europe. One struggle in American politics has been over how we respond to this. Do we continue with our policy of conformity and homogeneity or do we celebrate and nurture diversity? The debates over bilingual education, English as the of-ficial language of the United States, affirmative action, and specific protec-tions for the rights of some citizens have often divided along concerns about what makes us one nation, and what it is that actually guarantees freedom and equality.

It is crucial that a theory of disability as oppression comes to grips with this "real" inferiority, since it forms a bedrock upon which justificatory oppressive theories are based and, psychologically, an immense impediment to the development of political consciousness amongst disabled people. Such a development is systematically blocked through the naturalisation of impairment. (p. 234)

The liberal phase of naturalizing impairment hoped to remedy the "handiphobic" phase of stigmatizing people as defective. But, as Abberley pointed out, this in turn inhibits the development of self-determination and self-definition. Abberley, a self-advocate, sounds shockingly like a voice from a discredited past. Recognizing this, I hope, helps us get past objective measures of political correctness to recognize whose life we are talking about and who has power over that life. There is a world of difference between me speaking for people as an advocate and them speaking for themselves as citizens.

Compared with racism and homophobia, the anxiety that underlies handiphobia seems less likely to be expressed as overt hatred than as the more subtle degradation of pity.[4] Pity is often fear expressed in a more socially acceptable form—distancing. Many well-intended people find it hard to recognize that pity is as good as a kick. The battle between people with disabilities and Jerry Lewis's telethon, featuring "his kids," probably confuses many people who think "those kids" should be grateful for the charity. This attitude fits well with a medical model that sees a "wheelchair-bound victim" of misfortune or illness. This condescension undermines the perspective that people with differences are first and foremost citizens, not eternal children or victims. People who rely on the "Jerry's kids" understanding typically have the best intentions in mind, but they also need to recognize that good intentions are not acceptable substitutes for responsible behavior.

---

[4]I emphasize this seems to be the case only because people are more open about pity than hatefulness. For example, in 1993, DeAngelis reported about the American Psychological Association's updating of its biographical membership directory to include information about disability. Some responses as to what *psychologists* reported as their *own* disabilities included "bad handwriting," "male WASP," "ugly," "tired," and "mother of boys."

"As disabled people, we have been struggling for a long time to liberate ourselves from the chains of an able-bodied culture which does not value us, and which tries to teach us to accept an unequal status in our societies" (Mason, 1992a, p. 222). "We need to declare ourselves 'disabled people' with pride and not shame" (Mason, 1992b). In this area, people with disabilities—disabled people—are in the same position as everyone else: Our consciousness may be growing, our attitudes of respect and optimism may be deepening, but we are struggling with how to understand, interpret, and still respect difference. Until we achieve consensus, we will have volatile and unsettled terminology.

Furthermore, labeling (as we do with conditions) and diagnosis (as we do with illnesses) are not merely the objective, scientific activities they might first appear to be. We sometimes forget the politics implicit in science. Science has always been an available tool to prove the inferiority of the oppressed as part of the overall rationale that, somehow, oppressed people deserve their lack of status. Scientific literature long ago "proved" the irremediable inferiority of African Americans and women. Homosexuals were for a long time thought to need therapy for their immature and "pathological" sexuality. Now, though, people who demonstrate prejudice against these groups are themselves seen as having a social disease for which, as yet, we have no cure. As Fee (1979) wrote: "As long as there are entrenched social and political distinctions between sexes, races, or classes, there will be forms of science whose main function is to rationalize and legitimate those distinctions" (p. 430).

Whenever a group lacks a history of self-identity, the mainstream culture defines it with a projected image. Which came first, rigid clinicians with standardized tests and machine-like interpretations of those tests or the description of people labeled retarded as typically dependent on routine, incapable of abstract reasoning, and not able to generalize from experience? Although many people with labels fit this stereotype, I wonder if they were taught to do so by the routines and structure we professionals have unquestioningly built into people's lives. Psychiatrists regularly prescribe drugs for people who are "agitated" and "dangerous." Many service providers seclude people who paid helpers want to get away from and sedate people who make them anxious.

We professionals have consistently projected our own assumptions and prejudices onto those we purport to serve. For example, we sometimes describe parents as not accepting their child's disability and pityingly refer to their efforts to find the cure. But in fact, we do not accept people's disabilities all that well ourselves. Training people to get ready for work or community living implies our eagerness to change people rather than to accept them. I now believe that people with different abilities really are that—differently abled. Especially in the areas of employment, professional assessment tends to focus on what a person cannot do rather than on the often marketable skills the person already has or, just as crucially, on how the person wants to spend the day. If someone found a cure for Down syndrome or a simple surgical procedure to cure autism, I suspect most professionals would regard this as a Nobel prize–worthy breakthrough—one that people with those diagnoses should immediately embrace.

I was surprised when I first read Tomacek's (1990) declaration that she would reject a cure for her schizophrenia. I had just assumed anyone with schizophrenia would happily be rid of it. Although her schizophrenia has its bad hours, she points out that it is also a part of who she is.

> My schizophrenia makes me be in such a way as I can accept myself, and it is not my fault if the rest of the world will have little to do with it. To speak of "elimination" is rather strong and reminiscent of Nazi philosophies. I do not wish to become a so-called "normal" individual at all. I have tried for many years, and fairly successfully, but I have found it impoverishing, artificial, and damaging. To me, normalization and conformity are not acceptable because they would necessarily reduce my creative abilities, my potential to find the joy in life that I now experience according to my personal modes of learning, communicating, and living. (p. 550)

Similarly, John Limnidis, a deaf football player from Canada, a country whose citizens understand the difficulties of living with linguistic diversity, said, "Deafness is not a handicap. It's a culture, a language, and I'm proud to be deaf. If there was a medication that could be given to deaf people to make them hear, I wouldn't take it. Never. Never till I die!" (Shapiro, 1993). Dr. Temple Grandin (Sacks, 1993) talked in the same way about her autism; without it, she would not be Dr. Temple Grandin.

After reading these statements, I now wonder how people labeled retarded would respond to an offer of a cure. How many would choose to be "normal"? My own fantasies, however, of a medical miracle include a simple medication that would permit me genuinely to accept others for what they already are. I suspect that given the choice of taking a pill to become normal or giving normal people a pill to accept differences, most people with disabling labels would choose the latter.

It takes courage, though, to choose who you are over who you are supposed to be. The tendency of oppressed people is to internalize the oppressor. Some women, apparently, see themselves as succeeding when they are masculine, and failing when they are feminine; "light" African Americans are (even in their own community) sometimes thought to be better than darker-skinned people, and in the male homosexual community "straight acting" is, for some people, superior to more effeminate behavior. All of these liberation movements have had to reject these received values of what is superior (i.e., walking, talking, white, heterosexual-appearing male) as oppressively irrational. Will people with disabilities reject similar attempts to make them normal in this way?[5]

As usual in these situations of changing values, good ideas compete and clash. For example, the Special Olympics have been one way to provide competitive sports for people

---

[5]Temple Grandin, who has worked tirelessly to understand and to explain autism as an inner experience, is described by Sacks (1993): "At a recent lecture, Temple ended by saying, 'If I could snap my fingers and be non-autistic, I would not—because then I wouldn't be me. Autism is part of who I am.' And because she believes autism may also be associated with something of value, she is alarmed at thoughts of eradicating it . . ." [Temple wrote]: "Aware adults with autism and their parents are often angry about autism. They may ask why nature or God created such horrible conditions as autism, manic depression, and schizophrenia. However, if the genes that caused the conditions were eliminated there might be a terrible price to pay. It is possible that persons with bits of these traits are more creative, or possibly even geniuses. . . . If science eliminated these genes, maybe the whole world would be taken over by accountants" (p. 124).

with disabilities. Yet the opportunity to compete as an athlete in a segregated event also raises the ghosts of racial prejudices embodied in baseball's Negro League. If the Special Olympics were held in a society that welcomed people with disabilities with economic equality and social justice, then these "special" events might have the same meaning as, say, Scottish games where people gather in kilts to compete in tossing logs. At the moment, the role of people with disabilities is that of an oppressed minority rather than that of an equally valued ethnic group with its own heritage and traditions. People with disabilities might yet become such a group. The argument about the Special Olympics—as with segregated activities for people generally—is not so much about the segregation as about the context of the segregation.

This vision might prove, in the long run, to be true of education as well. It might happen in some future, currently hard to imagine, that people with learning disabilities might well be seen as different in a way that carries no stigma and no pejorative connotations in the same way that children with red hair or brown eyes are generally perceived as different. Clearly, a child with brown eyes is different from a child with hazel eyes, and yet it is doubtful that most people would be able to say what the difference means. If we discovered that children with brown eyes learned most rapidly with one set of instructional techniques and children with hazel eyes another, then it seems likely most teachers would use these different methodologies. But even then, would they necessarily need to be in separate classes?

If there were separate classrooms divided on these lines, then some other meaning of difference would be inevitably projected onto them and some other value would soon come to be placed on the children. We would hear how children with brown eyes were naturally superior in verbal abilities or how children with hazel eyes were most likely to excel in athletics. The specifics of the stereotyping are less interesting than the mechanism of its creation. Children can be trained into this perception. Children artificially separated by physical characteristics have been successfully persuaded that these differences matter. Dividing people into groups for arbitrary reasons eventually creates—and requires—a mythology that explains why the groups really are different.

Just as any technology is value-free until it is used, the act of labeling a person would be, in some absolute sense, a neutral activity if only it happened in isolation. But as professional diagnosis never does occur in isolation, it always has some social, cultural, and political context. When the values of a culture change, the distinctions within it must change as well. For example, at the beginning of the 20th century, IQ scores were used to help scientifically prove that American immigrants from the Mediterranean and eastern Europe were intellectually inferior to native stock. When the intellectual abilities of new immigrants were no longer of such concern, the need to categorize people on the basis of arbitrary and culturally linked intelligence tests lost its political rationale. Periodically, this old use of IQ testing makes an encore appearance to bolster an even older American enthusiasm—racism. As with most systems of ostensibly objective measurement, IQ testing serves the political agenda of the testers far more than it serves any of the tested.

Objective external assessment criteria, such as IQ, aptitude, and national achievement tests, are tools traditionally used to maintain distance and control over people. The psychiatric tradition of labeling people (e.g., paranoid, grandiose) gave way to the behavioral tradition of labeling activity (e.g., noncompliant, attention seeking). Both of these systems stigmatized their patients. When we guess the adaptive reasons that a person acts in a certain way and use that person's perspective as the basis for understanding, then we are much more likely to act in respectful and really helpful ways *with* the person rather than in strategies that work *over* or *against* the person.

Unless people explain their motivations to us precisely, we can only guess how their behavior is adaptive. Typically, the better the relationship we have with someone, the more likely we are to guess correctly about the person. One of the essential features of positive approaches is that permission to work with or for people is contingent on having a mutual relationship with them. It is hard to trust our intentions unless we have some regard for the person we hope to help.

This mutual relationship contrasts sharply with the tradition of objective observers who use diagnostics in a hierarchical social system. Most assessments are done with standard measures, quickly, and usually by strangers. It should come as no surprise that these measures support and reflect the values of the testers, whose status in turn depends on supporting the culture in which they work. Oppressed people often object to these measures intuitively, not realizing how radically professional work would have to change if the professions considered oppressed people as people, not to mention if they considered oppression as an unconscious tool of cultural maintenance.

The objective science of diagnosis in industrialized society contrasts sharply with the practices of the Native American medicine men and women working in more collaborative, lateral societies. In writing about the Teton Sioux medicine man, Fools Crow, Mails and Crow (1991) consistently referred to the people to be healed as patients, even after they explained:

> A customary and natural routine was followed with every patient, and I repeat here that while I am using the word "patient," and have even put it into Fools Crow's mouth, he never did use it. He referred to those who came to him as a "person," or more preferably by name. He intuitively knew that calling someone a patient did something negative to their sense of personal worth, and that it impaired and weakened the otherwise strong relationship between his patients and himself—a relationship he considered essential to success. (pp. 152–153)

One of the most common "difficult behaviors" is aggression. Most people do not like to be hit or to live or work where violence is a common occurrence. But labeling a person, or even a behavior, as aggressive in a clinical context has a radically different dynamic from respecting the reasons a person might be legitimately angry in a social context: being bossed about, being sexually frustrated, being insulted or rejected, or any of the dozens of other real and individual reasons anyone might have for being angry. It seems strange and perverse to persist in seeing these reasons strictly in our own terms rather than *also* in the ways the person who is angry sees them. The pretense of objectivity distances us from people who scare and confuse us (which is one political use of taking data).[6] At the same time, objectivity masks our own fears and hurts, which could beneficially serve to guide not only others but our own healing as well.

When people are understood only in terms of the lowest common denominator of their labels, they are at risk. Their behavior is often seen as inexplicable, or their motives are demeaned. Many times we interpret what others do as being "only" to get attention, especially "staff attention." I know a number of people like Vincent, for example, who prefers to spend time with staff rather than with other people with disabilities. He can even be quite rude about this, interrupting conversations or dominating social situations. Sometimes, too, Vincent might even take on the role of manager and tell his co-workers or housemates what they should be doing. The response I have seen most often used is, "Vincent will be told he is not a staff person and will then be redirected to working/socializing with peers." My friend Jo Allard Krippenstapel translates this to mean: "Keep acting retarded so we'll know how to respond to you" (J.A. Krippenstapel, personal communication).

Unfortunately, people are ignoring what Vincent is telling them when he acts this way. His behavior says that he does not consider the people living in his house to have the same status as the people who work in it. I assume that Vincent is like most of us and will imitate a person with more status more quickly than a person with less status. Most of us try to approach the people we work with with respect, but this respect is, as in any relationship, negotiated.[7] Negotiating the boundaries of mu-

---

[6]This is not to suggest that using data is necessarily an oppressive activity, though it often unintentionally is. If this helps people sort a confusing situation into a more understandable one, then it could be helpful, but whenever people need to do this it seems the problem is not just that the people don't understand the behavior; more significantly, they don't understand the person as a person very well. In this instance, data are unlikely to set you free.

[7]Many of us think of ourselves as working for people. Because I am paid either directly by service users or have the professional freedom to see them as my primary customers, I speak of working for people with disabilities. Alas, this kind of semantic shift is easier to make than changes in staffing practices, and the reality is that many people do not work for people with disabilities, they work with them. In fact, they work for an agency

tually acceptable behavior can be a continual process in any relationship, whether personal or civic. Most of our positive relationships are with people who are not physically aggressive or frightening. When a person gets to the point of frightening or hitting others, instead of looking for ways to help, we often feel empowered to take charge. This fosters the idea that the people we work with are ultimately incapable of governing themselves, that they can have typical opportunities until we get nervous and take them away. We might respect a person's opinions so long as these opinions do not prove inconvenient, but if this person's actions should disturb us, we feel we have the right to abruptly overrule the individual.

Every now and again, a stranger will phone me for advice about someone I have never met. Someone called recently: "Hi, my name's Phyllis, and we've got this 21-year-old autistic who's really assaultive all the time. He was looking around the refrigerator last night and we told him to shut the door so he hauled off and belted a staff. We're going to have him checked for frontal lobe seizures, but if that isn't it, *then* what are we going to do?"

"What is this man's name?" I asked.

"James," she replied.

"Who calls James other than his family?"

"No one."

"Who are his friends?"

"He doesn't make friends."

"Why was he looking in the refrigerator?"

"He likes attention."

There was a time I would have found this conversation infuriating. I still flinch when I hear someone called an autistic, and I would be pretty condescending (if only in my heart) to anyone thinking that people look for a social life in refrigera-

---

and if they should fall out of favor with their employer, it doesn't much matter what the people they are working with think. They are often fired outright or encouraged to leave. As it stands, some agencies allow service users a voice in this process but given the often highly personal nature of our service, people should at the least have the power to veto workers. Until people who use services ethically hire and fire those who help them, what they will have is rhetorical empowerment rather than the real political power implicit in having control of money.

tors.[8] Still, if I really want to see a world where James is taken seriously as a person, then—I have only slowly come to recognize this—I have to begin with myself. Would my abrupt dismissal of this woman be any different from her misunderstanding of James? I am constantly discovering how I have yet to learn to listen not only to people's words but to their larger meanings as well. I am still learning how to listen to learn.

It has always been too easy for me to respond to my own reactions and judgments first and last. I find I am happier with myself and my work, though, when I remember that 1) most people are doing the best they can. If they see a way, they will often change to do better, but most people won't see new possibilities if they come from hostile critics, and 2) Phyllis did not call to get my opinion of her. She was desperate. People were getting hurt and she was scared.

As we talked, she recognized that people had been giving James orders when they might better have asked him questions and that they had not been as thoughtful toward James as they were toward one another. By the time we finished talking, Phyllis decided that James probably had a lot of reasons not to be happy about his life. He lived with six other people he didn't choose to live with. He worked for very little money at a job he didn't like. As this perspective became clearer to her, she concluded, "We can do better!"

Just because the people working with James had not done as well by him as they might have did not mean they did not want to do better. (Even though we cannot measure intention, we know it exists, and, although the outcomes may be identical, we feel the difference between ignorance and malice.) Similarly, when he acted the way he did, maybe James didn't know any other way. Phyllis and I agreed that

---

[8]Lumping people together by diagnosis might make some sense in a hospital, but in a residential service this robs the person of identity. Teachers often talk about children in similar collective terms like TMR, EMR, SBD. This not only takes away an essential ingredient for education—understanding each child as unique—it also supports the illusion that there are rehabilitations and therapies for such diagnoses. If children got better in such a segregated world, the movement toward inclusive education and supported community living would never have taken on the urgency and imperative it has.

the next time he was staring into the refrigerator, people could just as easily ask, "So, what do you feel like eating?"

Just as we have forced people from general society with the blunt instrument of intelligence testing and robbed them of ordinary consideration, we have also taken people's behavior out of their social and personal contexts by labeling that as well. The ways we label behavior simply extend the ways we have been trained to label people. Once people have been identified as schizophrenic, they are at risk for being seen as engaging in schizophrenic behaviors. Similarly, when people "are" retarded, their behavior is interpreted with the lack of respect that this label has come to signify.

Dismissing people as attention seeking, for example, almost always comes from not taking them seriously as real people. James might have wanted to start a conversation and knew that holding the refrigerator door would soon get somebody talking, but he also might just have been hungry.[9] When we don't love people or take them seriously, we tend simplistically to dismiss their motivations. I have long been fascinated by the phenomenon of how *I* am good at managing my money, *you* are a little tight with a buck, but *he* makes Scrooge look like Santa Claus.

Our use of language and labels has a powerful effect on people's lives. I have sat through hundreds of meetings about people whose behavior has been troubling. I have found that asking people to speak in ordinary English is a useful ground rule for the conversation, although I have just enough of a clinical background to be the first offender against it. Leaving the jargon of our work behind, I am surprised at how much I can learn. When people say, for example, "Ellen needs a one-

---

[9]With people who have no clear way of expressing themselves, I start with the most obvious when guessing about someone's behavior. With the advent of facilitated communication, the most obvious thing is to ask James what standing with the refrigerator door open means to him. Sometimes, people with autism have explained, their behavior is confusing to them as well. So if James finds himself doing things that confuse him, he could let people know what might help him. As with everything else that might be construed as a positive approach, there is no right way to respond as much as a set of attitudes to act upon. Even if James doesn't use facilitated communication or spoken language, we can still ask, "How can I help?" This enables him to understand that our responses to his behavior are not to control him but to respond to him seriously.

to-one," I have learned to ask them what exactly that means. Sometimes it means that Ellen has a fascination with fire and needs someone to be around in case she decides to light one. Sometimes it means that Ellen is really bored and just likes to have company. If one-to-one were not translated, it could lead to assigning just anyone at all to work with her. Jargon expresses our needs as professionals, so it addresses our professional concerns. People don't need a one-to-one, agencies do. People might well need others around for a social life or need individual help to get through the day. One need is personal and can only be met personally. If someone's social preferences involve sports, crowds, and constant activity, this individual is very different from someone who enjoys staying at home and watching TV but who needs someone around in case of a bad seizure. The first person needs someone who enjoys doing those things—it's no fun trying to enjoy something with someone who doesn't enjoy it too. The second person needs someone compatible who enjoys staying inside and watching television.

The translation from jargon to English requires some speculation about what Ellen really wants. If Ellen likes fires, then maybe she wants to spend more time where there are things burning, which could mean anything from lighting votive candles in a church to watching fire fighters at work. Almost invariably, jargon draws us deeper into the system that Ellen's behavior might be protesting in the first place. When we use ordinary English, though, it can lead us back to the person.

The term *attention seeking* was a shorthand description that behaviorists used in order to be objective and to develop a technology for behavior change. Although this term initially helped in understanding how people learn, it has also become a way to devalue the needs of those people. A group of psychiatric survivors stated the following:

> Beyond the sale of all the pseudo-medical paraphernalia supporting it, the basic economics practiced by the mental health system and held in place by its oppressive structure is the state of attention. Utilizing their authority as "therapists," psychiatrists and psychologists continually promote the idea that adults should not pay attention when children demand it. We

are all familiar with the dismissal of a person with the sneering comment, "She's just doing that to get attention." By continually stressing the importance of ignoring people who are demanding attention, the "mental health" system creates the conditions most profitable to itself. The system "corners the market" on attention. Attention becomes a commodity to be controlled and sold like gas and electricity and water. This monopolizing and sale of valid, government-approved attention is bolstered by the mass media. Projecting stereotypes of "murdering crazies" running loose through society acts to keep people scared of each other, further increasing the value of "official" attention in the marketplace. The myth is fostered that only highly-trained, certified experts can provide attention, and that for a lay person to attempt to pay attention to someone who is hurting is highly dangerous and irresponsible. "Expert" attention, meanwhile, commands a very high price. Millions are made off of our continued oppression. (*Second revised draft policy statement for mental health system survivors.* Rational Island Press, n.d., pp. 4–16)

To put this into more personal terms: I have many friends in the field of human services. Most, like me, have had training in behavioral shaping. From time to time, I find myself too bored to watch television or too restless to read. It's too early to go to bed, and it's still too close to dinner to eat again—so I start phoning. I have nothing in particular to say, but I do want to talk. Perhaps you yourself have never done this, but certainly someone you know has done it to you. The only point of the conversation is the company. I have never (yet) had any of my friends say to me, "This seems like you are just looking for attention. What I will do now is hang up, but you can call me (tomorrow/next week/next year) when you have something meaningful to say and I will talk with you then."

Two other common and demeaning labels for behavior are noncompliant and avoidant. Some of us recognize noncompliant behavior at once as our own. Asked to choose which animal they would most like to be, few people would pick a sheep. Most of us identify, I think, more with eagles and weasels, seeing ourselves as people who can soar above it all or think of some clever way to burrow down and around unfair expectations. No one of my acquaintance has said, "I am proud to do what I am told without question." Many of us get away with bending and breaking rules because we are adroit enough to avoid notice. If, however, our evasions or authoritarian demands were not relatively sophisticated, or if we were already perceived as different, then we might well find ourselves further diminished by being labeled noncompliant.

The label of noncompliance not only dismisses any good reasons people might have for their behavior, it also sets us up to manage people in automatic and unthinking ways. Obviously, if someone's problem behavior is noncompliance, then compliance reflexively becomes the programmatic objective. As a result there are therapeutic programs to "teach" compliance. People are told to stand up and sit down, simply because they are told to, and then rewarded with a piece of sugar or treacly verbal praise.

Rather than asking why a person is unwilling to cooperate, services often choose this kind of coercive programming. Many of us avoid things when we fail to see the point of them, if we feel the demand is unfair or if it makes us feel inadequate. Few of us would feel that the remedy to this avoidance would be to have someone coerce us into doing as we were told without protest. Indeed, if we truly wanted to teach cooperation, we might try demonstrating it ourselves. Rather than training people to do our bidding, we could demonstrate cooperation by asking people what they want and how we can help them get it. This is not to say that we can necessarily deliver, but few people are insulted at being asked what we can do for them. This takes almost no time (compared to writing and implementing a program to coerce), and it takes no extra staff.

Avoidant behavior also seems to be a vice most often found in others. A service user who chronically refuses to leave for work can become the object of a behavior program that uses incentives for being punctual or a series of increasingly unpleasant consequences (from loss of pleasurable activity to being forcibly removed) for being stubborn. This strict standard is considered reasonable, apparently, because no dedicated, self-motivated professional would ever call in sick while enjoying good health. For one thing, that would be wrong. For another, we would expect our supervisor and a large assistant to visit us, determine if our claim of illness was really the case, and, if they found it not so, escort us physically back to work. If anyone did this to you, you would reasonably call the police or your lawyer—unless you are a client and your team has approved this sort of intervention for your avoidant behavior.

This is not to imply that a person's sudden decision to act independently may not be a problem. It may well be.[10] But just because the problem is real does not grant us the right to dictate a solution. The people I have met who refuse to go to work or who are avoidant always have good reasons for their actions. Often work is really just daycare for people with disabilities and is unpaid and meaningless. Or the person may have a medication schedule that makes him or her sluggish in the morning and would be better off working evenings. The reasons that these people might not want to go ahead with the day planned for them are as numerous as those anyone has for not wanting to go to work on any given day.

The argument I most often hear from staff members about this is: "I don't have a choice. If I don't go to work, I would have no place to live." This argument has no force, though. When people with disabilities have the same range of choices of where they work and at what, and when they have the same realistic opportunities to earn real money, then our guesses as to why someone would not want to go to work will be different. Since 1865, the U.S. Constitution has had provisions to protect people from involuntary labor—this right is still seen as a privilege for people with disabilities. Furthermore, I am concerned about anyone who feels a lack of

---

[10]Most people who use services do not get a day off "just because." In fairness, many people who use our services need some assistance if only for safety, and if no one is with them, they are at risk. This, however, points us toward two changes we need to think about: 1) Why is there no one else in their lives other than scheduled staff to spend a day with? Not all of us spend our mental-health days alone. Helping to make and sustain these kinds of friendships can be strenuous work, given the social vacuum in which many people with disabilities survive. Pending that kind of relationship, though, another question arises: 2) Why don't people have enough control over the money that is spent on their behalf to be able to hire someone on their own? Traditionally, agencies assume that their staff members are the only people who can be hired.

choice. If I have limited opportunities, I am better served by working for more opportunity for everyone rather than rationalizing that there should be less for others. The economic exploitation of service users is no less repugnant than the exploitation of service providers.

So, rather than getting people more consistently to do what they are told, better we ask: What would they rather do instead? The answers to that question may be hard to determine and even harder to provide, but this effort can put us into real collaboration with people in making the lives of everyone involved more lively.

When people are labeled retarded, their motives, wishes, and needs are not taken seriously, which can heap frustration onto a lifetime of frustration. In the midst of wealth (we spend billions of dollars on services), they often live in poverty. Surrounded by people (staff, therapists, and administrators), they are often lonely. Forced to live in close quarters, they are usually expected not only to remain chaste but, in some programs, not even to touch one another except to shake hands. I have heard too many people labeled retarded told without irony: Adults don't hug. Instead of attending to the basic needs we all take quite seriously in our own lives, we focus on people's behavior as the primary object of our concern. This shift has robbed people's lives of life. Instead of stories, we focus on incident reports. Instead of a person's history and personality, we give data.

A group was meeting about what was going on with Sandra, a woman who none of us knew very well. She had just moved into a group home with five other people who, like her, had spent many years in a large state institution. She and the people working with her were still learning about one another.

One Saturday, Lisa, who worked in this group home, suggested she and Sandra go out for lunch. The town Sandra lived in was fairly small so the choice of restaurant was easy to make. Their luncheon had been pleasant enough and when it seemed to be over, Lisa got ready to leave. Sandra sat resolutely in her seat. Sandra didn't use words so Lisa guessed that Sandra wanted another cup of coffee, which she ordered. When Sandra had finished it, Lisa again got ready to leave, but Sandra did not. So Lisa thought that if she just waited a bit, Sandra would get restless and want to leave. Sandra did get restless and started going to the other tables teaching people how to share. When some of the other diners were noncompliant with her task demands, she sat on the floor. After a couple of hours of coaxing, explanation, and general despair, the owner called the police—not out of anger—but just to get some help in resolving this. When Sandra saw the police, she calmly yielded to their authority, got up, and left.

It is interesting that no one did what I have come to expect. No one said, "You know why she does that? I think it's for attention." Instead, the people at this meeting decided that this would probably be less of a puzzle if they knew Sandra better. So they told some stories they had heard about Sandra—how a neighbor, now in his 80s, remembered Sandra as a child 50 years ago, sitting with her mother on the front porch; how the neighbors liked Sandra's family; how, when Sandra's mother died, her father had no help at home and felt forced to send her to the state school. We wondered what that must have been like because none of us had been doubly abandoned like that as a child. We were talking about life in the institution when someone asked, "Have any of you ever eaten in the cafeteria there? You come in with the other 30 people from your unit, you all sit at once to eat, and then when it's time to leave, you all rise to go back." It struck us, suddenly, that maybe when Sandra was in the restaurant, she was waiting for everyone to get up as the sign that lunch was over. When Lisa had said lunch was over, Sandra could see quite plainly from her 40-plus years of group dining that lunch was over only when all the food was gone and everyone in the group got up to go.

A couple of things occurred to us. Sandra might be a visual learner, and we might best teach her to know a meal was finished with some ordinary visual cues such as putting her knife and fork on her plate. We also realized how much time Sandra had spent lonely and lost among many other people. This isolation was still going on even in this smaller group home. This meeting disturbed Lisa. She had seen Sandra primarily as a client, but once she saw Sandra as someone who could have been her neighbor growing up, her perceptions of Sandra changed. Lisa started inviting Sandra to visit her house, which turned out to be something they both enjoyed. Lisa was divorced and her last child was moving out of state. So she invited Sandra to live with her and Sandra agreed.

Obviously, the services supporting Sandra were flexible beyond just responding to her observable behavior. The people working with Sandra had learned that if they were going to develop decent and *personal*[11] services, they had to listen closely and respond personally. Their understanding of Sandra's difficult behavior invited them to rethink and change their own behavior.

Just as labeling people evokes powerful, negative stereotypes, labeling behaviors can evoke programmatic clichés. When a behavior is identified as attention seeking, the next step is almost certain to be a way of ignoring it.

Since the 1980s, business managers have begun to recognize the obvious: Providing customers with what they want tends to result in more satisfied customers. American business ignored this for a long time—I think not because Americans are fond of rudeness but because the concept of good business used to imply a product. Now that about 80% of our economy is service oriented, we have come to recognize that a good service not only provides people with what they want but delivers it with an attitude the customer appreciates. Both as providers and consumers, we are all becoming more familiar and sophisticated about what good service is, and as we grow in this awareness, we move along predictable, developmental paths.

---

[11]Don Trites reminds us that individual does not mean personal. An "individualized program" or "individual service plan" might address people one at a time, but what makes such consideration valuable is a service's capacity to take a person's personal preferences into account (D. Trites, personal communication).

Invention is the mother of necessity. New technologies create needs that they alone can fill. There is really no *need* for air travel, telephones, televisions, computers, faxes, automobiles, space exploration, or for any of the other features of 20th-century life that we take for granted. Once these technologies exist, though, most people choose to have them because they expand the realm of the possible.

When technologies are new, consumers are grateful for what they get. Henry Ford famously offered the public a Model T in any color they wanted, as long as they wanted black. When television was first available, no one complained that the picture was only in black and white. For that matter, when radios were introduced, people failed completely to notice the absence of a picture. As soon as we take possibilities for granted, they become needs. Once we *had* to have a car, the color became more important; once everyone had a television, getting a color set made a difference. These things elaborate upon one another: Most people today can't imagine their cars without radios, for example.

Similarly, when we first realized we could do better than simply warehousing people with disabilities, we relied, fairly uncritically, on the newest expert technology: behavior modification. At first, this technology demonstrated that "untrainable" people could indeed learn. From this we discovered that "uneducable" people could indeed make informed choices. Now that we take these abilities for granted, services are starting to support people's lives with the same range of choices that the general public has. We no longer assume people need to live in an institution or a group home or spend their days in a sheltered workshop or an "activity center." Fewer and fewer of us are surprised to see people with disabilities sharing houses with friends, living alone, or working for paychecks larger than minimum wage.

This has put the technology of behavior modification in a new position. Behavioral psychologists first used people with learning difficulties to demonstrate the power of their teaching technology. Invariably, it was the psychologists—later the team of professionals—who established the goals that would be taught. More and more people with disabilities are deciding for themselves what they need and how they want to get it. Behavior modification programs are rarely considered or used when people are in real (rather than in name-only) partnerships with the people who are helping them.

This is a profound political shift. All technologies at first tend to make themselves more important than the people they serve, and indeed, initially, technologies use the person. Most of us with our first car or on the first day we had our driver's license probably found ourselves being taken around by the car. After a while, though, we used the car to do only what we wanted. At first, getting the car itself is the goal. Eventually we see it for what it is: something we can use for mobility and convenience. Familiarity and accessibility with the technology help us to focus on what we want from it. Similarly, behavior modification technologies were initially exciting because they were a novel way of thinking about and changing behavior. With our focus on the method, we professionals were not overly concerned about what they actually accomplished. Now, we can see their effects in a broader context.

Many behaviorists, having persuaded themselves that behavior modification is value-free, are in a poor position to see how control is a value, central and implicit, in behavioral technology. As people labeled retarded get an increasing voice in how their lives are to be lived, behavioral programming will probably be used as often for people labeled retarded as it is for the general public. At present, however, the clear majority of people labeled retarded find themselves at risk for being controlled in ways that range from irrelevant to life threatening.

By labeling people's behavior, we often feel that we have the right to act on how the behavior affects us rather than on what the person doing it might be trying to communicate. If James's behavior says, "I'm hungry," but we react to it as if it were attention seeking, we manipulate him socially and he will *still* be hungry. If Sandra's behavior says she doesn't understand how meals end, even when verbally reminded, she might find herself labeled a noncompliant client and on a program to force her to surrender to the judgments of others. Even if this program works, she will only have learned to leave the table because someone has told her to.

If James becomes violently upset when people ask him why he is looking in the refrigerator, then I would be inclined to overlook mentioning it to him when he has the refrigerator door open. If he eats everyone else's food or eats until he makes himself sick, I might offer to make him a snack he enjoys before he goes into the kitchen or find something he likes doing that doesn't involve eating. If it seems he is eating past the point of satisfying his appetite, then he might well be eating out of boredom, anxiety, or for any of the many reasons that the rest of us eat when we aren't especially hungry. Ignoring his behavior and the function it serves for him or redirecting him to something that is irrelevant to him seems pointless. The feeling and rationale that people need to be controlled distracts us from more compelling questions: Who loves this person? Is this person comfortable and happy living here? Are these the people this person wants most to live with? These questions can create so much stress for service providers that it is often simpler—and not necessarily conscious—to ignore what people's behavior is saying and control them simply to maintain business as usual.

Chapter 3

⌒

The Politics
of Behaviorism

The institution did not become obsolete because people found it immoral: People found it immoral because it had been rendered obsolete. Once behaviorism showed that every person can learn and that the environment can often be a person's most powerful teacher, institutions became irrevocably obsolete and immoral. It has, alas, taken a generation to appreciate this fully.[1]

Similarly, in the struggle to stop the use of pain as a way to control behavior, the moral argument is obvious, but the *why* lacks all compulsion until there is a *how*. As communities have come to recognize their inherent skills in helping people with exceptional needs and act on these abilities, the need for aversives has disappeared just as the need for institutions has.

One of behaviorism's early agendas was to show itself in

---

[1]Initially, the most progressive group of thinkers in developing services—the parent movement—aimed to improve the institution because keeping people comfortable and clean was the best that most people dared to hope for. Ironically, the rise in federal funding in the 1960s to improve institutions came at the same time that behavioral technologies were making such places—clean or dirty—irrelevant.

strict contrast to the dynamic models of psychoanalysis. While Freud developed an intuitive system redolent with Greek myth, hidden motives, and uncertain outcomes, behaviorists used empirically measurable models of modern science (especially physics) and rejected psyche as an irrelevant construct and emotions as fictional constructs. In this spirit, behaviorism has represented itself as morally and politically neutral and as a value-free technology.

Skinner's work on operant conditioning, however, stood in such contrast to the prevailing Freudian view and—particularly for people who had been thought to be ineducable—held such power that the concept easily appeared to be modern and scientific.

> The world view of modernity is dominated by science and scientific technology and the modes of thought peculiar to them (Gehlen, 1980). It is rooted in the ideal of progress, a faith in the power of human abilities to be equal to any problem, the quest for certitude, and a devaluation of the traditional past (Shils, 1981). The cognitive style of modern consciousness tends toward the pragmatic and the rational. The focus of evaluation shifts from the ends of activity to means and their efficiency, as technique and technical considerations achieve paramount importance. Utility emerges as a generally agreed upon value (Ellul, 1964). The aims of prediction and control and a style of planning and decision making in which emotional and aesthetic consideration are subservient to the rational and pragmatic are essential features of modern organizational direction, whether those organizations be communist bureaucracies or capitalist industrial corporations (Berger, Berger, & Kellner, 1973). Science becomes the ultimate source of knowledge and the model for all forms of intellectual activity (Hayek, 1952; Winner, 1977). [Woolfolk & Richardson, 1984, p. 778]

Since the 18th century, science in Western culture increasingly has become the ultimate arbiter of what reality is. The earliest examples of operant conditioning, as it turns out, were reported at the very beginning of this scientific era, but their appearance was too premature for the culture fully to absorb the implications. Almost 200 years before

Skinner was Bisset, a Scottish shoemaker, born in 1721 in Perth.

Bisset moved to London, married a woman of some wealth, and curious after reading about a "learned horse" at St. Germaine, tried his hand at animal training. His success was little short of remarkable. The former shoemaker had no trouble imposing his will on dogs and horses for simple acts of obedience. He next taught two monkeys an unusual routine. One danced on a tightrope while the second illuminated his brother's movements by holding a candle in one paw and providing musical accompaniment on a barrel organ with the other. Bisset next turned his attention to domestic cats, a species notoriously uninterested in school. The results inspired one of the Pinchbeck family, the famous showmen and builders of automata, to persuade Bisset to perform publicly in London. Although Pinchbeck dropped out of the proceedings at the last moment, Bisset's "Cat's Opera" was an enormous success. After the parade of horses, dogs, and monkeys, three cats proceeded to play tunes by striking their paws on a dulcimer and squealing in different keys, producing some pleasing feline harmonies, all the while staring intently at sheet music propped up in front of them. This performance garnered Bisset some £1,000 and encouraged his further efforts.

He taught canaries, linnets, and sparrows to spell by selecting appropriate alphabet cards, had a rabbit beat a drum with its hind legs (a stunt which goes back at least to the fourteenth century), and trained six turkeys to do a country dance (admittedly, he later confessed, by placing them on a heated floor . . .). He even taught a turtle to "fetch and carry" like a dog. After six months of training, the turtle with blackened claws, scratched out any selected name on a chalk-covered floor! It was only after these successes and the additional accomplishment of training goldfish—to do exactly what is never stated—that he applied his efforts to that beast of legendary stupidity and intractability—the pig. (Jay, 1986, p. 10)

Bisset trained and exhibited a "sapient pig" in Dublin, but the performance was interrupted by an outraged official who beat Bisset and "threatened the life of the pig" (Jay, pp. 10–11). Immediately after this, Bisset fell ill and died without publishing his technique. Apparently, the first monograph on the subject is *The Expositor; or Many Mysteries Unraveled*, by the conjurer William Frederick Pinchbeck (1805). This work was written as a series of letters (see Appendix A) that reveal the technology of training a "pig of knowledge" to answer questions by picking up cards.

Other such sapient animals had been reported. Leibniz, the German mathematician and philosopher, observed such a horse and reported that it could only provide answers known to its keeper and so he deduced, correctly, that the animal was not psychic or "learned" but simply responding to some undetected set of cues. Pinchbeck demonstrated that by rewarding successive approximations one can teach a pig to pick up lettered and numbered cards.[2]

One is a bit taken aback at how much was foreshadowed by these enterprising buskers. Pinchbeck's pig serves the same role as Skinner's pigeons in the sense that the power of the technique—if not the technician—is demonstrated with a species thought to be stupid. It is significant that neither the intent nor the result was to improve the reputations of the "stupid and intractable" animals as much as it was the "triumph of form over content, means over ends." In both the 18th- and 20th-century examples, the behaviorists were considered the remarkable elements of the phenomenon.

"Perhaps," said the Eccentric Mirror (London, 1813), "no period ever produced a more singular character than Bisset: though in the age of apathy in which he lived, his merit was but little rewarded. At any former era of time, the man who could assume a command over the dumb creation, and make them act with a docility which far exceeded mere brutal instinct,

---

[2]Critics have used this type of cueing in order to discredit the validity of facilitated communication. Certainly, the physical contact of the facilitator and the person has obvious potential for prompting, however unintentional it might be. The difference that critics fail to mention, though, is the work that goes into training the animals to respond and the time it takes to reinforce the appropriate behavior. Cueing seems far less probable an explanation for the numerous examples of people who demonstrate previously unsuspected literacy and cognitive abilities almost immediately. I can certainly appreciate the confusion facilitated communication has caused as it defies a great deal of the training most professionals have had. However, a great confusion can lead to an entirely new awareness while denial generally leads to personal, spiritual, and intellectual rigor mortis.

would have been looked upon as possessed of supernatural powers. . . ." (Jay, 1986, p. 11)

Rather than revise their low opinions of "dumb creation," "brutal instinct," or even the individual pig, the praise went to Bisset as a unique wonder. It would hardly have diminished Bisset's achievement to credit the pig as more perspicacious than the public had previously imagined. Similarly, Skinner was widely praised for training pigeons, yet it was the pigeons, after all, who did the learning.

Bisset's infamy has significant implications for the people whose lives have been powerfully governed by these controlling technologies, the most obvious being that when people learn something through behavioral instruction, the technique gets the credit for their accomplishment. Think of how different your own education was. Most of us went to schools where the honor rolls listed students. I don't recall any prizes for professors whose students had the highest grade-point averages. At commencement, the graduates are the ones congratulated, not the faculty.

This has been a striking and recurring difference between behavioral teaching and ordinary education. The unspoken assumption that the teaching technology is much more powerful than the learner has also taken an interesting turn in the study of animals' use of language. Ironically, it has been behavioral psychologists who have been dismissive whenever primates use signs in ways that appear conversational. This, they claim, is not language as we know it but merely imitative learning. Given the behavioral model of learning, this seems a curious criticism.

Behaviorism gave people skills with one hand, but withheld their dignity with the other. Kipnis (1987) found this good news/bad news process at work in three areas: work, social status and relationships, and personal growth and change.

Work is often the place where we feel our greatest competence, in the pleasure of making things happen and of just generally doing. For those of us who enjoy our work, pleasure can come from the variety of things we can make happen as well as from the obvious and sometimes immediate effects we can have on the external world. Many of the work opportunities for people with disabilities are severely limited and hold few possibilities for job satisfaction.

While jobs in the industrialized world have become increasingly individualized, the expectations of work for people labeled retarded still tend toward constant conformity. This is true not only for the clients but also for the staff as regulatory and funding agencies increase their demands. In most sheltered workshops, though, the clients form the base of the organizational pyramid and, as always, bear the greatest burden of conformity. To enforce this sense of conformity, workshops typically use behavioral technologies to exert control.

Kipnis (1987) "found that satisfactory work of employees doing routinized work was attributed by managers to the system of work, rather than to the skills, abilities, and motivations of the employees. The reverse was true for employees doing nonroutinized work" (p. 33).

> Managers attributed poor work in routine settings to their employees' poor attitudes and lack of motivation to work hard. After all, if the work had been so simplified that even a child could do it, and still errors occurred, the only logical explanation was that the employees were deliberately malingering. Equally poor work done by employees in nonroutine settings was attributed to the difficulty of the work, certainly a less hostile explanation. (Kipnis, 1987, p. 33)

Most work programs open to people with disabilities are based on routines involving simple tasks. It is not hard to see how the control implicit in behavioral technology drives a wedge between those supervising and those supervised. In this climate, staff members frequently ask, "How can we motivate the clients?" But when staff members themselves feel overwhelmed by their work, they rarely ask for help in getting themselves motivated as much as they seek help to deal with stress, burnout, and the demands of their own supervisors.

Environment can be stronger than will. Unfortunately, the same environments that are so frustrating and unfulfilling for people with disabilities work just as rigorously against their staff. As requirements for licensing and funding agencies become increasingly routinized and intrusive, a "good program" will be seen as the direct result of strong monitoring. This robs people—especially direct services staff—of any sense of responsibility, creativity, or ownership. If this analysis is correct, we can expect licensing agencies to ask, in genuine perplexity, "How can we motivate direct services staff?"

The essential link of feeling, based on actually being, responsible for excellence can easily be broken by paternalism, however well intended. Because bureaucratic systems typically respond to their weakest links with stronger regulation, mistakes by a less skilled person increase regulated routine and thereby alienate more competent people who will leave, opening the way for more incompetent people who will stay and make even more mistakes that will invoke even more memos, policies, regulations, and deadening routine.

When the quality of direct services is considered, the reason invariably cited for the high staff turnover rate, lack of staff ability, or lack of staff enthusiasm is money. Clearly, it is unrealistic to expect a committed work force for the salaries that most people in direct services earn, but money is not the entire reason. Much of the dedication one finds greatly exceeds what people are paid. What is often conspicuously lacking is basic respect for the ingenuity that people—both in direct services and client roles—bring with them to the job. Throwing more money at people who are not respected as intelligent and worthy simply creates a more expensive dysfunctional system.

Work is not only the place where most of us feel reliably competent, it is also where we make many of our friends. But the use of controlling technologies affects *social status and relationships* and can foster social inequities.

Kipnis (1987) found that managing people through controlling tactics sets up a cycle of estrangement. If success is due to the technology, then people are seen as needing external control. The more they are seen as out of their own control, the less status they have, the less they are taken seriously, and the more they need their helpers' assistance. Studies (Kipnis, 1987) of dating and married couples suggested that those who made decisions unilaterally expressed less affection than did couples who saw themselves as sharing power equally. The implications for the lives of people with disabilities and for those who would be their direct services partners are clear.

In considering *personal growth and change*, Kipnis (1987) wondered if therapists who use controlling technologies perceive their clients less favorably than those who use more nondirective therapies. This seems, intuitively, to be a good guess. One psychologist who has been an enthusiastic proponent of using pain to control the behavior of people with disabilities apologized for "anthropomorphizing" people with autism. The more inhuman the technology, the less human the subjects of the technology necessarily appear. As the humanity of people recedes, the technology itself assumes increasing allure and value.

Another distinction of behaviorism from the Freudian model was that it worked independent of insight. Because behaviorism did not require awareness, none was sought and none was found. To this day, there are people who imagine—contrary to the actual experience of many—that people labeled retarded lack insight. This myth, compounded with the lack of opportunity for many labeled people to make their own decisions, creates the dangerous moment when the well-meaning collaborate with the well-trained to "do what is best for the person." Sometimes, we actually *do* the right thing for people. But the ways in which we make decisions about other people's lives cannot do much to guarantee that result.

> What changes may be expected in day-to-day relations between friends and associates as people rely on the technology of social control to obtain compliance? One obvious answer is that with technology, influencing agents no longer have to beg, act polite, or simply ask. They can get their way now, by using the right combination of words, by using reinforcements in strategic ways, or even by changing other's environments. Although these increments in social power may make friends and associates more compliant . . . this added control will make influencing agents more arrogant. We move rapidly from a posture of gratitude to one of easy indifference and worse as we become the origins of people's behavior. (Kipnis, 1987, p. 33)

Behaviorism is clearly a powerful technology for teaching, but power is a difficult tool to wield. Indeed, control over others almost invariably slips from our grasp as a tool we use and becomes a goal that uses and controls us.

> From its inception, behavior therapy adopted that most modern of sensibilities . . . the *technological attitude* . . . or *technocratic consciousness* . . . Successful technologies, however, carry with them a number of potential drawbacks. One unhappy effect of the proliferation of technology and technological thinking within contemporary society has been to drive out other forms of thinking, often resulting in a triumph of form over content, means over ends, methodology over theory. . . . The ascendance of methodological and technical concerns can divert our attention from those troublesome questions that address the value of the goals achieved by the technology or that ask upon what basis such goals are to be determined. (Woolfolk & Richardson, 1984, p. 779)
>
> It is not surprising, then, that behavioral technologies based on persuasive influence tactics are found in all of the applied fields, including leadership training, jury selection, marketing, advertising, and psychotherapy. Books about how to get your way are psychology's updates of yesterday's ju ju beads, hex signs, and voodoo spells. [Kipnis, 1987, p. 32]

Although behavior modification aspires to the myth of scientific objectivity, it really is closely allied with some of the biases found in our culture. This myth of being value-free puts behavior modification at risk for being co-opted into a political system of "protector oppressors." As Woolfolk and Richardson (1984) wrote

> Behavior therapy contains few concepts that allow the therapist to take any perspective on the client external to the client's frame of reference. Freud, at least, could within his system unabashedly advocate the ability to love and the ability to work as universal criteria of competence in living. The behavior therapist has no analogous pronouncement to make. In the absence of such normative concepts as health and sickness, growth and stagnation, which in other systems transcend the preferences of the individual, the behavior therapist has fewer categories with which to evaluate client behavior. Thus, without an independent therapeutic compass of this sort the behavior therapist is always thrown back upon the preferences of the individual. One might, in fact, argue that this is a principal ideological vec-

tor of behavior therapy: to dispense with perspectives that limit the rights of individuals to pursue self-chosen goals in the most expedient manner science can produce. (p. 783)

This lack of a "therapeutic compass" was, potentially, an opportunity to use behavior modification as a tool to foster a person's actual wishes. But when behavior modification was first used in the field of developmental disabilities, the client was the service system not the person targeted by behavior programs. In this context, behaviorism unwittingly perpetrated a system of protective oppression that has effectively kept people with disabilities powerless to act in their own lives.

Many behavioral practitioners have militantly refused to recognize the driving, internal political values of behavior modification. Ostensibly, behavior modification relies on the values of the client, but, in reality, it relies on the values of the behavior therapist. For people who are assumed to be incompetent, especially people who do not use language to communicate, teams of professionals, parents, legal personnel, and advocates have allowed their own judgments to rule. When the goals of an individual are unclear or in opposition to the culture in which funding sources and therapists work, the one compass that behavior modification has—the person's wishes—is taken away. Without these wishes as a guide, the behavior specialist's choices become, *de facto*, the person's choices. Given the overwhelming political power of professional opinion and the dangers it can present, it is not surprising that what began as a technique for *teaching* rapidly became a technology for *controlling*.

Beyond the manipulation of rewards and punishments, behavior modification also relied on two forms of discipline presented in a new guise. The practice of "time out" from reinforcement was a reworking of the seclusion room, which in turn was simply a therapeutic version of solitary confinement. Similarly, observing people rigorously—both to establish a baseline for the behavior and to discern its antecedents and consequences—has a parallel tradition in the history of the prison.

An innovation in prison design was Bentham's Panopticon, a circular prison that placed the inmates in cells facing a central tower. The tower was designed in such a way that observers could not themselves be seen. The cells were backlighted with large barred windows so that an inmate's every movement could be detected. This arrangement is familiar to every student of psychology as the one-way mirror. Bentham had also tried to design a system of tubes in order to listen to the prisoners, but 18th-century technology did not permit this without the prisoners being able to listen to the conversations of their keepers as well. A microphone in the ceiling eliminates this problem for modern psychologists.

As Foucalt (1979) summarized:

> There are two images, then, of discipline. At one extreme, the discipline-blockade, the enclosed institution, established on the edges of society, turned inwards towards negative functions: arresting evil, breaking communications, suspending time. At the other extreme, with panopticism, is the discipline-mechanism: a functional mechanism that must improve the exercise of power by making it lighter, more rapid, more effective, a design of subtle coercion for a society to come. The movement from one project to the other, from a schema of exceptional discipline to one of generalized surveillance, rests on historical transformation: the gradual extension of the mechanisms of discipline throughout the seventeenth and eighteenth centuries, their spread throughout the whole social body, the formation of what might be called in general the disciplinary society. (p. 209)

This "disciplinary society" is pervasive in human services. Most services have recognized the punitive aspects of segregation and isolation, but people have been slower to see the culture of observation as punitive. Subjecting others to scrutiny is itself an act of power and dominance, and the fact that the observers themselves cannot be observed underscores the inequality of power. Bentham intended observation to be a part of the punishment: The prisoners had no power to observe or even know they were being observed. When psychologists observe, it is part of treatment as well. Generally, the more controlling and punitive the culture of the service, the more these one-way surveillance techniques are found. People with difficult behavior are routinely housed in discipline-blockade enclosed institutions and their constant exposure to the observation of others is generally taken for granted.[3]

Although observation is prone to obvious abuse, I do not want to be overly simplistic about it, either. Sometimes having hidden observers can be helpful. For example, children are sometimes more comfortable and better understood if they are with someone loving and familiar than strangers. Observing a child playing with a parent can give a more accurate picture of the situation at hand. A therapist or a teacher might well invite an outsider to observe someone as a way of getting a fresh perspective. The key element, of course, is the invitation and the collaborative nature of the process. Nevertheless, the idea of therapy or supervision while being observed by invisible others strikes me as a strangely artificial technique. I know of some places where a hidden mentor phones instructions to trainees during their work. Unless there is some serious risk of contagion, this kind of quarantine often attempts to disguise a crude political control with a flimsy mask of pseudoscience.

When I was visiting a "mental handicap" hospital in Europe, the head nurse was particularly pleased that I should arrive to see the new monitoring system. With a camera in the bedroom of each resident, a single worker could watch a bank of video monitors and thus monitor everyone simultaneously. The ostensible reason for this was the high incidence of seizures and sleep disorders, but nothing was mentioned about how the people whose bedrooms had been so improved felt about this gross intrusion into their privacy.

Objectively, observation and assessment are ways to control professionals as well. Generally, in the name of fiscal planning, professional activity is monitored and rendered into data. This kind of management externally imposes controls over services that, I suspect, are best provided by internally motivated people, who are the most likely to avoid or

---

[3]Obviously, people can be subjected to observation in what appears to be their own homes. People who live alone or in accommodations that appear homey find that their homes can quickly change back into institutions with professional practice. Staff observing and taking data, hidden cameras, or movement detectors can create the same atmosphere of surveillance as Bentham's large prison did.

escape this kind of regime. As creative people leave, less inspired people take their places. Attempts to improve or maintain quality through external control can, paradoxically, drive the quality of the service inexorably down.

This has been a failure of the behavioral perspective all along—a failure to take into account the sensibilities of people whose behavior is of concern. Even the most apparently innocuous of behavioral traditions, taking baseline data, can become a political tool. When we observe people objectively, we can gain insight that our subjective impressions miss, but danger comes when observing people objectively is all we do. We need to be more rigorous in analyzing our own behavior and recognize that our intentions have often differed from our actions.

When behavioral psychologists first began working in institutions, the people who lived in them were barely seen as people. The idea of collaborating with the wishes and needs of labeled people was not as much ridiculous as unthought of. One might just as well have proposed consulting with the sideshow pig or the laboratory pigeon. Without mutually respectful relationships, power becomes dangerous. We can hardly be surprised at violence, against one's self or others, in the loveless and sterile environments we have provided for people with disabilities. Where there is no mutual respect, the only right is might. Where there is no love, power becomes the object of desire.

Chapter 4

◆

▬ The Hierarchy of Control ▬

"Positive" Reinforcement

Behavioral programs often appear in the context of training people for "independent living." Independence is central to our American identity—from our celebrated declaration of it to the lone cowboy of the American frontier. Henry Thoreau, having written about his solitary cabin by Walden Pond, became an emblem of this spirit, although people sometimes forget he was hardly a recluse, living only a mile from town. His project in independent living was only selectively so and his life was more social than not. In any case, even if most people really did live independently, it is hard to imagine how they would achieve this by systematically submitting to the judgments of others.

Rosemary Dybwad once visited an institution in England where a woman in her 40s was dressing age inappropriately as a teenager—as if most ordinary people in their 40s struggle to look middle-aged. In any case, the clinical staff had discerned this as a problem, developed a program to address it, and trained the staff to say emphatically, "I am a woman. Can you say that back to me? I am a woman." For several weeks, the woman simply stared at the people rehearsing this unusual conversational gambit, but eventually she repeated, somewhat haltingly, "I am . . . a woman!" The staff members reinforced this accomplishment immediately by saying, "Good girl!"

Oddly, people don't see the paradox of training people to "act like adults" while reinforcing their behaviors with childish and irrelevant "rewards." I feel a strong mixture of sorrow and anger when adults present a behavior card with checks or stars or stickers on it showing they were "good" during certain intervals of the day. One colleague was dissuaded only with great effort from having people in a group home wear their behavior cards on strings around their necks. Her logic was that the general community seeing these cards would naturally praise the people for their accomplishments. Of course, tokens and star charts are only the crudest examples, but earning food or "privileges" that every other adult in the world takes for granted is just as insulting in its own ways.

I visited a day program to meet Norma, a woman who seriously hurt herself. Other than hitting her head frequently and forcefully, she did nothing particularly exciting. Norma had beaten her forehead so hard and for so long that she had permanently altered her appearance. When time allowed, someone would take her in the agency van to go shopping, run an errand, or just drive around town. During these excursions, a member of staff brought along a cooking timer set to ring at 15-minute intervals, at which time, if she had not hurt herself, she could "earn an edible reinforcer." The program psychologist called this "a community-experience program," which in a way it was, but what in the world was the community likely to conclude from the experience of seeing a woman in her 30s going about town and getting candy from other adults who had been prompted to do this by a cake timer? And even more to the point, what was this woman supposed to think of herself from what was happening to her? These sorts of half-baked ideas are often tagged as "positive programming."

The tradition of using edibles came directly and uncritically from animal laboratory experiments. Its overuse suggests the absence of any of the ordinary things that might motivate ordinary people. Generally, edibles and artificial praise are used when people are in highly segregated settings and asked to do things that don't make a great deal of sense to them.

Every now and again, people point out that behavior therapy has become a lot more sophisticated than these outmoded practices suggest. The problem I have encountered is that the political basis for behavior modification is immutable and, until people with disabilities are in a position to decline these therapies, no amount of sophistication will remove the elements of control and coercion implicit in the theory supporting these practices. Beyond that, however, I have yet to see such sophistication put into practice. I have yet to see behaviorism actually used in a social context of equality and regard.

The use of unusual reinforcers is a good way to alert ourselves to unusual social circumstances. We rarely have to reinforce people for eating foods they enjoy or being with people they love. So, as a general principle, it seems sensible to ask if what we are reinforcing is so important that it requires this odd kind of intervention. In addition, we often forget to think about the political implications of such interventions. Essentially we are coercing people to do our bidding, and, more often than not, their submission is more for our convenience than theirs.

People often react to this observation with guilt, as if they were accused of intentionally oppressing those they serve. Although I think these kinds of programs *are* generally oppressive, only rarely does that oppression seem to be a conscious effect. Instead of hectoring people about their practices, I am much more comfortable inviting people to look at what they do (and inviting them to help me see what I do) without debasing their often decent motives.

Would I ever use an edible reinforcer? My hunch is probably not. It wouldn't make sense given the way I work. But just because I don't see how it would be possible to be respectful and use an edible reinforcer hardly rules out the possibility. I have had, several times too often, the sobering experience of denouncing something only to find—within hours—a good reason to do it. Besides, this argument is not meant to be dogma about practices as much as it is about the political context of their application. Still, it is hard to see how using an edible reinforcer could occur in a spirit of equality and collaboration. Too often I have seen reinforcers of all kinds used simply as tools to enforce compliance.

Indeed, other than to prove how powerful the teacher—and how powerless the student—is, it is hard to see the pleasure or value in such exercises. If the person to be trained already enjoys standing up and sitting down, then something the person doesn't enjoy is sometimes chosen as a way of making the point: Do what you're told. Yates (1990) wrote of a consulting psychologist who had developed a "guaranteed compliance program," in which a person is physically forced to do something and then rewarded for it. This at least has the honesty to show plainly the lesson of the person's powerlessness. I also know people who have made training videos demonstrating exactly this kind of compliance procedure. They claimed it helped people who couldn't focus long enough to learn to do so. This training would teach the person a basic skill—attending to directions—and, from that, the pleasure of having learned it. I appreciate their intentions, but coercion is not necessary in effective teaching. Some of us have had teachers who thought so, but these are rarely the ones we recall with affection, if at all.

I have listened to groups of people who have been subjected to such "positive" programs talk about what they thought of them. Their reactions ranged from bewilderment that they should somehow change anything about themselves for such piffle as stars, tokens, pennies, and snack foods to indignation that their lives should be so unfeelingly manipulated. People have described how they had to feign indifference to ordinary pleasures: "If you like ice cream, you have to pretend you don't. Otherwise, they make you do things for ice cream." More than one person has complained of these demeaning practices. I remember one man, especially, who mockingly parroted, "Oh! Here's a dollar! Isn't that *great?* Here's your *reward* for the *week!*" Another man sarcastically observed, "Maybe they think I should go out and buy a *dolly* for myself? Or maybe a nice toy *truck!*"

Ironically, behavior modification, which once went to such lengths to distance itself from psychiatric tradition, now works comfortably within psychiatry's medical-hierarchical model of "special units," "special schools," and "residential treatment." A highly trained shift staff, even one with a high turnover, can indeed provide decent acute-care medical service, but by now we know there is almost no hope of this model's ever giving people anything useful for an ordinary life.

This is a hard saying, and I emphasize that it is the model of service that lacks all hope, not the people who work in it. This can be a complicated argument but, having worked in an institution, I took a long time to realize that the energy and goodwill of my co-workers could not give people decent lives so long as they lived in the institution. By working in institutions, we were also supporting a system that enforced the unnecessary isolation and social segregation of the people we worked with. However, we worried that, had we left, we would leave people in an even worse situation. Over time, though, it became clear to me that if the people living in institutions had no need to be living there, and if the people working there had the energy and commitment to support them with respect, then the only barrier to including them in ordinary places was the model of the institution itself. When People First groups have considered this problem of good person–bad service, they have come to this same conclusion that models of service that hurt the service user are often unfair to the service worker as well and that an alliance to change this situation is more useful than either group blaming the other.

Again, most of us who provide services do not actively intend to control or demean those we serve. Indeed, the people who provide services directly are often the people who know an individual the best and most personally. But often the unspoken expectation is that direct service staff will control behavior.

Aides were found to be the most coercive and it was suggested this was because they were allocated so much responsibility for

direct patient care, security, and order. Psychologists, psychiatrists, and social workers on the other hand were generally permissive, but unlike the aides, were detached from this intense
and direct responsibility for the patients. (Tognoli, Hamad, &
Carpenter, 1978, p. 143)

In a real community, though, the "permissive professionals"
would be as responsible to the people served as those providing direct support. I have found that some of the more punishing suggestions for behavior modification come from
those who know the people best: the people who are in daily
contact with a person. I used to think that this was because
they did not have "adequate training" to know how they
could work with people without hurting them. Sometimes
that has been the case, but direct service staff need assurance
that they themselves will not be punished when the people
they serve appear out of control. Too often, direct service
staff are not respected or trusted much more than the people
with whom they work. We will not make the bureaucratic
pyramid any more efficient or open to change with increased
regulation or monitoring. We need to find a spirit of mutual
respect and equality in our work—both for those we serve as
well as those with whom we serve.

The monitoring and control of teachers is a similar concern for schools. The recent trend to connecting teacher pay
with "excellence" is a good example of this. Excellence, of
course, is defined by the results that the teacher's students
achieve on standardized tests. One natural consequence of
this is for schools to "educate the best and shoot the rest."
This does not result in any kind of excellence I would recognize. Because no one, in principle, is opposed to excellence,
the question arises as to how this could be defined in human
terms and in a collaborative way. I imagine that the process
would be at least as interesting as the answers, but I can't
imagine how excellence could be uniformly defined across an
entire country. What kind of an educational system would we
have if teachers and students began each year with a few days
of defining what they wanted to accomplish and if the results
of these efforts were then handed up the administrative lad-
der to inform the servant-leaders at the top? This might be

more compelling, not to mention more effective, than having an education czar prescribing excellence as if it were a medication. Indeed, no such prescription—in any sense of the word—exists because nothing is good for everyone. Yet policies and teaching technologies are chosen in remote offices as solutions for people who are never spoken to or in any real way consulted. We cannot mandate excellence; we can only work to inhibit carelessness and indifference. But these are matters of the heart and of caring and intuition, not matters of standardization.

Of equal significance is the question of why people hunger for and achieve excellence. In 1992, the national press widely reported a British schoolteacher's filling in a student's examination book and handing it in for grading. The teacher was not quoted as to his motive, but for whatever reasons he achieved the essential purpose in a system whose ultimate concern is outcomes: Results are more important than how they were achieved or even what they represent. Naturally, the teacher was cited for unethical behavior, but he could just as honestly be considered an effective teacher for responding so directly to what national policy demanded: measurable results or progress.[1]

Devotion to an abstract sense of efficiency seems inhuman. I have occasionally been brought to visit programs with the description "You'll like visiting here. Fran runs a good house. Never any problems." In other words, if Fran created an environment where people were alive and honest, with all the problems that this entails, she would be at risk for being

---

[1] These kinds of arguments about what education should be are often cast, dishonestly it seems to me, as either–or. *Either* we have an open-ended process in education that has no measurable goals and no direction except the learner's wishes or an individual teacher's preferences *or* there are national standards by which students are measured at year's end, clearly showing what they have learned and what they have not. Of course, education could include both, striking a balance between giving the confidence and competence to keep learning and instruction in specific disciplines of knowledge. Because this balance is impossible to set except in the context of each learner, it has no value for people who use hierarchical management structures. However, if we assume people generally want to learn, and teachers typically strive for excellence, then the need for standardized and remote control would be reduced.

dismissed as incompetent. The only way to run a house with no problems is to keep it uncluttered with the problem-prone living. Fran herself may want to provide a service that has some tolerance for human quirkiness, but not only is her reputation in the agency at stake, licensers also exert pressures. To give just one small example: Some staff were talking about how the house they worked in had become oppressively controlling for several people. The licensers cited them for failing to label all the leftovers in the refrigerator even though they were wrapped in clear plastic. Conceivably, some people might benefit from this labeling, but how sad that the licensers essentially assumed that people in this house had nothing better to do with their time. In a way, if I were invited to help people think about what a good home requires, I would be more concerned about why these people had so much time on their hands.

People working in direct services often are under pressure to control difficult behavior not only for their own safety, but for their professional reputations as well. This does not allow a great deal of latitude in which to assess a person's reasons for acting in ways that are troublesome. An initial attempt at positive programming, an effort at a benign form of control, often does not work because the incentives for the person are either trivial or demeaning. And when these bland inducements to change fail, instead of escalating to more powerful reinforcers, people often abandon reward for punishment and adopt negative reinforcement as their intervention styles.

Although people are—quite properly—insulted by candy, tokens, stars, and other childish treats, they are not extravagant in their pleasures. What people with disabilities seem to want most is what most people want: a loving home, good food, sleep, relationships, something sensible to do with the day, and the opportunity to make the rhythms of all these fit their tastes. It seems perverse to turn these ordinary experiences into programmatic rewards when any decent service would make them available noncontingently.

What is really at stake is the opportunity for pleasure, which cannot be controlled and usually threatens those who want to control others. Pain can be reliably quantified[2] and inflicting it on another takes power from the person receiving it. Pleasure, however, is unique to the person, is hard to measure, and gives power to those who receive it. Some people argue fervently for the power of positive reinforcement, yet I have never heard of people seriously escalating reinforcers to bestow large sums of money or trips to Paris by way of Tahiti, though people who believe in this form of control would do this more often if they practiced as emphatically as they preached. In actual practice, rather than getting increasingly powerful rewards for good behavior, people too often find the exact opposite happening to them.

—

Helen, a woman in her 40s whose chief pleasure in life was shopping, made the serious mistake of hitting a psychologist, who promptly wrote a behavior program about it. With this program, Helen could earn "shopping privileges" only after 3 days of not hitting anyone. The psychologist thought that using shopping in this way was positive reinforcement, although Helen, who had been used to going shopping whenever she liked, probably did not think this was very positive at all.

This story is striking in two ways. First, Helen was living in a community program that prided itself on its compassionate support for "special people." Very few adult women in North America consider shopping a privilege. Some intentional communities control the actions of their members, but these are acceptable only to the degree that these communities are voluntary and do not use public funds.

The second issue is the psychologist's unquestioned assumption that Helen's hitting required a behavior management program. Although anyone getting hit is something to

---

[2]By quantifying pain, I am suggesting that an electric shock of a certain intensity can be reasonably expected to cause most people pain. How much pain may vary from person to person, but few people are likely to find it pleasant. Similarly, the severity of loss may vary from person to person, but most people would consider losing their freedom through a prison term a painful experience. Nevertheless, we can't realistically "sentence" someone to a term of pleasure by uniformly assigning him or her to any one activity or place.

be taken seriously—violence is a problem that needs to be addressed wherever we find it—it seems unjust for the psychologist who had been hurt to be given such a free hand in return. Nowhere else in our society is the person offended allowed to punish the offender.

This behavioral program was deemed a success. Helen stopped hitting the psychologist, largely it seems because the psychologist learned to stay out of her way. No one else seemed to have agitated Helen quite as much. No one had asked Helen why she had stopped hitting, or, for that matter, why she ever had begun in the first place. In any case, the program seemed to be working so well that people decided that Helen might now be able to go 4 days of not hitting before earning the privilege of spending her own money. Using this sort of logic, Helen's behavior might become so good she would never go shopping again.

One of the pleasures and difficulties of adult life is that it so often requires us to recognize opposing ideas as simultaneously true: Although control is implicit in reinforcement technologies, so is the potential for liberation. Behaviorism has been a powerful educational technology, and yet true education widens a person's range of abilities, which diminishes the possibility of being controlled at all. The argument here does not concern the technology of behaviorism but the politics of its application.

I hope this point is obvious: There is no such thing as a value-free way of working with others. The challenge is to keep ourselves honest and to consider what values we actually use in our work and not just the values we say we use. One of the sad and painful ironies of psychology in the field of developmental disabilities is that we psychologists have judged (and often hurt) people on the basis of their observed behavior. We, however, have overlooked, excused, and even congratulated one another on the basis of our intentions.

Overcorrection

Ann was a 50-year-old profoundly retarded female, IQ of 16 and hospitalized for 46 years. She also had several physical disabilities including epilepsy, impaired hearing, chronic asthma, no muscular control of her left hand and only thumb and index finger control of her right hand. Her verbalizations were limited to the single phrase "I want to eat" randomly repeated during the course of a day. Ann had been a major behavior problem throughout her long hospitalization, primarily because she damaged furniture by throwing and overturning beds, chairs and tables. This behavior was first recorded at age 13 and continuously appeared thereafter in her hospital records. The high frequency and unpredictability of object throwing made it impossible to include Ann in off-ward educational activities and caused the ward staff to spend considerable time repairing and straightening up furniture. Several reductive techniques had been used in attempting to eliminate furniture throwing including time-out, physical restraint, and requiring Ann to restore overturned furniture to its correct position. None of these reductive techniques had been successful in eliminating the behavior.

A behavioral program that required Ann to correct the disturbance by righting the furniture was in force when the authors were asked to intervene. She was also chastized [sic] after each offense. These programs remained in effect as control procedures during an 8-day baseline period. An attendant on each shift was given the specific role of continuously observing Ann and recording all disturbances. Daily checks by the trainer confirmed the reliability of the baseline records.

After the baseline recording period, the Restitution program began. When Ann turned over a bed, she was given Household Orderliness Training and Social Reassurance Training for a minimum of 30 minutes. Household Orderliness Training required Ann to turn the overturned bed(s) back to its correct position and remake the bed completely and neatly; she turned beds over with such force that the bedding was usually strewn all over the floor. She then smoothed out, straightened, pushed against the wall, and fluffed the pillows, of all other beds on the ward. When Ann turned over a chair or table, she was immediately required to straighten all tables and chairs on the ward, wipe off all furniture with a damp cloth, and empty all trash cans. When she turned over a table containing food, she was required to clean the entire dining room after sweeping and mopping up the debris. Since she failed to follow the trainer's requests initially, Graduated Guidance of her limbs was given. Also, she did not appear to know how to make beds and arrange furniture. Consequently, the Graduated Guidance procedure was instructional as well as motivating. Social Reassurance Training required Ann to apologize to the individuals whose beds or chairs she had turned over and to all other individuals present on the ward, all of whom were usually apprehensive because of her episodes. Although she was essentially non-verbal, she was able to move her head in the appropriate direction (up and down or sideways) when asked if she was sorry for what she had done and whether she intended to create another such disturbance. . . . (Foxx & Azrin, 1972, pp. 18–19)

. . . Ann often remained passive or kept her limbs rigid during the initial training efforts and therefore required frequent Graduated Guidance Training during the first few days. As training progressed, Ann became more active, stopped resisting the manual guidance and became quite proficient at making beds. The Graduated Guidance Training was rarely needed after the 7th week of training. (Foxx & Azrin, 1972, p. 20)

As we have seen with all systems for behavioral control, the context of the person's behavior and the ways the person has found the behavior satisfying are overlooked in favor of eliminating the behavior because of its apparent maladaptive qualities.

This brief report does not tell us a great deal about Ann or where she lived or what she was like as a person, but we can make some inferences. We might well ask what kinds of lessons Ann's life had taught her. Just as her behavior seemed out of control, it is not hard to see how her life might have seemed out of her control. People who live in institutions, especially since the age of 4, have not had most of the ordinary experiences of growing up. As typical children mature into adults, they gain greater control in making decisions about their lives, not just in where to work and where and with whom to live but in everyday matters such as when and what to eat, when to bathe, and when to go to bed. People who live in institutions are not given these choices. As a result, people growing up in such places learn that their lives are determined by others. Ann also had other challenges to making choices and gaining competence. She had little control of her hands, which limited activities available to her. She had a seizure disorder, which many people experience as something that happens *to* them, often unpredictably and uncontrollably. She had chronic asthma, which can make even air inaccessible. How powerless she must have felt with no control of one hand and only limited control of the other, no speech that was taken seriously, and virtually no life beyond the locked ward she had lived on for 46 years. The one competency she had seemed to be throwing furniture around. Her most dramatic choice in life seemed to be choosing when to do this. Had the authors speculated about what her life was like when she was *not* overturning tables and beds, it is not hard to imagine their seeing it as stale, flat, unprofitable, and dull.

Given this narrow life, what would Ann herself be likely to want? It is hard to know where to begin; there is so much she might have reasonably asked for. Ann could certainly have used some time off this ward with people she chose who liked her and could be role models for ordinary behavior. With 46 years of training and practice in unusual behavior, it is not surprising that she was quite skilled in behaving unusually.

If the quite understandable concern was about her throwing furniture, why couldn't she have gone for walks outside where throwable furniture is easily avoided? Going for a walk is a socially ordinary way to get to know people— just because a person does not use words does not mean that he or she cannot converse. Many people who do not use words express opinions and feelings with the way they move their eyes or the way they hold or move their bodies. Parents, who often know their sons and daughters better than anyone, are good at interpreting the meaning of this body language. In any case, spending time with Ann away from her ward would have given people interested in working with her a chance to know her better.

We sometimes forget that our work often involves significant personal change and, equally dangerous, we forget how such change happens in our own lives. Many of us have changed because "life happened"—events and the people in our lives significantly altered the way we saw the world. Sometimes this is an abrupt turning point, sometimes a process occurring over years. Sometimes—but this is only a small part of how most people actually change their behavior—we elect a formal relationship with a therapist to help us change, but no therapist (I hope) would presume to launch a program for change without taking time to get to know the person's background and personal style. This kind of groundwork is essential in forming a therapeutic alliance. Why should Ann be given a service any less thoughtful or thorough? Instead of family and friends, Ann had only these formal relationships, and the absence of any personal consideration for her makes it hard to guess why—and for whom—she would want to change.

This might be why none of these reductive techniques had been successful. If previous efforts had not changed her behavior, perhaps staff had not been successful in forming a working relationship with her. If we really see people with challenges as people first, then this is a remarkable therapeutic oversight.

Indeed, Ann's plan that had chastised her after each offense might have better addressed Ann's need for relationships. Perhaps the only time she had dependable social contact was when she was chastised. Not surprisingly, a person as isolated as Ann might well choose unpleasant connections with people rather than none at all. It would be interesting to know if anyone had ever spent time with her in a more relaxed way and been more open to her socially. The authors of this account began working with her by observing her. Although it is useful to see what her life was like, it seems that observation was strictly limited to her behavior. With this focus, the program of overcorrection ignored her as a social being and responded to her only as an emitter of behavior.

The authors pointed out that because she learned how to make beds and arrange furniture, the procedure was instructional. This instruction obviously included these skills, but one wonders what social lessons were taught. Less obviously, it would seem that Ann had been taught the Stoic virtue of compliance.[3] Foxx has said that one prerequisite for overcorrection is that it takes a "trainer" who is physically

---

[3]One central dictum of the Stoic way of life is Epictetus's dictum: "Discern the inevitable and submit."

more powerful than the "trainee." This makes the procedure clearly one whose purpose is to teach uncritical submission. It teaches that control is something "trainers" have and "trainees" don't. Explicitly, Ann had learned how to make beds. Implicitly, she also learned how to live more quietly in an institution. Most important, it is hard to see how she could learn from this therapy how to express what she needed or how to get it in a socially ordinary way.

Finally, I wonder what the 7 weeks spent in this overcorrection program might have led to had staff spent the time instead just getting to know Ann as a person, learning how to appreciate her for who she is, and finding out what she might enjoy doing.

This overcorrection program has a parallel in the lives of all of us who as school children were made to stay late to copy out a hortatory sentence, such as "I will not talk out of turn in class," some arbitrary number of times. (I remember 1 million as the usual assignment.) My teachers might have defended this kind of punishment as an opportunity for me to improve my penmanship but, if this was the case, the intervention failed. I did not, alas, learn good penmanship until years later when people stopped demanding it of me. What I did learn was that people with power over me can make arbitrary decisions and that neither I nor my reasons for talking out of turn needed their consideration.

The authors' apparent rationale for this as a procedure—"to educate the offender to assume individual responsibility for the disruption caused by his misbehavior" (p. 16)—overlooks the mutual responsibility of teaching. Holding Ann entirely responsible for her unusual behavior fails to acknowledge the role of her teachers. If the environment is a powerful teacher, then why would we hold Ann solely responsible for having learned what living in an institution necessarily teaches? To blame Ann for her choices in an environment that offers virtually no choice is really to blame the victim. Ann could have learned more adaptive behaviors, but this would have taken a special effort on her part. And if she had, would she have had people in her life to acknowledge the great strength she had demonstrated? But that Ann made a choice that was not appreciated by others cannot be seen as her deficiency alone.[4] Her "behavior problem" was not solely her creation, though she had, however unwittingly, been taught that it was.

We can ignore the interdependence of our lives more easily in an institution but only at the price of teaching compliance, passivity, and dependence. When we teach people to be dependent, we gain very little compared to what we lose. What was lost for Ann was the chance to be more aware of how she could make decisions about herself and her life. The quality of Ann's life may not seem like much of a concern to a busy world, but it surely meant a world to Ann.

One wonders if the people who asked Ann if she were sorry for what she had done asked themselves as much. Ann overturned furniture. They helped incarcerate a woman for life solely on the basis of her disabilities. This brings us to an important characteristic of positive approaches. Positive approaches do not rationalize or minimize the difficult behavior of people with or without disabilities. Positive approaches encourage us to see clearly and honestly the good reasons and adaptive qualities of even the most troubling behavior, no matter whose it is. While these approaches are not about blaming, they are not about blithely forgetting. Positive approaches are not about being right, but about being whole. We need active reconciliation not just for Ann but for those of us who have hurt people with our intentions to help. Just as Ann did not deserve or need to live in an institution, the people who worked there did not need such a place in order to realize their good impulses. Everyone involved with institutions is diminished by them; we need opportunities to admit our error, forgive and be forgiven when possible, and then move on. For me, at least, the ordinary correction essential for personal awareness and growth is enough. Like many people, were I to be overcorrected, I would stop working on changing myself and begin to work—aggressively—on changing my overcorrectors.

---

[4]In reading this over, I wonder why she was not suicidally or homicidally depressed. Choosing to vent her spleen on inanimate furniture seems to me an ethical choice that I'm not entirely sure I would have made had I been in her shoes.

"Ignore and Redirect"

Many people who rely on human services for help find themselves routinely ignored and redirected by systems that do not pay much attention to their wishes, much less their basic needs. Those whose behavior is particularly troublesome often find themselves the objects of programs that intentionally ignore and redirect them.[5] Discussing these technologies is difficult because the same name can be applied in very different contexts. For example, if I am really upset about having had a frightening car accident, people who redirect me to think about something more pleasant are not really helping me if I need to talk it out. If I get confused and mix up the facts of my misfortune or keep repeating myself, my friends will overlook this and attend to my emotional needs first. People who care about me will keep me and my immediate concerns in their focus rather than impose their own needs of the moment onto me. This mutual back-and-forth sharing, of listening through someone's bad hours and knowing that over the years they will take the time to hear yours, is one of the fundamental gifts of friendship.

One common version of ignore and redirect in polite society that I have observed is found in the etiquette of dining with people who don't know each other very well. Every now and again, we all find ourselves eating with someone who gets a bit of food on his chin, and it bobbles about as he is talking. Unless I know this person fairly well, I have a hard time saying, "You have a distracting bit of food on your chin." Instead, I ignore it and politely dab at my own chin, which seems to be the universally recognized sign for your fellow diner to do the same. Of course, the right side of my chin is on his left so the question arises: On which corner of my chin do I dab? Some of us, having taken this sign as a hint, wipe our napkins over both sides, for certainty's sake. Then there

---

[5]Just as the sideshow gave us Pinchbeck's learned pig long before Skinner's pigeons, so too does vaudeville provide us with an early example—I would guess this was invented by noon on April 16, 1865—of "ignore and redirect": "But other than that, Mrs. Lincoln, how did you like the play?" Humor often at once reveals the source and resolves the anxiety provoked by the otherwise incomprehensible.

is the problem of the person who is merely rubbing his chin because it itches. Ignoring and redirecting in this context is socially acceptable, but the older I get, the more I have decided that it's considerably simpler just to ask at the beginning of this ritual, "Do I have food on my face?" I have also learned to overlook certain things with some people. Generally, I can overlook minor temporary annoyances. But in the long run, ignoring the people I care about or the problems they care about does not help them or me.

Many of the people we work for, though, have had their wishes constantly thwarted and have had to fight, sometimes violently, to make themselves heard. The ignore and redirect technologies I have seen literally ignore people's very real emotional concerns as well as redirect people to activities that do not make the staff quite so anxious. For example, I have a friend, Michelle, whose father died suddenly. Michelle had the experience common to those who have had a sudden and wrenching loss: It makes other people uncomfortable, and they do not talk about it for fear of upsetting the grieving person. But if the saddened person herself brings the topic up or begins to cry, then it is obvious she is already upset and could use some recognition of her distress. As often happens to someone living with a sudden loss, Michelle found herself getting agitated, sometimes abruptly, and, to people who did not know her, without apparent reason. Unlike most people, though, Michelle found herself on a program where people ignored her distress and redirected her to something much safer for them, with phrases such as, "It's time for you to go back to your work," or "We really have to get these chores done first."

This obviously—and dangerously—ignores what the behavior is telling us and redirects it to something irrelevant for the person. I also understand and appreciate the inhibiting fear involved. For example, someone might well be reluctant to talk to Michelle about her father's dying if his or her own father had just died. The lost opportunity, though, is the healing that can come from sharing pain. But no one can talk about everything with everyone, and Michelle might be just the person you would least want to talk this over with or she

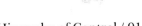

picked a bad time for you. Why not just say that? At least it lets Michelle know the problem is in her timing or your own painful feelings and leaves her knowing that her own hurt is real—and so is yours. Changing the subject implies that grief (or whatever feeling we are ignoring) is something inappropriate, trivial, or shameful. Another person's feelings can be annoying, embarrassing, confusing, or hurtful to me, but it is hardly my business to imply, much less label, them as inappropriate, shameful, or trivial.

Some people, for example, were nervous that once Michelle began talking about her father's death she would never be able to stop. I know I have had that fear in dealing with some people, and I certainly had that anxiety when I began to confront my own fears and rages. But this hypothetical calamity has yet to happen to me. For better or worse, nothing lasts forever. To be sure, Michelle might take a long time to talk about her father's death or she might need to talk about it a lot over a long period of time, but eventually she (or her behavior) will say, "There, I've said it." This can only happen when, at the same time, she finally feels, "And there, you heard it!"

If Denise wants a cup of coffee or a break, it is hard to understand why someone can't provide this for her. If Aaron's uneasiness shows the people who know him that he would rather go for a run or a swim than sit and do a puzzle, then it seems self-defeating to persist in praising him for complying with something that is neither interesting for him nor of any earthly use to others. When people tell us (or our experience with them has taught us) they want something we can provide, then the most positive approach is simply to provide it.

The biggest challenge I find in spending time with people with labels is generally not their behavior. The people themselves are often quite pleasant to be with. Yet, the things they are expected to do (and that I have been expected to do with them) are often bone-wearingly boring. Personally, I welcome someone's demand for a break, a walk, a snack, or a ride around town as a real opportunity to get out and to do something enjoyable. Just doing ordinary things spontaneously has been a useful way for me to "assess." What sorts of things catch this person's eye? Does she like activity with people or does she enjoy being quiet on her own? Does she like being indoors or outdoors better? These kinds of questions can give us practical directions as we help people construct days that have some meaning for them. When we ignore people's requests for things we really can provide, we set up discouraging power struggles that end up defeating everyone involved. Each time we fail to take someone's stated needs or implied wishes seriously means that these ordinary opportunities for us to learn together are lost.

Many people with learning differences have had virtually every hope or wish so frustrated that they have rarely been able to say for themselves, "Now I am satisfied." Instead, they often hear from those around them, "You've had enough." This is often just a way of saying, "I'm tired of listening to you or dealing with you." If we told people our honest feelings, even though they would not get what they wanted at that moment, they would at least have the dignity of being treated as equals. Instead of this honesty, we often turn things around and tell people there is something wrong with them, that it is they who are inappropriate. Few of us would find our dinner companions all that companionable if when the dessert menu arrived they announced, "No need. You've had more than enough. It would be inappropriate for you to have another bite to eat!" There is only one person in the universe who can really know if you are hungry and when you are full.

Ignore and redirect shows up frequently as a solution for difficult behavior, and its frequency reveals how easily we lose awareness of how naturally we technologize and routinize ordinary life. Most of us overlook the little quirks and the lesser irritations of our friends all the time. Occasionally, I catch my friends doing this for me, and I am usually charmed by their generosity. I might, however, think very differently about it if they were to say, "Oh, of course we do it because we believe ignoring and redirecting will gradually improve you." Suddenly they would have shifted me from the social world of friends to the clinical world of therapists. And yet this is precisely the direction—from the social to the clinical—that we use so naturally and uncritically to rationalize much of our work. The problem is that what happens to us—when friends overlook our quirks—happens in a purely social context. The parallel activity in services—ignore and redirect—is completely clinical and has no social context.

We use the parallel argument to rationalize positive reinforcement. Whenever I object to giving adults demeaning, extrinsic reinforcements such as tokens or trivial rewards, someone invariably points out that I get paid (or hope to) for my work. What they fail to see is that I get a somewhat different level of financial compensation and, harder to calculate but nonetheless significant, I get considerably more social status for my behavior than the betokened person will. The fact that we are both given something for our behavior is all that these two activities really have in common.

As long as everything is going our way, we treat people as if they were our friends. I have seen any number of people working in a genuinely friendly way as they help others out. But often as soon as we service providers are even slightly troubled, we become clinical. We do not do this with our friends and we certainly do not even think of doing it with people who are not in a very close personal relationship with us. Many times, troubling behavior alerts us to a pressing need, but our response focuses on making the behavior go away rather than on satisfying the person's intentions or desires.

In fairness, this practice of ignore and redirect reflects a wider cultural reference. Whenever we do not have a relationship with someone who frightens us or who is difficult to understand, we rely on an external control. Many people avoid strangers whose behavior is just a bit odd. When people we do not know fail to agree with us, we are inclined to resort to the force of law. Given the ways much of our culture has changed from primarily family and community relationships governed by a personal history of experience to professional relationships governed by professional ethics, it is not surprising to discover the increase in lawsuits and court actions. Misbehavior or violation of a community standard might once have led to complete social ostracism, but in a more mobile, less personal culture those sanctions are weakened. Consequently, in order to determine what is just and then to obtain justice, we are forced to submit to impartial, but also impersonal, third-party reviews by licensing agencies, professional review committees, and the courts. So when a person we are trying to serve disturbs us, we are often quite comfortable in resorting to an outside agent—for example, a behavioral consultant or a behavioral technology.

Burton Blatt has been attributed as saying, "In the absence of feeling and belief I resort to data." In the absence of mutuality in a relationship, the more powerful take control of the less powerful. There is no therapy without politics and whenever we resort to pre-arranged and controlling techniques in working with people, we implicitly admit our failure of heart, imagination, or will. Overlooking behavior as a way of establishing friendships is quite different from ignoring behavior to make it go away. Our energies are better put to eliminating the *need* for difficult behavior than in trying simplistically to eliminate the behavior itself.

Negative technologies (something is withheld in order to eliminate a behavior) often point to a larger need in the person's life; but, for whatever reasons, we tend to take away what the person needs most. Just as people who need wider access to the community in order to learn ordinary behavior often find that access withheld, people who need more social contact often get ignored. One of the most common characteristics of people with difficult behavior is the absence of friends—people who are in their lives "just because." It is easier to ignore people who are difficult to be with than to find people who want to befriend them.

Typically, what begins as a problem with the person becomes more clearly an interactive problem of the person's needs and the service provider's capacities. How to help people make wider social circles is a far more personal challenge than is "extinguishing behavior." Some service providers are content to be the entire social life of those they serve. They have agencywide vacations, socials, parties, and sports. Of course, some staff work so closely, warmly, and well with some people that they over time come to feel like friends. When I have found myself in this position, I have been tempted to refer to us as friends, but I have been wary of doing this for the simple reason that I am sensitive to the fact that staff people, no matter how friendly, tend to quit and, once gone, to lose contact. Ordinary friends, too, can drift apart. The difference is that these friendly staff often comprise the person's entire social universe. This is a real problem, of course, if everyone you like keeps leaving with 2-weeks' notice. The message becomes clear to people over time: The people I can rely on have to be paid to be near me. And sometimes even money is not enough.

Some services discourage staff from getting "too close." This can leave people with very little social warmth at all. Alternatively, some agencies encourage people to socialize wherever they are comfortable, to visit staff homes, to meet their friends, and to become as much a part of one another's social lives as is mutually satisfying. I know a number of people, many in direct services, who are gifted teachers so that when someone they are working with comes to their homes and meets their families and friends, this person naturally learns how to make friends in socially ordinary ways. When staff see themselves as bridges to a wider social life, people are more likely to be seen as individual personalities. Too often people with disabilities are first encountered in large groups rather than as individuals.

Some services now have community integration workers to help community presence become personal participation. Unfortunately, these two concepts are often confused and much of what is described as community experience is tantamount to babysitting. People are passively led to a movie or around a mall and then taken home again and this is documented as community experience. Very little in the way of connection goes on during such events. (Sometimes when a person tries to engage someone they do not know socially, it is seen as "inappropriate talking to strangers.") Because we hide people with differences away, most people are awkward at first when encountering someone who does not speak clearly or perhaps does not speak at all.

We can use a technology such as ignore and redirect to support the status of people with disabilities as invisible beings. Or we can begin to recognize that this status is unacceptable and that such a technology supports something we no longer believe. We can use a person's difficult behavior as a way to rationalize our own, but we can just as easily decide to use the same behavior as an opportunity to learn.

When we discard technological responses to personal problems, we leave a world of some predictability (the primary reassurance that technologies provide) for a world of uncertainty. The good ideas that I have for helping Helen make more friends might be irrelevant or irritating to Robert. So recognizing the personal qualities of the helpers is essential to respond to the individual preferences of those being helped. With a technology in its "purest" form it doesn't much matter who implements it (my car should start for you as promptly as it does for me), but with social relationships, none of us is wonderful to everyone.

This invites us to consider a new world for professionals too—one in which what we know is inextricably linked to who we are. In this new arrangement, personal growth, awareness, and the capacity for change leave the realm of unilateral assessment and rehabilitation and enter the realm of mutual engagement. Some professionals would perhaps prefer to ignore and redirect these new working attitudes and practices, but for those of us who welcome this "revision," it becomes an opportunity to make our invitations to change trustworthy and genuine.

"Time-Out"

I visited a school where Paul, a 9-year-old boy labeled retarded, attended a general education class with other children his age. The people who had accomplished this pioneering bit of integration were understandably pleased with themselves: Paul was one of the first children in their system to be moved from separate special-ed classes. But Paul was not only labeled retarded, he suffered from a severe reputation as well.

The school principal guided me around the large open classroom and quietly pointed out Paul, who was sitting in a singing circle. Whenever I visit to help a specific person, I try to act as if I am visiting everyone, so I did not look at Paul any longer than to connect a face with his name. This huge room was alive, sunny, and bright with (appropriately enough) primary colors. The several teachers and the 40 children all seemed to have something engaging to pursue.

"This is Paul's time-out chair," the principal said. It was just an ordinary chair off to one side.

"How do you use it?" I asked.

"Well, when Paul gets agitated, he sits here and calms down," the principal replied.

Many kids find it easy to get overexcited. Giving Paul a chair off to one side seemed a reasonable—and not particularly punitive—response.

"Time-out from positive reinforcement" is commonly shortened to "time-out." It has come to mean so many different things that when people tell me they use time-out, I have learned to ask them what they actually do. Sometimes it means nothing more than asking people if they need to take a break: "We notice Joanne gets agitated from time to time so we ask her if it wouldn't help to stop work and have a cup of coffee and just relax." Or a teacher notices a potential problem: "Billy gets restless and rather than leave him in a position to get into trouble, I send him on an errand to the principal's office." That seems thoughtful enough and often quite helpful.[6]

Few people really want to feel excluded or ostracized, but many of us do need time just to be by ourselves. From an external observer's perspective, suggesting a quiet break can appear to have the same outcome as sending someone away as a punishment, but there are real differences between an invitation and a command and between solitude and loneliness. Operationally, they might be indistinguishable but, as is often the case, what appears to be happening matters less than what the people involved think is happening.

---

[6]The critical distinction is the spirit in which people are responded to as well as their apparent interpretations and emotional reactions to the time-out. Various "nonexclusionary" time-out schemes can sound less punitive and may be offered in hopes of being less intrusive, but the recipients of these techniques are still quite capable of understanding their punitive and infantilizing nature.

Time-out from positive reinforcement began as a way of decreasing unwanted behavior with the fundamental logic that if reward increased behaviors then deprivation of reward must decrease them. Although the history of time-out is primarily institutional, this technique gained credibility because it seemed so reasonable. One early rationale for time-out was its apparent similarity to parents' sending children to their rooms as a punishment for misbehavior: If the environment is reinforcing a behavior, then removing the environmental reinforcement should decrease or extinguish the behavior. In theory, people have tantrums in order to get others to look at them, and if no one looks, they will stop having tantrums.

The comparison to parental behavior, however, comforts those using this intervention more than those to whom it is done and, unfortunately, overlooks the social context in which most people with disabilities live. Ordinarily, children sent to their rooms do not have virtual strangers guarding the door and do not have bare rooms without windows except for a pane of Plexiglas in the door that their punishers can observe them through. (I have visited some places where newspaper has been taped over the window in the door so the person inside feels completely isolated.) Most critical of all, the relationship between a parent and a child is significantly different in virtually every way from the relationship between an individual using services and those providing them. One of the most commonly recognized, complicated, powerful, and, almost always, inviolate relationships in our culture is that between parent and child. The relationship between parent and child is ordinarily disrupted only by death or legal review. However, the relationship between an individual who uses services and staff is often casually disrupted, almost always at the instigation and convenience of the staff as if there were no possible importance to the relationship at all. At the simplest level of economics, most children are not a source of income for their parents. Indeed, parents do not depend on their children for much beyond the convoluted and emotionally intense relationship itself. This is in precise opposition to the relationship between those providing services and those who use them: Staff typically do not depend emotionally on the people who are the source of their income.

Many people providing direct services are dedicated, even loving, but rarely is there the same I-would-die-for-you passion that many parents unquestioningly have for their children. When a parent punishes a child, it is often in the context of nurturance and love.[7] A parent sending a child to his or her room really does not compare to the context in which most time-out programs are carried out.

Although this kind of intervention has cultural support for parents and children, it bluntly disrespects people with disabilities. If we really valued our relationships with people, we would find it hard to force them into a bare room as part of that relationship. And if we really see ourselves as capable of teaching and the people we serve as capable of learning, then this kind of control is unnecessary, or worse, destructive. What are we teaching people when we do this? When we use time-out, our behavior—whether we acknowledge it or not—communicates *our* frustration, *our* inability to teach, and *our* limitations.

Service cultures that rely on control for behavior change presume that the controllers are the prime sources of everything, good and bad. Just as good behavior can be the result of a good program, difficult behavior can be blamed on the inappropriate social attention of parents or staff members. In discussing the use of time-out with people who hurt themselves, Carr (1977) noted:

> Curiously . . . there was no measurement of the frequency of the occurrence of social reinforcement. There was no demonstration that ward staff, for example, were in fact attending to such behavior at any time. Yet, when self-injurious behavior occurs at a high

---

[7]As with all generalizations, there are particular exceptions. Sometimes people living in the extreme environments of institutions develop friendly and loving relationships with staff members. Just as obviously, there are parents who have either an absence of caring or an active malice toward their children. Punishment, when done "for the child's own good," by abusive parents, can be seen for what it is: abuse. And those staff members who have had loving relationships with people with different abilities generally do not, in my experience, use punishment much. These exceptions, then, prove the rule: Where there is no love, there is control.

frequency, the assumption is often made that somebody must be attending to such behavior, thereby reinforcing it. (p. 801)

The world of unilateral control makes it impossible to see the person with a disability as capable of demonstrating feelings or of protesting independently. Because feelings and preferences can be systematically ignored, they are not attended to and all that is left is the work of extinguishing the problem behavior.

Controlling others is ultimately an impossible task, and we have often seriously compromised our ethics and basic respect by trying. Any success that depends on the compliance of others inevitably will be frustrating and inspire resentment. Hence, time-out might be described as a removal from reward, but its appeal is its function as an active punishment. Carr (1977) pointed out,

> Time-out procedures may actually constitute aversive stimuli, that is, self-injurious behavior decreases, not because of the removal of social reinforcement, but because of the punishing aspects of being confined to a chair or being forced to wait in a barren room. (p. 801)

Depending on the point of view, time-out can result in two distinctly different experiences: My putting someone into time-out is likely to be reinforcing for me. If someone throws things and I am unpleasantly startled, I can time the person out. I now feel better: My sense of order is restored, an unpredictable person has been removed from irritating me, and I am back in control. This is a negative reinforcement procedure because the removal of something unpleasant leads to my feeling better. What has been reinforced? Using behavioral principles, it is my timing-out people who annoy me.

Conversely, my being put into time-out is likely to be quite a different experience. If I am so angry that I throw my work, I might be protesting something specific or many things in general. Especially if I do not have words with which to communicate, it is a challenge for me to express myself in detail. Perhaps being without speech irritates me. In any case, if I am feeling discouraged or upset, throwing my work can be my most emphatic expression of those feelings. If I express these feelings and people react by forcing me to submit to their wishes, my senses of inadequacy and frustration are deepened even further.

Of course, if we think a person is literally acting out frustrations, being timed-out can easily increase that frustration. A person using time-out reacts to the behavior alone and does not respond to what an individual wants changed. If I bang walls out of desperation, frustration, anger, or pain, and all I get is time-out rather than help or comfort, then my reasons for my behavior will not change, my behavior will not change, and I will be timed-out again. In this kind of system, everyone gets locked into a cycle that is often literally vicious.

Often the same people who have been assaulted are the ones who decide to use time-out. This makes this procedure even more clearly punitive than the phrase "time-out from positive reinforcement" suggests. While the people using this intervention might see it as a way of changing behavior, the person being timed-out can easily see this as a punishment for wanting or asking for something. This intervention is commonly used in "community services" that do not recognize how institutional it is. How can this practice be defended as socially ordinary? It is especially disturbing to see people who are kicking and screaming forced into a time-out room. This humiliation often occurs in front of co-workers or visitors. Most private homes and ordinary workplaces manage to exist without time-out rooms. If we are sincere in our efforts to teach socially appropriate behavior, then we might provide socially ordinary places and ways in which to teach it.

Most of the people I have worked with in this field want to be helpful. Time-out is usually presented as helping those who are out of control. If so, much depends on your understanding of what help is. But out of whose or what control is the person? Time-out is supposed to help people "understand limits." It does. But who sets these limits, and what has been limited? This method really teaches that might makes right. Is this the sort of social message we want to promote?

Time-out is sometimes presented as just another neutral application of a value-free behavioral technology. This theoretical lack of judgment and emotion allies with the numerous prescriptions to "avoid eye contact," or to "use a neutral tone of voice"[8] when timing someone out. The reality is that most people involved in time-out programs feel anything but neutral. This sort of therapeutic neutrality is artificial and makes the people implementing these plans themselves seem even less real as people. While attempting a robot-like neutrality, the people they are timing-out are handled as objects, like toys that can be put back into the toy box when they cease to amuse. This is an especially tragic scene for people whose misbehavior is often their only noticed communication. Such programs further disrespect with the presumption that staff have no feelings either. The emotional neutrality of time-out is everywhere present in theory and nowhere visible in practice.

Time-out is sometimes presented as a positive intervention for the person being excluded, but this has rarely been the focus of research. Typically, studies have explored different aspects of the procedure such as the most effective length of time to be used—assessing the effectiveness, for example, of a 5-minute time-out compared with a 30-minute period. If the point of these procedures is to allow people to calm down, then researchers would be investigating how long it typically took people to regain their composure or different ways people found it helpful to do this. People might compare the opportunity to exercise with the chance to sit and calm down. Emphasis on the quantity of the punishment clearly indicates that concern lies more with the procedure than with those proceeded upon.

As a rule of thumb, I find it helpful in sorting out the intent of a program to see how it is written. When people write that they use time-out to offer informal opportunities for the person to get away from stress, then I tend to trust they are just giving the person a timely break. If the plan specifies the time that a person will be excluded, then the plan is likely to

---

[8]The idea that one's voice can be neutral in a crisis strikes me as highly improbable. I have purposely tried in a number of emotionally tense situations to achieve this neutrality and have failed to fool anyone as to what my feelings were. Similarly, I cannot recall not having a guess, right or wrong, about what others meant when they spoke.

be about serving staff members and not the person. For example, if the stress of work regularly causes me to lose my patience, the obvious first consideration is to wonder if I have the right job. We tend not to ask this of service users because they have so few choices of what to do during the day. Even nonpaying and boring day programs have waiting lists, so people are expected to accept what they have. For people like me, this lack of choice is itself stressful. Knowing I can leave the kind of work I do and find a completely different way to support myself gives me greater tolerance for the things that occasionally irk me.

Even though I have a great deal of choice not only in my career but also in the specific things I do in the course of a week, I still have peevish moments because of the mood I woke up with, the moods of the people I am working with, or because I am overly hungry, tired, or anxious about something completely unrelated—we are all familiar with how life works. Given this variability of reasons for behavior, it seems highly unlikely that any pre-arranged set of reactions could necessarily help, although such a program would consistently give the unambiguous message: Who cares why you're doing this. Stop it. This is different from saying, "We don't know why you are feeling out of sorts—would taking a break help?"

I might negotiate that I will just take a brisk walk around the block while I calm down. I might walk for 2 minutes or 20, depending on my mood, the weather, or whatever strikes me as worth paying attention to that day. However, if people arbitrarily decide not to talk to me for 10 minutes whenever I irritate them, it is hard for me to miss the shift from my choice to control by someone else. Both plans might sound positive, but they wouldn't be equally calming for me.

The real function, if not the actual intent, of time-out often seems to be revenge, however obliquely this might be acknowledged. One feckless behaviorist, though, did recommend giving ice cream and cake to all the people on a ward so that the people locked in time-out could see exactly what they were missing. Of course, I wonder what life in such a place would be like for people to be surprised with ice cream and cake to give one person grief rather than everyone pleasure.

People labeled retarded are often mistakenly thought to be too stupid to know what is happening to them, even though they are often well aware of their plight. Indeed, their most significant handicap is that, far too often, no one around them grasps the depth and totality of their understanding, much less their expression of it.

Institutions were based on the discredited assumption that, lacking any ability to control themselves, people labeled retarded needed to be controlled by others. In this model of therapeutic control, a time-out room makes sense. But if we take the abilities of people seriously, if we trust in our capacities as teachers, and if we really believe in the social equality of people with disabilities, then this technology of control has no role in our work. Unfortunately, many behavioral technicians have not been as adroit in adapting this theory to community life as they have been in adapting community services to the theory. Increasingly, behavioral technology as a therapy has become a political instrument to control people rather than the powerful tool for teaching it was first developed to be. This is particularly relevant for schools.

So, when the principal explained how they used Paul's time-out chair, it seemed more like an opportunity for him to quiet down than a punishment with which to ostracize him. But the tour continued. "And this is Paul's time-out desk," the principal noted.

This desk was in a dark corner behind room dividers that faced what turned out to be charts documenting Paul's behavior for the last quarter. Apparently, this desk was an interim strategy because the principal then told me, "If he doesn't settle down in the chair, we sometimes take him here. But if he bites or hits someone, he goes directly to his time-out room." The principal was obviously proud of this architectural accomplishment, a closet with gray carpeting, gray walls, and no light. As I squinted into this void, trying to think of just how to respond, two women rushed up with Paul between them, dropped him into the closet, and shut the door.

It is one thing to talk about a time-out procedure, but quite another to see it actually happen. I could easily imagine what it would have been like for me at that age to have two adults swoop down on me. "What happened?" I asked. "He hit someone during singing circle," one of the women replied. I remember the great reverence I felt for group singing as a 9-year-old, but it was difficult to imagine Paul's respect for it when I recalled that he had been born without hearing. I acted—no, reacted—rather badly. I announced that I was too angry to talk coherently about this and that it would be best if I left at once.

As I was simmering on the front stairs (I had to wait for the person who had driven me), the principal gently explained that there was going to be a meeting to discuss this program and that given what I would probably be charging for my advice I might want to be in there to give it. I was unmoved. Like a lot of people, I would sometimes rather suffer before giving in to bribery or intimidation. But he also pointed out to me that unless I came up with some alternative, they would probably keep doing what they were doing now. This persuaded me.

Sitting back a bit from the conference table were two women I had not yet met. They introduced themselves as neighbors whom the local service agency had hired to help out Paul's mom in the afternoon. Still feeling a tad cranky, I asked them if they perhaps had time-out coffins in the backs of their cars so they could keep the program consistent throughout the day. Unlike me, they were unfailingly polite.

"No," one said, "we have our own way of dealing with Paul. When we notice he's getting nervous, we offer him something else to do. When we're on the playground, you can just tell when he's going to get upset, so we ask him, 'Do you want to play on the slide? Should we go get some juice?'"

"And what do you do when he does get fussy?" I asked.

"We wait him out. It usually means he needs some extra time or that he's tired and needs to go for a nap. After a while, you just know," the other replied.

This is the sort of strategy that sometimes is described as ignore and redirect because these women were ignoring Paul's behavior and redirecting him to a safe place. It seems more to the point, though, to describe this as paying attention to his needs and overlooking his temporary behavior.

This is not just a matter of playing with words for the sake of word play. The difference being not so much the outward, observable behavior of the women, but the attitude that their behavior expresses and affirms.

When a person does not communicate with words, we often have a hard time explaining how we know what he or she is feeling and means. It makes sense that if a person is communicating nonverbally, then we do not have the words to describe it either. Sometimes people who know how to "read" behavior are dismissed as projecting or making up reasons for the person's actions. I think we need to respect this process more than we have. People who live together or know one another really well do not need to be told how someone is feeling when that person comes into a room. We have all taken one look at someone we know well and asked, "What happened?" because an expression or posture so clearly showed that something had. This form of communication, though, even in the best of circumstances is subject to serious misinterpretation.

Nonverbal body language strikes me as fairly difficult to break down into clearly defined and behaviorally objective terms because it is a language we know without speaking, having—I would guess—learned it before we could talk. Of course, when people from different cultures rely on gestures, misunderstandings can arise. Simple and natural gestures such as waving hello and thumbs up for O.K. have different meanings around the world. Each culture has its own body language, and I sometimes wonder at the impact of this when people of different cultures meet and these differences aren't recognized.[9]

---

[9]The study of nonverbal behavior as communication was already well established when behavioral technologies gained wide currency. The use of behavioral analysis in services for people with developmental disabilities was most impersonal and technological. Howell and Vetter wrote in 1976:

> In contrast with this rigorously statistical, judgmental, task-oriented approach to the study of non-verbal behavior . . . [there is] the procedure of *contextual analysis*. . . . The meaning of the behavior emerges from its function in the larger systems, not in the event itself. The experimenter does not ask what this gesture means, but rather how it fits into the interaction of the larger system. He [sic] does not measure and count behavioral events *per se*, but rather looks at the

One example of a cultural difference I have seen commonly cited is the distance that people comfortably take with one another in Arab and European cultures. Although there are differences within nations and classes, in general, Europeans stand further apart than Arabs do. It is one thing to note the typical European or Arab. It is another thing not to be able to transcend that stereotype and perceive the real person behind it.

Reflecting on this meeting about Paul later taught me some things I had only briefly thought about previously. Occasionally, in our enthusiasm to find what is wrong with our service systems, we scapegoat one group or another. "If only direct service staff were better trained," we complain or, "If only we had parents who would comply with our recommendations," as if we could place the blame for our general distress onto one group. I share in this fantasy, by the way, because it would make life so much simpler if one group were responsible for everyone else's misery. But this would require one group to be bad and another to be better, if not good. Most of life is not so much about good and evil as it is about the interplay of strengths and weaknesses within ourselves and among others.

One division made from time to time is that between professionals and the community. It seems to me that this parallels the differences we traditionally assign to our heads and our hearts: professionals taking on the role of cerebral and potentially heartless scientists and the community acting as all-caring, but not necessarily well-informed, enthusiasts. Just as no one functions very well or for very long without the active interplay between heart and head, neither do our services work very well when only one kind of knowing dominates.

---

larger picture. Instead of charts and statistics, the results are simply descriptions and abstractions. . . .

The traditionalist watches behavioral events in restricted interactional processes, but the contextual analyst interprets the behavior only in its full structural context. The discrepancy between the theories leads to a second split in methodology. The traditionalist counts and quantifies behaviors in statistical presentations, whereas the contextual analyst gives behavioral descriptions. (pp. 63–64)

The professionals in Paul's life had all acted professionally, but they had failed to see the real child behind his behavior. The principal provided an environment for all children to be educated in and had understandably left the classroom as much to the teachers as he could. The teachers, finding a pupil whose behavior was troublesome, had reasonably turned to a behavior specialist for help. The behavior specialist, like me, had no personal connection with Paul and responded to his aggressive behavior by writing a program in the tradition of the practice in which he was trained. Yet even with all the good training and good intentions the professionals brought to their work, their efforts still resulted in a time-out room, which was a failure of imagination or of caring or both. I say this without blame. I once wrote time-out programs, too.[10] But some crucial element is missing when bright and well-intended people can turn with clear consciences to so punitive a practice.

Yet, the women helping Paul's mother by taking care of him during the afternoons were professionals, too. If it had not been for the service system, it is unlikely they would have spontaneously dedicated their afternoons to him as conscientiously as they did. I am not saying they would never have helped out, but there is a real social difference between helping a neighbor once in a while and the sort of dependability paid employment demands. The difference between these women and the other professionals was that these professionals worked in such a way that they had a personal relationship with Paul and acted on it—personally. The lesson they taught me was not that professionals are hurtful, though they can be, but that in using our skills as caring and competent people, a real and respectful relationship is essential if we hope to help.

This interconnection between the personal and the professional is critical. Looking back, I now see that without my professional connection with Paul, I had nothing. It was only by using my expertise—my experience in having worked for

---

[10]Even so, I found identifying with this 9-year-old boy and his hurt far easier than identifying with the psychologist. Although I have been in both roles, it has taken me some time to recognize that I need to respect both sides in such difficult stories.

people with difficult behavior—that I was able to have an effect on his support system. In other words, only when everyone involved in this boy's life used their heads and hearts to
collaborate could we create a practical and respectful alternative to time-out.

Occasionally, one hears professional bashing as if, somehow, anyone who is paid is necessarily compromised. The
history of professional services, like history in general, is a
harvest rich in folly. Failures of service come when people
love what they do more than the people for whom they do it.
We professionals need contact with the people we work for,
their families and friends, and their places of work or school,
and we need to meet with people in their environments and
not in strictly professional settings. I used to have an office
where I saw people for therapy, but I gave it up. It has forced
me to meet people in their homes or where they work. This
has helped me use my training, experience, and expertise in
the context of people's actual lives. Too often the only influ-
ences on professional behavior come from other professionals who themselves are similarly isolated. Conferences
and training for professionals are fine ways to transmit information, but our work requires us to use our power with more
subtlety than results from simply relying on technique. As we
have collectively learned, schools of therapy do not help,
therapists do; therapists do not change behavior, people
themselves do.

Similarly, the horror stories of what parents have done—
or what they have allowed to happen—to their daughters
and sons occur most often when they have abdicated their
common sense and parental love in favor of professional
opinion. Some parents have allowed their children to go
through terrible times in the name of fixing them. Other parents have known precisely what their sons and daughters
needed yet have been forced to give them something they
knew was inappropriate. The kinds of mistakes that parents
make tend to be opposite to the ones professionals make. In
the name of loving their children, of doing what they have
been taught is best, parents sometimes stray from their own
strengths of love and knowledge of their child as a real person with a unique personality. I am wary, particularly with

young parents, of giving advice that could interfere with their basic parent–child relationship. Instead, I have found it more useful to ask parents what their dreams are for their child and what they think they will need for those dreams to come true. The ambitions that I hear are remarkably like the ordinary dreams most of us, in our optimistic communality, share.

In any case, the solution to Paul's time-out program was not for me, as another consultant, to write yet another plan for people I had only just met about a child I didn't know. Neither was the solution for me to observe the class for an hour or a day and come up with recommendations. The solution began to develop when the behavior specialist and the teachers consulted with the two helpers about how to read Paul's nonverbal signals.

In retrospect, what I find so informing is that when I spoke personally about how I really felt, no one cared. No one knew me well enough to care what I felt. As a professional, though, I had the power to jiggle the system a bit. Wisdom is truth lovingly spoken. Without the engagement of both head and heart, we see dangerous practices heartlessly unleashed or people loved blindly without their whole selves taken into account. We professionals can function as the thinking brain of our services, but without the life-giving heart's blood of people who daily stand by the people with needs, we cannot have wise services.

There is a larger lesson that people with disabilities can help us learn: We, as a society, need to listen to people other than knowledgeable experts. We need to hear not only from academics, theoreticians, and the whole range of the intelligentsia that we have attended to in the past, but also from people who are living the lives we sometimes so casually discuss. In recent years, more services are responding to people who use their services as the heart of their work, moving from an empty rhetoric to a rich reality.

It is also important to respect Paul's teachers. How could they be most comfortable and most effective in helping Paul recognize his anxieties? How could they help him learn how to manage those feelings? They started by offering him choices: "Would it help if you sat over there?" or "What about going over with the reading group for a while?" This was not done in the spirit of segregating him as much as simply giving him some respectable options. Rather than expecting the teachers to mechanically implement an inflexible behavior management program based on Paul's observable behavior, this approach freed them to be spontaneous, to respond to their best guesses as to what Paul needed most at a given moment.[11] When people honestly try to get along, they are less inclined to need technological control. When people have more choices, they have more responsibility, and the more sense of responsibility a person feels, the more likely there is to be a sense of ownership. This change in perspective can set off cycles of success where strength can lead to strength.

My indignation and accompanying tantrum were shown to be even more inappropriate when this group of professionals reconvened after I left, rethought how they had been working, and found a way to deal with Paul so that they now use the time-out room to store gym equipment. I am, alas, quicker to judge than to trust. As it turns out, the adults in Paul's life were fairly quick to change. Some years after all this, I am still more nimble in leaping to judgmental conclusions and clumsy in my understanding and respect.

———

Carol's workshop had had no work for the past 2 weeks so the directors decided to spend mornings doing "fun activities." On Wednesday, Carol and some of her co-workers went to a local park and had a cookout. Halfway through the lunch, Carol told Kristen—a staff member—she wanted to go back to the workshop. Kristen said, "Carol, there are 20 other people here and they all want to stay. You can just wait."

---

[11]One benefit of technologies is that they increase predictability and make error part of a program rather than a component of the human condition. With this way of working, the teachers could misread Paul and offer something that would aggravate him more. This is the unavoidable price of being in a mutually responsive relationship. Here the errors are personal and human and offer us the chance to learn. With control technologies, the errors are impersonal, programmatic, and give us almost no room to behave as people and no formal opportunities whatever to apologize.

Carol got upset. She decided to walk back on her own, so one of the supervisors decided she would have to wait in the van if she could not be trusted to stay. Carol resisted this suggestion, and two people "escorted" her back to the van. After another hour, the group was ready to leave. Carol refused to buckle her seat belt. When Kristen angrily buckled it for her, Carol hit her on the side of her head.

Because Carol's treatment plan called for her to be timed-out for physical assault, she was taken to the time-out room at the workshop for "hitting a staff member." Once there, she took off her clothes and screamed to be let out. The person monitoring her threw her clothes back in and told her that when she was ready to dress and keep calm she could come out.

As it turned out, Carol got out of time-out at the end of the afternoon break. Seeing everyone else relaxing, Carol lit up a cigarette. But about a third of her way into the cigarette, the buzzer signaling the end of break sounded. Kristen took Carol's cigarette away from her and told her to get back to work. But when Carol got to her workstation, there was no work. Instead, people were expected to sit quietly until it was time to go home. Seeing this, Carol picked up her chair and was about to throw it when two people rushed over and physically escorted her again to time-out.

Later, in talking this over, Carol was asked why she had had such a bad day.

"It started with the cookout," she said.

"What happened?"

"I was sitting next to Walter and I hate him."

"And?"

"And so I wanted to go home."

"And what happened?"

"They wouldn't listen to me so I decided to walk. Kristen and Paul chased me and took me back to the van. They made me sit in there alone. It was really hot," Carol complained.

"And then you hit Kristen?"

"Yes. I'm sorry I did that. But she made me wait in there while everyone else was sitting outside."

"Well, how could you have handled that differently? I mean having to sit next to Walter."

"I could have told him to go away."

"You could. What else could you have done?"

"I could have moved somewhere else."

"Yes. Do you think the next time it bothers you to sit near someone, you could move somewhere else?"

"Sure."

Technologies to control behavior fail to ask people why they do something and without that vital information, we find ourselves trying to control something we do not properly understand. Because hitting another person is a serious matter, we might better respond to it seriously, not mechanically. If a person is automatically timed-out for hitting, then we are regimenting ourselves when we could be thinking flexibly about constructive options. For example, if Carol started running on a wet floor, fell, and broke her leg, would we say, "You know the rule here is no running"? Of course not. We would immediately help her to get her leg set. Perhaps later, when she was no longer in pain, we could discuss how dangerous it is to run on wet floors, but we would delay making our observations until Carol was ready to hear them. If we really respect a person's judgment, we will wait and give the person the chance to say, "I won't run on wet floors again—it's too dangerous!" When a person strikes out, I assume it is in response to some emotional distress. Do we think that because we cannot see emotional pain the same way that we can see a broken leg, it is less important or less real?

Just as a person with a broken leg presumably wants it set and the pain relieved, a person overwhelmed enough to hit another person needs to have the source of the anger resolved. Regaining control is part of this process, not the point of it. Most people get upset for a reason and we need to find what that is if we are really going to help. But if a person is so upset that we cannot determine the reason immediately, then making the situation less tense is a first step. It is asking too much of anyone to be angry and articulate at the same time.

Helping others calm down is only the first step to listening, not a way of saying, "Be quiet and leave me alone." Some people find that taking a break or working at something else is helpful. If a person is too upset or cannot tell us what will help, we can suggest: "Would taking a walk help?" "Do you

want to go for a cup of coffee?" But we can make these offers
only if our friends know we will eventually return to work on
the original problem.

Some people have objected that going for a cup of coffee
reinforces inappropriate expressions of anger. In theory this
is true, but in practical social reality it simply and effectively
models a helpful and caring relationship. Much depends on
how we understand a person's behavior. If we think of it as an
isolated phenomenon we need to change, then we have a different response than if we see it as a person's nonverbal expression of anger. Surely, most of us have had the experience
of getting so angry as to be incoherent. Sometimes I can get
so caught up in my irritation that I say things I might have
thought better of. My real friends at work might try to remove me temporarily or redirect me, but they will not automatically time me out by ignoring me or snubbing me. If we
go for a beer after work to help me calm down and talk about
what has happened, I do not think any of us will think of that
as reinforcing my being obnoxious at work.[12]

My experience with most behavioral programs has been
that the person's target behavior does not immediately respond to a few exposures to the reinforcement. Indeed, the
standard advice for people beginning a behavioral program
is to be patient, that these things take time, that a person will
not necessarily associate the reinforcer with the behavior
right away, and that a behavioral plan might require weeks
before the desired result occurs.

Assuming that the people we work with are quick to
learn maladaptive strategies but take months to learn a social
courtesy is simple prejudice. It might take many demonstra-
tions of giving coffee to a physically aggressive person after
each assault for the two events to be associated. Even then,
one would have to be careful not to provide coffee without

---

[12]Many people make the assumption that if something is pleasant, it is
rewarding and if it is rewarding, it is reinforcing. We can call something a
reinforcement only if it actually causes an increase in the antecedent behavior. Until this is demonstrated, we have to assume that we are being
supportive of a person in need. But if it turns out that a person really does
use physical aggression simply to get a cup of coffee, then we have a point
of negotiation with that person and can explain that there are more efficient ways to get refreshments.

the person's having been physically aggressive first. By spending time with an angry person, we can show concern and model ways that problems can be solved. As concerned helpers, we should be able to persuade others to consider socially ordinary ways of expressing anger.

Social relationships often begin with a thoughtful and well-timed gesture. Just listening to someone in crisis can be powerful and helpful. We often respond to a small kind deed with great and genuine gratitude. Having someone listen to me when I am distressed has been one of my life's saving graces. From a strictly behavioral viewpoint, however, the people who were taking time to pay attention to me could have been reinforcing my feeling upset. In a technical sense, this could well be true. But I assume that I am like most others in that I would rather be happy than sad and that I prefer to be at ease rather than locked in turmoil. But what has really happened in this situation? What has actually been reinforced? I do not think I have been reinforced for telling my troubles. What has really happened is that my sense of trust and respect and my feeling of being understood have been reinforced. I have also had the opportunity to be in an actively caring relationship. This models for me, if nothing else, considerate behavior. Having seen it and felt it, I am in a better position now to show it and help others feel cared for. Mutual consideration is hardly compatible with physical aggression.

Carol's story is rich with lessons we have not learned. If we really want to support people with disabilities in learning ordinary social behavior, it would help if we model that behavior ourselves. The people working with Carol were responding primarily to her label and not to her as a person. If a person without a label at a picnic had said she wanted to go home, the typical response would have been to ask why. Carol's bad day might have been avoided with a word in the simple question: Why?

Physical Restraint

"Behavior modification . . . is limited mostly to hierarchical interactions in which more powerful persons seek to modify the behavior of the less powerful through the control of sanctions" (Kipnis, 1987, p. 30).

The hierarchy of least intrusive interventions is based on power and the exertion of power over others. The use of tokens, ignore and redirect, and even time-out are sometimes seen as "reminders" for a person as a way of gently controlling one aspect of a person's life. My life would be changed dramatically if I lived where such things went on, even for other people. I have seen architects' plans for residential community services that include time-out rooms as naturally as a laundry room or a storage closet. I can't imagine that anyone would confuse such a place with a home.

Fortunately, many of the people at risk for having to live in such places don't confuse these places with a home either. When they are told they need to go into time-out, they rebel. People who are subjected to control technologies often find their more passive protests ignored and should they actively protest, they find themselves physically restrained.

Once again, the act of physical restraint is less informative than the context. If someone were about to walk into the path of an oncoming car, then common sense would lead most of us to grab the person's arm to restrain him. Most of us doing this would not be satisfying an urge to restrain people as much as responding impulsively to a temporary danger. Programs that teach restraint techniques could be useful for any of us because we all run the risk of being inattentive to ordinary dangers from time to time.

The danger for people with disabilities is that such restraint technologies are used not as emergency interventions but as routine programming. The use of physical and chemical restraints is so common as hardly to be noticed in most institutional cultures. Mechanical restraint is somewhat less common but still used with surprising frequency. Yet, the literature on these interventions is virtually nonexistent. Psychologists have been slow to examine these interventions, and yet many of us have written programs that incorporate intrusive measures with no more justification than the unquestioned tradition of using them. Curiously, one of the claims that control technicians have consistently made is the empirical basis for their work, but one rule of thumb in human services is that *the more intrusive the procedure, the less empirical evidence there is to justify its use*.

Steve was a tall strong man who lived in a group home with three other men who also had autism. He spent his days in a vocational training program. This program had begun as a special school, but as the children grew to adults, the program staff began to struggle to find ways to support people in ordinary work. Steve appeared to become anxious when meeting new people, and the way he most reliably expressed this was to pull people's hair. When I first started consulting for the agency running this program, I would sometimes stop by Kay's class. Steve would become visibly agitated. Kay offered him a chance to take a break from whatever he was doing and relax on the couch, but one day my presence was so upsetting to him that he ran over and was about to pull my hair. Kay held Steve from behind, led him back to the couch, and reassured him that I was not there to hurt him. Steve quickly calmed down. It was clear that Kay's strength came from her relationship with Steve rather than from any physical strength she might have had because Kay was about a foot shorter and 60 pounds lighter than Steve. Had Steve not trusted her, Kay could never have restrained him.

When I left, Kay had a talk with Steve. Steve did not use words, but he did use some signs and had a wonderfully expressive face. When Kay asked him why he was so upset, he signed "Ted," the name of a former teacher.

"Did Herb remind you of Ted?" Kay asked.

Steve nodded.

"Did you think Herb *was* Ted?" she continued.

Steve nodded again.

"Then you need to know that his name is Herb and that he is not Ted. Do you want to learn a sign for Herb?" Kay offered.

Steve agreed.

Kay taught him the sign for H, and said, "The next time you see Herb, you can sign his name as a way to say hello."

Kay was a natural teacher. Without particularly thinking about it, she had given Steve a way of greeting me that reflected his style. Because the way he had learned to approach new people was with his hands, she gave him something else to do with them. If Steve had learned to scream at people, she might have respected that by teaching him some other sound that would give him a more ordinary way to relate to new people. Kay had not taught him a "competing" behavior as much as she had given Steve a socially ordinary way to get to know me. People with autism often respond to situations with many of the same sequences each time they are in a similar situation. Sequencing may be an adaptive way of organizing information for people with autism given their perceptual challenges. Perhaps Steve had learned that when he met someone new, the proper thing to do was to pull hair. Learning to sign H gave him a different sequence to use with me. Many people are now using sequences to teach people with autism new skills. People with autism find that ambiguous or unclear situations make them anxious and this contributes to their acting out. One obvious way to prevent acting out is by using visual cues and sequences so that people are able to predict more accurately what is going to happen next.

Kay also wanted Steve to have more control in social situations and to have some experience in getting his wishes respected. She thought that Steve had learned that his life was primarily controlled by others and that new people were threatening to him because he was unsure what demands they might place on him. She reasoned that if Steve could see that he was respected in a cooperative relationship, then he would feel less pressure to act out. If new people made him anxious, then he should have some way of asking them to leave or of leaving himself. Kay taught him a gesture of waving away as a sign that he needed to be left alone and the sign for break as a way to show he needed to leave. This gave Steve some choice in whether he wanted to be with a person and an easily understood way of expressing himself. The next time I dropped by Kay's class, Steve tapped his upper arm with the sign for H as a way of saying "Hello, Herb."

Steve's reputation for pulling hair was based on fact. He really had hurt people. Because many of the teachers in this agency substituted for one another, virtually everyone had worked with him at one point or another. Other trainees had reputations for occasionally acting aggressively, and one teacher, Chuck, argued that physical restraint was a necessary component of any training program and that, if the teachers were expected to work with "violent clients," they should have professional training in restraint techniques. He argued that using standardized holds would lessen the chance of anyone being injured.

Kay had no formal training in restraint techniques, but she had found that holding Steve gently and briefly helped him stop pulling other people's hair. She had talked about this with Steve, and she felt they both understood this as an effort to help more than it was an arbitrary demonstration of authority.

Some of the teachers considered various programs of physical restraint techniques. This proved frustrating for them because they felt that many of these training courses focused too much on techniques that made them feel uncomfortable. Still, they persisted with them because they also worried that they might be accused of being irresponsible for not learning some standard system of restraint holds. Eventually, they resolved this by asking Kay to introduce them individually to Steve. Kay taught Steve a sign for each of their names, and she showed them Steve's sign for feeling anxious. Kay also explained to Steve that if he felt the need to pull people's hair, people would be likely to hold him until he stopped not as a punishment but as a way of preventing harm. This worked fairly well. By getting to know Steve and his typical wishes, people saw that his behavior was communicative. Instead of seeing him as a management problem, they saw the need to be more responsive to him. When people were more actively and obviously listening and responding, Steve apparently felt less of a need to be frightening in order to make his points.

If we want thoughtful, responsive services, then we need to discriminate between what we do in unforeseeable emergencies and our responses to more predictable difficulties. The danger of being trained in restraint techniques is that it gives us the power to control difficult situations with no incentive to look at the bigger picture of what is actually going on for the person. Being trained to respond automatically can limit our creativity and depth of understanding. Had Kay automatically restrained Steve because that was all she had been trained to do, she probably would not have had the same fresh approach to him that she did.

Steve's behavior was consistent. Almost every time he met a new person, he responded with hair pulling. This consistent response suggested his need to learn new ways of expressing his anxiety. Curiously, when a person's behavior is consistently difficult, some services react with a consistent program of control. How, then, does the cycle get broken? If Steve does not know how to act with strangers and we do not teach him, how will he ever learn? If the teachers had been trained in physical restraint techniques simply to control this behavior, then all that would be maintained would be Steve's pulling hair and the need for several people to restrain him.

Unfortunately, much more energy has gone into controlling violence than has been spent asking why anyone, regardless of label, would resort to physical aggression. Some service organizations pride themselves on the comprehensive training they provide to new employees on how to handle physical assault. These techniques have many names, although they all train the same thing: ways to restrain people from doing something or ways of forcing people to move from one place to another. All of these techniques assume that, sooner or later, we need to know how to respond to violence from the people we serve. Agencies that routinely train staff in these techniques generally do not spend comparable time considering how the restrained person finds this behavior adaptive.

Much of the physically aggressive behavior I have seen from people labeled retarded has been the logical extension of not having been taught how to express ordinary needs and wishes in ordinary ways or of having those needs and wishes systematically ignored. People in direct service who have been trained to wrestle clients to the floor when they do not do what staff want often have difficulty in seeing such extreme measures as cruel and unusual: "Walter has to learn he can't just do whatever he wants in life. I can't. Why should he? He needs to learn we're in control."

If we are serious about modeling social skills, and if we really believe that our actions speak louder than words, then how can we justify the routine use of restraint? Except in the most dire of emotional emergencies, how often is a typical person physically restrained?

The use of physical restraint reflects a passive acceptance of institutional history. Many people labeled retarded formerly lived in places such as state hospitals that were primarily designed for people with psychotic disorders. Even today, it is not uncommon to walk onto a locked state hospital ward and find someone in "four point"—tied by the wrists and ankles to the corners of a bed. This unfortunate procedure is made even more abnormal if the bed is placed in the hallway by the nurses' station, which makes it more convenient for staff to observe the patient without having to leave the safety of an enclosed office or a protective counter. People with psychoses can be extremely challenging, but physical restraint is usually unnecessary except among strangers. A person's aggression is often like a forest fire: Once started it can be difficult to stop, but with some simple precautions, it can be prevented in the first place.

As people labeled retarded moved out of these institutions, the habit of using restraints too often moved along with them, but restraining people only reinforces for everyone the stereotype that they are beyond reason and cannot control themselves. However, such institutional habits can be changed.

When Gordon was about 3 years old, he was labeled severely retarded, and his parents were encouraged to put him into a state school. When he was 15, he was admitted to a state psychiatric hospital because he had become so large and aggressive that the school staff couldn't control him. At the hospital, he assaulted an aide, who pressed charges. This created an administrative problem that was resolved by transferring him temporarily to the state prison hospital for the criminally insane. After 20 years, this "temporary admission" came to the attention of the local court, which decided that it was unconstitutional to incarcerate a person who had never committed a crime. Although everyone agreed that Gordon was inappropriately incarcerated, no one was especially keen on his release. One plan called for him to live in a group home with other people labeled retarded. A number of experts explained to the court that Gordon was too violent to tolerate this freedom. They pointed out that it regularly took eight corrections officers to restrain Gordon when he got upset.

One agency thought that Gordon might well tolerate life beyond this prison and that what he needed was to start getting some practical experience with how ordinary people lived. Gordon had made some friends in this prison, so people knew that he could make and keep friends and that he would probably best learn to adapt to a new environment with the help of a friend rather than with a series of trainers. The agency hired Phil, a young man with little experience in human services but interest in Gordon's plight. His first assignment was to visit with Gordon and see if they were likely to get along. At first, Phil and Gordon got to know one another in the prison, which was where Gordon was most comfortable. It had, after all, been his only home for most of his life. As Phil and Gordon got to know and appreciate one another, Phil began to feel comfortable enough to invite Gordon out for a drive, or a walk around some of the little towns near the prison, or just to go out for a cup of coffee. Phil was not a large man. Gordon really was. If Gordon had become violent, Phil would have been at risk for serious harm. All Phil had was some genuine regard for Gordon.

Phil made it clear that when he and Gordon ventured out of the prison, Gordon would decide where to go, what to do, and when to come back. The obvious focus of these excursions was to show Gordon what the world was like, or could be like. The not-so-obvious focus was that Phil was teaching Gordon how to be comfortable and relaxed when he was not locked up and to check out the kinds of things Gordon might like to do with his days. Because Gordon had never worked, it was not clear what kinds of jobs he might want to look for. During several months of these trips, Gordon never once hit, or came close to hitting, Phil. If they talked about something that agitated Gordon, Phil listened and empathized.

Phil had never really talked about physical restraint with Gordon. It was obvious that Phil would never have succeeded in restraining Gordon even if he had tried. Besides, Phil thought correctly that it would be an odd friendship that required a plan for physical restraint. What was not obvious to the staff in the hospital was the power struggle that had been set up. Like most people when outnumbered and pinned down, Gordon struggled to break free.

When it became clear that Phil and Gordon were becoming fairly good friends, I had the small hope that the agency might find a way for them to live together. Phil would probably need a lot of help in supporting Gordon, especially at first, but I thought perhaps this relationship would be a good anchor for the next stage of Gordon's life. As it turned out, Phil was getting married at about this time and having Gordon as a roommate would have been quite a bit different from having him as a friend. Given Gordon's reputation, the agency was having a hard time finding people who were interested in having Gordon share their home. This agency, though, did not think it was impossible to find such people, just that it would take time. Given that the state had allocated almost $100,000 for Gordon, I thought it would be only a matter of time before someone found an incentive to get to know him. I don't want to be unnecessarily cynical about this, but people who are "impossible" to serve sometimes become more appealing if there are strong compensations attached to them.

The court grew impatient to meet its deadline, so Gordon found himself with a new agency whose plan was to use the money allotted to Gordon in order to fund a group home for three other people as well.[13] This is a common story: A person has been seriously disserved, a state government recognizes this, allocates much money as a way of making amends, and then the service provider treats the money as its own rather than as belonging to the person. In this case, Gor-

---

[13]Gordon's new "home in the community" was really a little institution. The agency would not have needed permission from the town council to move into the neighborhood if establishing this home had been truly seen as a community effort. The neighbors protested vigorously, but the town council, fearing a discrimination suit, granted permission for the agency to operate the home. As a consolation to the townspeople, the local government authorized the police department to train a SWAT team "just in case." As an extra precaution, a number of neighbors took out gun permits to "protect themselves" should Gordon or his housemates trespass.

don's money bought him a room in a house with three people he did not know. As it turned out, he got to know and seriously dislike one of them. This did not matter. Gordon was expected to adjust. He was also assigned, because they had a space available, to a vocational training program where people were given the opportunity for endless training but not for ordinary jobs in ordinary places. Gordon was not happy.

One evening, he became upset and hit the housemate he disliked. As a result, the staff met with their behavioral consultant who decided that Gordon's behavior needed to be "nipped in the bud." As a result, Gordon found himself on a new behavior program that rewarded him with one cigarette per hour of good behavior, that is, for not hitting anyone. Anyone who has spent much time in almost any institution knows that two of the major activities available to the people who live in them are drinking coffee and smoking cigarettes. After 20 years in a forensic hospital, Gordon was typical in his high consumption of caffeine and nicotine. That he should go from about 40 cigarettes a day to at most 16 might please anyone concerned for his health, but it did not please Gordon. Furthermore, at his day program he had already found himself on a behavior plan that restricted his coffee to one cup at each break, morning and afternoon. Anyone who has a fondness for (or, in clinical terms, an addiction to) caffeine or nicotine knows how hard it is to cut back. If anything, those of us who have ever developed dependencies on these two drugs know how our use of them is linked to stress. So Gordon had abruptly moved from a culture he understood to a completely new one, had found himself moved from living with people he knew and liked to living with people he neither knew nor liked, and one set of rhythms in his day had been changed to a completely new set of patterns set by others. In short, he had left a life that was far from ideal but had at least been familiar and his, for a life that was neither pleasing to him nor in any meaningful way owned by him.

One afternoon, Gordon came home on the van. He was tired and cranky and demanded a cigarette. It was 3:15 P.M. so the people working in the house told him that if he could remain in control for another 45 minutes, he would earn a cigarette. Gordon did not remain in control. He got upset. Using good sense, the people in his house ran out. Gordon ran after them. They ran back into the house, locked the door, and, while Gordon was banging on it, they called the police. The police, who had been prepared for just such a contingency, sealed off the street, forced Gordon face down on the lawn of the home his money had bought, handcuffed him, and took him back to the forensic hospital.

Sometimes people are thought to "need" physical restraint to regain control, but this usually only helps service providers, who know no other way to help people calm down. Having taught people to expect physical restraint whenever they get angry, we then see them as deficient when they know no other strategy for regaining self-control. We can teach alternative responses to anger, but we can, somewhat more simply, make restraint unnecessary by making it irrelevant. By having no way to enforce such a scheme and by diminishing the need for it, Phil helped Gordon discover more ordinary ways to express his anger and to trust that his opinions would be listened to.

In discussing control techniques as part of a continuum—progressing from positive reinforcement to behavioral surgery—it should be noted that none of these control procedures explicitly defines itself as such, and the people who employ these techniques do not think of being controlling but of helping. Frequently, these systems of control are seen as "humane alternatives," often to one another. Some people see physical restraint as less restrictive than chemical restraint while others see chemical interventions as less restrictive. However, the debate on less restrictive begins and ends with the idea that people with developmental disabilities need external controls.

I have visited many hospitals, group homes, and workshops where the people working in them insist that physical restraint is the only way to handle most of the patients, residents, or workers. The rationale for this is usually espoused this way: "They really *need* the sense of control that the restraint gives them. It's a kind of security for them to know who's in charge, knowing that we won't let them do anything bad." The language and logic of protector-oppressors can almost sound like caring. But who really needs the sense of security that comes from knowing who is in charge, the people served or the people serving them?

Sometimes, the procedure of physical restraint is used so often that those who use it forget that it is ostensibly to help a person regain control. Instead, it becomes a ritual of punishment bordering on abuse. A group working on a locked hospital ward once asked me to find an alternative to restraint for one woman because, as they indignantly explained, "She seems to get *sexual* pleasure from having us hold her down." In other words, preventing harm is acceptable only if it is unpleasant. This calls to mind Macaulay's observation of the Puritans that they objected to bear baiting not because it gave pain to the bear but because it gave pleasure to the spectator.

> Burton Blatt (1970) had made history when on May 2, 1967, he addressed a special session of the Massachusetts Legislature which had convened at the Fernald State School to try and face up to the State's responsibilities towards its institutionalized retarded citizens. . . . "I have irrefutable evidence, from 18 years of clinical experience in the field of mental retardation, that NO RESIDENT needs to live in a denuded state, needs to be a head banger, or needs to be locked in solitary confinement. I have irrefutable evidence that practically every resident can be taught to live among his fellows without being of danger to himself or others and without the use of physical restraints." (Dybwad, 1985)

More than 25 years later we have yet to put Blatt's irrefutable evidence into practice. Armstrong (1992), writing about Massachusetts, reported:

> Each year hundreds of mentally ill and retarded people in state institutions and community programs are tied to beds or chairs with leather or cloth cuffs—ostensibly to prevent violent or abusive behavior.
>
> Yet former patients and mental health advocates argue that the physical restraint of patients often leads to abusive situations or serves only to punish uncooperative or aggravating patients.
>
> Patients who have been restrained describe it as a terrifying experience.

"Restraint is terrible. You feel like you are being raped," said Rose, a former patient at the Metropolitan State Hospital. "It's like being assaulted. You are fighting for your life while they are holding you down."

After being restrained, the client is usually placed in a bare seclusion room, isolated from staff and peers.

Rose estimated she was put in restraint and seclusion a dozen times during her most recent yearlong stay at the hospital.

For more problematic patients or clients, restraint can be an everyday occurrence. A retarded man was put in restraints 92 times during the month of March alone.

The positive approaches described in this book present a major challenge to service providers and practitioners: to abandon a familiar, straightforward technical system for an unfamiliar process of working by trial and error. But all this really involves is accepting the power of relationships for fostering personal growth and recognizing that forming any close relationship is full of potential for understanding as well as misunderstanding. This challenge requires that we renounce consistently dominating others in favor of working cooperatively with them, often by using nothing more (or less) sophisticated than intuition and guesswork. Indeed, what is often called for, as in Gordon's story, is a complete shift in the structure of service. We cannot expect to work positively with people as equals in hierarchical services that systemically define them as "less than."

Chemical Restraint versus Medication, Medical Models versus Personal Support

Classical psychoanalysis defined people exclusively in pathological terms. As the old joke went: Patients late for their therapy appointments were resisting; if early, they were anxious; and if on time, compulsive. Like most old jokes, it reveals some truth: Externally defined, people cannot be understood on their own terms or taken seriously as real people.

People who are given psychotropic medication to control their behavior often find themselves in the same position. When I was in training, I got to know Mary, a woman who had occasional manic episodes. When she took her lithium she appeared to be a fairly ordinary person, but she complained of the drug's side effects.[14] She was distressed by the 25 pounds she had gained and by the sluggishness she felt. She recognized that her adventures while in a manic state distressed others immediately and herself eventually, but she still wanted a drug holiday. Mary had a group of family and friends who saw themselves as supportive, but they were all opposed to her decision. As she pointed out, "I can't win. If I'm quiet and depressed, everyone's happy to leave me that way because I'm no trouble to them. If I feel and act O.K., they tell me, 'See? The drug really works for you.' And if I have a few days where I manage to feel energetic and cheerful, everyone's on me to get my levels checked to see if I shouldn't increase the dosage."

Medication can have the same controlling role in the lives of people with difficult behavior as behavioral technologies. When the medication works, the drug gets the credit. When it does not work, the person is then further labeled as an especially difficult case. In retrospect, I would guess Mary's objection to the drug was in part due to her frustration with her powerlessness over her own life. At the time, I was busy helping her tread the sometimes narrow path between mania and depression. Today, I might still do some of that, but I would also be more concerned that she find some part of the world where she saw herself as she mostly was—a strong and intelligent survivor of real difficulties, capable of taking care of herself and helping others, too.

Now, I see that I was unintentionally working for her to accept a fundamentally passive role when she was looking for an active one. This conflict between what the person wants and what helpers *think* the person wants happens whenever we see people as incapable and as needing us to take over their lives. Helpers can too quickly generalize from "You need help" to "As a prerequisite to getting help, you need to allow me to determine what that help should be." This some-

[14]Properly speaking, lithium carbonate is a naturally occurring salt and not a major tranquilizer. But the political context of its prescription and use of lithium is not very different from the use of psychotropics to control people's behavior.

times subtle shift in professional focus turns liberating support into oppressive control.

Finding the balance among what the person wants, what the helper wants to provide, and the risks inherent in those choices really strikes at the heart of the political structure of services. Typically, most of us see that others need someone to take charge or need to change their behavior more readily than we see any such need in ourselves. When people have experienced an apparent loss of self-control and have relied on others for help, it can be hard for them to demonstrate that they need less help. Having seen people at their worst, services can forget how to recognize people at their best. Having taken care of people in emergencies, service providers can have a hard time making the transition to partnerships that support people in their real lives, which are not emergencies.

Maintaining focus and a sense of purpose can be exceedingly difficult with the use of any technology. As with everything else we have reviewed, what begins as a way to support a person can invisibly become a way to support a service system. People whose behavior changes while taking a drug, especially those who do not use words to communicate, often find themselves taking the drug indefinitely rather than "risk a regression" by discontinuing it. In addition, if the behavior should recur or become more dramatic, then the dosage is likely to be increased until the behavior disappears. I have known an alarming number of people who have been prescribed dosages well above the manufacturer's limit and have been nearly killed by this relentless determination to control the behavior chemically. This danger intensifies as we shift our focus, often without noticing, from the person to the behavior. When we are known personally, few of us are seen as just a set of behaviors; we are known by our personalities, our histories, and in a personal context. In contrast, some people may be known only as "head bangers" or "hitters." Few of us would be happy if we were known to everyone in these ways. If an ordinary person's behavior becomes extreme, family or friends try to put these puzzling new behaviors in the context of personal history. "Uncle Fred has always been so considerate, this anger is just not like him." Clinicians, however, put the behavior in the impersonal context of other extreme examples. "These Alzheimer's patients can present a real management problem for staff."

The lives of people in distress can take very different directions depending on who is asked to help. A common problem for people providing services is figuring out who to call when they are confused about what to do. For example, if Denise has started hitting people, any number of things can happen to her depending on who is asked to respond first. A medical practitioner might want to give her a drug, a psychologist might assign a behavior program or a therapy appointment, an occupational therapist might want to assess her styles of sensory integration, her family might want people to punish or placate her, the program administrator might want to increase staff time with her, and her service coordinator might want to send her to a residential treatment center out of state. Much of Denise's future will rest on that first telephone call, but how do we know who to call first? Ideally, any one of these key people is comfortable with giving a preliminary opinion and asking for further consultation to help rule out (or in) other contributing causes, but sometimes consultants insist their expertise is the only information needed and will try to "own" Denise and her situation. Too often professionals work in isolation and rely entirely on a single way of understanding and responding to behavior. When they proceed to personalize their struggle to "conquer" a behavior, this narrow focus can lead to the excesses that have killed people in the name of therapy. At this point, we recognize controlling and authoritarian ways of working for what they ultimately are—inhuman.

People labeled retarded were for a long time thought to be incapable of having emotional difficulties because they were presumed not to have emotions at all. For example, many professionals thought that people with intellectual disabilities could not become depressed. Today, this strikes many people as an unfortunate lapse in clinical understanding, but the social implications of those mistakes linger. For example, many families assume it is not necessary to inform people labeled retarded when a family member dies or to include them in the funeral or in any of the less formal grieving processes that families go through. The sad presumption is that "they wouldn't understand." Many people labeled retarded have stories about how their emotional lives were either trivialized or assumed to be nonexistent by people who meant them no malice. In addition, there are people who have been regularly abused, physically, sexually, and emotionally, and both their abusers and those around them assume they will just forget about it. That people are able to keep going in a world that routinely ignores their feelings is testimony to the persistent strength of the human spirit.

Beyond these gross neglects, some people with developmental disabilities also have mental disorders such as bipolar disorder and schizophrenia. There is a problem in that many psychiatric services see their interventions as too cognitive to benefit people with intellectual disabilities, and many people with training in developmental disabilities feel that psychiatric disorders are beyond their expertise. The simple answer to this problem is for both sides to learn more. I can think of nothing that psychiatric survivors have found helped them that would not help people labeled retarded as well in similar situations. As it is, there is no dominant therapy (beyond medication) for most psychiatric disorders, and it is mainly by trial and error that a match is made between a person and a treatment.

For people labeled "dually diagnosed" (both emotionally disturbed and developmentally disabled), psychiatrists and specialists in developmental disabilities often feel equally at a loss to help. Psychiatrists feel that intellectual handicap is a specialty with which they have no particular expertise, and services for people with developmental disabilities typically feel that the nuances of psychiatry are best left to psychiatrists. For good reasons, each profession refers the person to the other rather than learning to collaborate with the other.

Fortunately, more and more professionals in both fields recognize the benefit of a second opinion and that sharing responsibility has the potential to make everyone more responsible. (It also has the potential either to make everyone so professionally cautious that nothing happens or so confident that someone else is paying attention that anything can happen.) But even in cooperative and balanced working relationships, some people are so isolated by their training, or lack of it, that they don't know which questions to ask or where to find answers to the questions presented to them.

Many professionals are still sufficiently overconfident to venture well past their expertise, answering questions and consulting about problems that they should have referred to others. Typically, when professionals are confused or unknowledgeable about an issue, they work to reconcile the person to the service rather than work to see how services might better meet the person's needs. I know of neurologists with no experience in education who advise on classroom placement; clinical psychologists who, contrary to any scientific or ethical logic, predict a person's future; and behaviorists with no medical training who diagnose people's medical needs. These people presume that having a solid background in one area somehow makes them wise in related disciplines as well.

Even when people use their expertise, over-reliance on a single technology to control behavior obviously sets the stage for over-rejection. Having seen drugs used inappropriately and too broadly, some people have adopted the position of completely rejecting their use. This error in the opposite direction misses the point: The debate over effective technologies is fundamentally about what is meant by effective and who controls their use.

Psychotropic medications (usually major tranquilizers) are most appropriately used to control auditory hallucinations. Abuse of these medications resulted when they were used to control behavior. Of course, just because some psychotropics are an efficient—perhaps even the most effective—way to control auditory hallucinations does not mean that they are necessarily the *only* way to respond to a person who is hallucinating. Many psychiatric services focus on a set drug, dosage, and strategy to enforce patient compliance as the way to respond to people who hallucinate. Psychiatric survivors themselves have found a variety of ways of responding to this problem, but one common starting point I have consistently heard mentioned is that they be treated with respect. Psychiatric survivors, in my experience, do not assume that just because someone is hearing voices she is out of control, or "crazy." When a person's behavior is out of control, we rarely trust the person who has "lost it" to know how best to regain it. Obviously, the middle of a crisis is a poor time to ask someone how best to help, but when the person is calm—and we are, too—is a better time to talk it over and make some reasonable guesses about how to help the next time the problem arises.

This faith in people to know themselves is one leap many of us professionals cannot see how to make, and so we ourselves suffer a serious learning disability. Fortunately, for those of us who wish to learn, there are plenty of psychiatric survivors who will take the time to teach us. Many professionals do not trust or respect the people they serve. Again, many labeled people are generous and are willing to help professionals overcome this debilitating and progressive emotional disorder.

For most people, the term psychosis implies an impairment of judgment and a loss of control, which moves other people to act for the person. Typically, families and professionals collaborate (although families can be co-opted by professionals) in deciding what is best for the person. This usually well-intended process would be harmless if people met only to establish a consensus and to determine how best to respond to the person's crisis. A problem develops if this group acts to enforce its decisions irrespective of the person's preferences.

The ability to make a truly informed decision about the use of psychotropics is really beyond anyone's capability. Typically, the physicians who prescribe a drug do not know what it is like to take the drug, and no one can ever really know what taking that drug is like for another person. No one can predict which drug will be most effective for which individual. No one can predict when or if the hallucinations or delusions will return if the medication is discontinued. No one can predict when or if a person will develop permanent side effects, such as brain damage, as a result of taking the drug. With so many uncertainties about the risks and benefits of taking these medications, I have found that people with psychoses are likely to know as well as, or better than, the professionals which drug might help them and how long they will need to take it. This might be considered a type of intuition based on experience, but people with these difficulties often have a nonverbal dialogue with their bodies and learn to anticipate hallucinations as well as how a given chemical will affect them.

Professionals can direct people to the medications that are *probably* the most efficient for their specific conditions and can explain the range of potential benefits and risks, but it is really the individuals who have to decide if they agree with the recommendations. As is so often the case in life, we are forced to make serious decisions with incomplete and often inaccurate information. The expertise we professionals can bring to decisions comes from our clinical and academic ex-perience, but no ethical and responsible professional will or can predict with complete confidence how an individual's story might unfold.

Given all this uncertainty with which professionals work, it would make sense to invite people to collaborate actively in the ways they are served, but most people find themselves ig-nored or patronized once they have been labeled crazy. For people with developmental disabilities, this disregard for their sensibilities is so socially pervasive as often not to be no-ticed. Even when people of good will struggle to know a per-son's wishes, they are often unsure they have guessed cor-rectly. And if they are sure they know, they often find a system that has no real interest in hearing about it. If John has been prescribed a major tranquilizer, then he will take it. Getting him off this drug can be a long and delicate process because clinicians are usually better trained to find reasons for main-taining or increasing dosages than for discontinuing them.

Small wonder then that, once sufficiently manageable on drugs, people find themselves on them indefinitely. This as-pect of the medical model is not restricted to psychiatrists or to the use of drugs. When people are on behavior plans, es-pecially intrusive and painful ones, and their behavior is judged to be under control, there is a great reluctance for the practitioners of the behavior management plan to stop the use of pain. Indeed, when they do, people often revert to their former ways because being hurt has taught them nothing except to submit to external control. The use of pain, as the earliest behaviorists knew (see Appendix A), is a poor teaching strategy and usually leads a person to avoid, escape, or rebel.

Because many services rely on control, this status quo is virtually impossible to change when people no longer have behavior problems. As long as a group feels it is responsible for another group rather than responsible to them, its peace of mind necessarily depends on the passivity of the controlled people. A positive approach, however, invites us to ask, "Why do you need to act as you do?" and, "How can I help you get past this difficulty?" The context for this inquiry is a mutually important and responsible relationship, which makes it less likely one person will consistently control another. Most of us know that these kinds of relationships are filled with the potential for errors and misunderstanding. For those for whom professional or personal competence depends on being "right," this kind of mutuality can be threatening. In most important relationships, however, it is the fidelity to the relationship, the capacity for "being there," that can make the difference as much as or even more than what we know and what we do with people. In a mutual relationship, we allow people room and encouragement to change and grow. Sometimes people respond to the responsibility and invitations of a relationship immediately, sometimes never. And there's very little predicting who will be friends and who will not.

For those of us whose training was defined by efficiency in making things better, this way of working can be frighteningly uncertain. Some people find this way of thinking too far from what they have been taught, but few people with and for whom I have worked have found it much different from what they know and respond to best in their own lives.

In our own lives, if our best efforts do not work, we sometimes radically change what we are doing. More typically, perhaps, we just keep on doing the same thing with even more determination, and this often leads us to focus more and more on what we are doing than on why we are doing it in the first place. This common and human error is easy to make when working in human services. If a person does not respond to our first attempts to help, we sometimes intensify our effort rather than rethink our plan. It is a little harder to lose perspective when working collaboratively as a group of people who respect one another, have different perspectives on life, and who can each speak freely as individuals. Many interdisciplinary teams are really small wind ensembles with an exacting conductor who determines the program, the tempi, and every aspect of phrasing.

Positive approaches are not about "fixing," and their "success"—for human services as well as for the earth itself—rests largely on our learning to live with and accommodate one another. This is usually an ongoing effort and rarely a permanent certainty. The criterion for success is not just about results—it is also about how we stay with people while they change and grow.

If a plan doesn't seem to be working well, I am less interested in pathologizing those involved than in asking what we can change, how we can invite ourselves to look at this in a different way and perhaps try something new. The steadiness of relationships combined with the flexibility of planning can give us strength. Again, I need to emphasize that this way of working is not about being right; it is about being helpful.

This way of working is also about understanding and accommodating the people for whom we work as well as those with whom we work. If a job coach has worked for 3 months to track down a job and set up the necessary supports for Jan to work, it will be hard not to feel disappointment and anger if Jan wants to quit by lunch the first day. Sometimes, Jan's wanting to quit is just saying, "I need reassurance." But sometimes Jan might be saying, "I will never like this job!" and if we ignore her wishes, we may force her to act in extreme ways before we recognize Jan really means what she says: She wants to quit this job. Until someone is fairly extreme in his or her demands, we tend to find ways of adjusting the person to our services rather than adjusting our services to the person.

One of the basic premises of any positive approach is that, if we faithfully attend to what people need, want, and wish for, then we will find them more amenable to change, and they will change in the direction of more ordinary behavior. If what we are doing is ineffective, it can be explained as our not having paid close enough attention to what people need, want, and wish for. In that sense, those who want to help others are in large measure responsible for understanding what people need and want. At the same time, I do not think it helps anyone to be told, "You should be able to figure this out," or "You should be able to provide anything a person with disabilities might ask of you." That sort of expectation is self-defeating because it drives away genuinely caring but confused would-be helpers. Instead, a positive approach invites people to enter into the same sort of relationship that most of us have and treasure: ongoing, with mutual affection and regard. In such relationships, we all make mistakes, are all in some ways inadequate, and yet it is not the level of success that makes the relationship so satisfying to the people involved; it is the ongoing commitment. In the context of relationships, the success and failure of our work becomes harder to assess because the key elements no longer involve simply quantity but the more complex issues of quality. We professionals have routinely overlooked the significance of relationships. Not only do we not have many established strategies for having personal connections with those we would help, we have deputized parents, who do have this connection, into professional and paraprofessional roles. Oddly, we have maintained a double standard: When parents have difficulties with their children, we ascribe this to some deficiency of their caring or skills. When our own, relatively impersonal efforts fail (by our own precise standards), then we forgive one another because those children were beyond hope. We need to put this kind of rhetoric and blame management into permanent retirement.

———

Anticipating certain difficulties is a common-sense way to prepare thoughtfully for a situation and can eliminate having to improvise in the heat of a crisis. There is a risk that this preparation stops our thinking rather than develops it. Rather than paying attention to what is actually happening with the person and responding to that, we pay attention to the program and try to get the person to follow it. Means overtaking the ends happens easily to the best of us, so that often the best we can do is be aware of the possibility and work in ways so that others can point it out to us when it happens.

Program for Wendy
Target behavior: Assaultive behavior

1. If Wendy becomes verbally assaultive (shouting, swearing, etc.), she will be asked what is bothering her.
2. If she refuses to talk this over calmly, she will be told she is being verbally assaultive and redirected to another task.
3. If she refuses, she will be asked to go to her room to calm down. If she refuses this request, she will be physically escorted to her room.
4. If she becomes physically assaultive, she will be taken to the time-out room and held by three staff. Because she can be very assaultive with hitting and kicking, two staff people will hold her arms extended out from her body, another will hold her feet. They will keep her in this position until she has regained control.
5. When she says she is calm, she will be held another 5 minutes and then asked to stay in the time-out room for another 15 minutes to make certain she has regained control.
6. If she cannot regain calm after 30 minutes, she will be given an emergency medication.

This program for Wendy, a 26-year-old woman, is typical. These procedures—even with the many variations I have seen—have a weary sameness of approach that assumes, as we often do, that Wendy's distress needs management. The tradition of behavioral control has focused far more on consequences than on antecedents. For example, one state requested proposals for an anger management course for 12 angry service users. This struck me as an odd request given that no one seemed to know why these people were upset. Given a choice between a course in anger management and less to be angry about, I can safely predict which I would choose.

The plan outlined for Wendy is often thought to be a reasonable, step-by-step progression that gives Wendy the opportunity for appropriate expressions of distress. Unfortunately, this plan gives Wendy very little room to express her anger compared with the wide range of possibilities most ordinary people have—and use.

Step 1 of this plan gives Wendy the opportunity to explain what is bothering her. People labeled retarded often have a hard time expressing themselves clearly in ordinary circumstances, and, as we all know, it can be particularly hard to be articulate and effective when angry. Most of us have had the experience of being so upset as to be speechless or so angry as to throw things or scream. When I have been in this state of mind or, more precisely out of my mind, I might appreciate someone asking me what is the matter or I might not. It would never be of help for me to know that I had better come up with an answer or else I will be expected to calm down. I think the most infuriating words I can hear when I am angry are "calm down." An angry person often needs to be reassured to take time, that there is no hurry in saying what the problem is because those who care will wait patiently.

Suppose Wendy is upset because she has lost the key to the cabinet where she keeps her compact discs. Frustrated that she cannot listen to her music, she starts shouting and blaming her roommate. We could employ Step 1 by saying, "Wendy, you seem upset. What's bothering you?" Or we could say, "What is it now, Wendy?" Depending on our relationship with Wendy or our own mood at the moment of her distress, we could be heard as supportive and helpful or as irritated and uncaring.

Even if we are seen as trying to help, it might well be that Wendy has had a hard day at work and has lost the little patience she had. She might just stomp around and swear loudly. This plan urges us to go to Step 2 (i.e., If she refuses to talk this over calmly, she will be told she is being verbally assaultive and redirected to another task.) In Step 2, we would say, "Wendy, you seem upset. Why don't you watch television for a while and take it easy?" This might be well-intended, but the problem is that Wendy wants her compact discs. She might shout "No!" and kick a chair. Because she has not told us we do not yet understand that she is looking for a key. One approach to her problem would be to stand out of striking distance and wait, hoping she will be able to let us know what is bothering her. But the plan moves us to Step 3 (i.e., If she refuses, she will be asked to go to her room to calm down. If she refuses this request, she will be physically escorted to her room.).

We might still be seen as friendly in saying, "Wendy, you seem upset. Would it help if you went to your room and calmed down for a minute?" If she continues to shout and swear, we could correctly surmise that she does not see this as a helpful suggestion. Again, one sensible response would be to wait until she has calmed down enough to let us know what is bothering her or how we could help. If Wendy does not use words to communicate, then we could try to guess what is wrong. Many people who do not use language are able to indicate yes and no. In any case, we could still say to Wendy, both in word and deed, "You seem to need something. How can I help you get it?"

But after the potentially helpful first two steps, this program directs us to become bolder, more controlling, and to act in ways that I could never imagine as helpful. Step 3 says, in effect, "We will help you as long as you meet our standards. Now you must either regain control to our satisfaction or we will take control of you." Even if a person were to comply in the face of this display of power, what have we taught? We have taught that control is something *you* lose and *we* give back. I do not think that is the lesson we want to teach. It is much more to our stated purposes to demonstrate that self-control is something we all can lose, but with practice and patience, we can learn to get it back.

This is a dangerous message. When we are angry, we often feel overwhelmed either by the outside environment or by a tumult of feelings and thoughts. To have another person take away—or even just *try* to take away—what little sense of control remains can accelerate the problem. I find it hard to feel self-respect when I am incoherently upset. I would find self-respect impossible to feel if someone were to escort me to my bedroom. In fact, it is absurd to think that anyone could do that to me. No one should have that power over me. Of course, if a group of people knew that I literally could not call for help, or would not be taken seriously if I did, then anything could happen to me.

Escort is a euphemism for many displays of authority; people under arrest, for example, are escorted by the police. But in ordinary social situations, a display of authority can provoke resistance as well as compliance. Some people react aggressively only when they feel crowded. By simply standing out of reach, patiently waiting, we can prevent ourselves from getting hurt and lessen the likelihood that a person will be able or need to strike out. This approach requires only one person to maintain safe and ordinary social contact with the agitated person. Physical restraint requires many people and puts everyone involved at risk of serious injury.

Through the use of physical restraint we teach that power is the basis of permission. We are saying, "If you really want to get angry with someone, find someone less powerful than you." I have met with many people who routinely use physical restraint and complain, "Kate is really just a bully (or is manipulative or sneaky). She only picks on people who won't strike back." Such people rarely see that they have taught Kate how effective this strategy is.

It is not hard to make the emotional progression from being angry and being told to go to your room to being made even more angry. If someone tries to escort you and you would rather not be escorted, isn't it also likely that in order to get away you would become assaultive? The rest of this intervention for Wendy really just elaborates on the basic message: Do as we say or we will *make* you do as we say. This message is bitterly emphasized with a little revenge by demanding that you must demonstrate our criterion of being calm for 15 minutes in a room with nothing in it. This reliance on a standard time rather than on a sense of the person's perceived need seems unnecessarily arbitrary. Because I cannot predict for myself how long it would take me to calm down in a specific situation, I cannot honestly gauge this for someone else. But this underscores the message that we know better than you do what you need to feel and when you will feel it. Instead of asking others how they feel, this sort of plan tells them. I think this intervention requires superhuman effort not to continue feeling enraged. Of course, if Wendy had been given a "chemical restraint," then she might not have the energy to act on this fury though the fury might remain.

Chemical restraint or emergency (p.r.n.) medication has been a staple of psychiatric crisis intervention. As with almost every other aspect of our service, this strategy has its partisans, and, in fact, some people respond well to medication. Technically, the decision to give emergency medication can only be made by a psychiatrist, but in practice this often gets decided by the direct service and nursing staff. Because these are often the very people who have just been hurt by the person, their objectivity is likely to be at a low point. Even when psychiatrists are actually called for permission to medicate, the conversation is usually fairly brief. For obvious reasons, psychiatrists take the word of the staff without serious question because they identify more with the staff than with the person. I wonder how often psychiatrists ask to speak with the person to be medicated. Indeed, I have known psychiatrists sufficiently protective of their time as to sign blank forms authorizing medication that nurses fill in as they decide it is needed. These medications are often given by injection. I have known nurses to take pride in their ability to make this "treatment" as painful as possible for "especially bad cases."

Even more sinister is the idea that once permission for physical restraint or time-out has been given, less restrictive steps are only superficially tried. For example, some staff decide that Wendy is only going to end up being timed-out anyway, so they run through the preliminary steps only perfunctorily. When Wendy starts to yell, they say, "O.K., Wendy, what is it this time?" When she fails to respond to their "concern," she is told, "If you don't stop acting bad, you'll go to your room." When this does not work, Wendy ends up held on the floor by three people while a fourth calls the nurse for a shot. I have known other *caregivers* to be even more direct. If a person can be timed-out for hitting someone, then staff intentionally provoke an assault by pushing the person so that when the person hits back, he or she has become assaultive and needs to be timed-out.

This approach inhibits all who work or live with it. Do you have any ordinary relationships where you think of your responses as Step 1 and Step 2? This routinizing of social life not only makes the subject of such routines feel the lack of personal contact, it makes the people carrying these out feel programmed and anonymous. The implication is that any of the people in this plan can be replaced by any other. In contrast, real relationships are unique and irreplaceable.

There is another fundamental flaw to the rationale behind this kind of strategy. This technology is typically used to control ordinary feelings such as anger or irritation. I have never seen a plan that would teach someone like Wendy how to enjoy another person or a person to appreciate her. In spite of its professed reliance on positive reinforcement, this kind of technology focuses on problem behaviors. One of the joys of having friends and significant others in our lives is the spontaneity in our time together. Both in good times and in bad, we rely on the inspiration of the moment. Sometimes we guess correctly, sometimes not. When we do something that helps another, we share the pleasure of that. When we guess wrong, we can apologize, ask for more information, or just try again. Would we ever think in an argument: Step 1. Try humor; if that fails, go to Step 2. Cajolery; if that fails, go to Step 3. Serious sulking. We may have followed this plan but not, I hope, through pre-arranged programming. The choices we make come from our involvement *with* a person and our relationship, not from a calculated program of control.

Mechanical Restraint

Mechanical restraint is the most anomalous of the control technologies. Even though it is used in places whose assumed function is therapy, such as hospitals and state schools, it is not clearly understood as a "treatment." There is virtually no literature that articulates mechanical restraint as a coherent therapeutic intervention, that is, who should be restrained, or how, or when, or for how long. In practice, mechanical restraints seem to be not overtly intended as punitive, but of all the control technologies, mechanical restraint is mainly done for the satisfaction of those restraining rather than for the person being restrained.

The routine use of control technologies creates a climate where people lose their identities. Instead of being known as Frank and Rita, Frank and Rita are known as behavior problems. In this context, the behaviors are seen as independent of the people, and the behaviors are often seen as occurring "for no reason" or for the reason that these people themselves are beyond reason. Once the behavior is seen as out of control, then struggling to regain control becomes the logical goal.

The routine use of mechanical restraint is justified in terms of service needs, rather than in terms of personal needs. "Sometimes Frank just gets too out of control to be dealt with in any other way" is really a way of saying, "We need to treat him this way in order for us to run our business as usual." We rarely ask, "What do *we* need to change so this person could be served more respectfully and directly?"

I forget to ask this question enough. I used to accept what I was taught, that if I were working in a hospital emergency room and a large, loud, and aggressive person began to throw furniture, I would have only a few choices: send her away (which would be unethical if she needed medical attention), hold her down (which might take more people than are working at the moment), or tie her to a bed until she calms or can be assessed. As long as I accepted this problem in terms of the existing service climate, I considered mechanical restraint to be both necessary and ethical. If, however, I looked at this situation from the person's point of view rather than just my own, I might more aggressively consider what this mental health service needs to avoid interventions where everyone ends up scared and exhausted.

People who live with problems often find personal and workable solutions. In human services (as in other areas of our society), we have forgotten to ask the people who use services for their opinions. I visited the Ruby Rogers Self-Help Drop-In Center (founded by the Former Mental Patients' Liberation Front) in Cambridge, Massachusetts, to ask people about their experiences. People talked about how they had been helped in intense moments of crisis by simply having someone they trusted listen to them.

Even brief conversations, they said, helped them defuse their feelings of being out of control. People talked about feeling scared or angry and going to the emergency room because it was the only place open at 4 A.M. and, instead of being given a chance to talk, they found themselves tied down and drugged up. Again, having a relationship where one is known personally makes the difference between the enforced control of straitjackets and the chance to calm down over a cup of coffee. *For people who need help, not being known personally and not being taken seriously by those who can provide help is itself the emergency.*

The use of mechanical restraints in human services has a mostly secret life. Although none of the standard literature advocates the use of such restraints as a treatment of choice for behavioral difficulties, people with developmental disabilities are still at risk for being chronically tied up, shackled, or held in restraint cuffs. Ironically, use of mechanical restraints sometimes comes from the understandably humane impulse to prevent self-injury. In one way, the decision to restrain says, "We don't know why you are hurting yourself. We just need to stop you." This sounds like a reasonable first step. Unfortunately, it is often the only step. Instead of considering the person's life and how his or her preferences and wishes are met or frustrated, we are liable to fail in our understanding. Although people's troubling behavior often results from their difficulties in communicating or from their frustrations with life, we service providers have spent a disproportionate amount of energy on changing the person's skills rather than on changing and adapting what we do for people and how we do it.

Instead of looking at difficult behavior as the concern and responsibility of everyone involved, we tend to label the person as a severe behavior problem and look for ways to manage *the person as a problem* better. Because efficiency holds high value in both behavioral thinking and institutional management, mechanical restraint becomes a predictable way to conserve expensive staff time.

Control technologies are essential to maintain the oppressive congregation of people with similar labels. Congregation can be practical and efficient for people with treatable and curable conditions in medical settings. Putting all people who have coronary disease on one ward makes sense if the staff have an expertise in treating coronary disease. Especially if the treatment is good, people on the ward will only be there for a relatively short time before getting on with the rest of their lives. However, segregating people with non-medical conditions such as developmental disabilities produces the opposite result: People will become more, rather than less, developmentally disabled. Environment is more powerful than will.

The kinds of diagnoses that many people with challenging behaviors share are more categorical than explanatory. We do not understand the causes of schizophrenia, autism, or idiopathic mental retardation, and these labels do not explain much about where a person's behavioral challenges come from or what to do about them once they do develop. Whenever we have failed to recognize why people are different, clinical tradition has tended to enforce outer conformity at the expense of the person's actual reasons for being different.

What literature there is about mechanical restraint generally presents its use as ultimately teaching a person socially more ordinary strategies for self-control. Unfortunately, the ways in which this is done are socially unusual in themselves. Hamad, Isley, and Lowry (1983) provided one example:

> The subject was a 41-year-old profoundly mentally retarded, nonverbal man living in a state institution. He was admitted to the institution at the age of 6, and his records indicate that self-injurious behavior (SIB) began when he was 8 years old. Initially, the topography of SIB was predominantly hands or fists to head. Occasionally he would bite his arms. Later in life hitting the area around the eyes with either knee became the sole topography of the SIB. Four years prior to the study the behavior caused detached retinas and blindness in both eyes. At the time of this study he received 10 mg of Haldol (haloperidol) each evening. Medication remained constant throughout the study.
>
> During waking hours the subject wore a brace-like restraint device attached to his hip and knee which prevented knee to

head contact. The device permitted the subject to walk, stand, or sit without interference.

The study was conducted in an apartment consisting of a large day room and bedroom, at a large institution for mentally retarded persons. The apartment housed the subject and three other residents in a staff ratio of 1:2. (pp. 213–214)

The authors described their intervention:[15]

The subject was released from the mechanical restraint device for one 15-minute trial at noon time on the first day of the intervention. Additional 15-minute restraint free trials were added at 8 and 10 A.M. and at 2, 4, 6:30 and 9 P.M. across the next ten weeks. Assignment of 15-minute restraint release times was decided on an arbitrary basis. When the subject exhibited no attempts at SIB during any 15-minute interval for 3 consecutive days, the amount of time out of restraint was increased by 15 minutes for that trial. For example, if no SIB was observed at the noon trial for three consecutive days, time out of restraint was increased for 15 minutes for the noon trial only. The time out of restraint was decreased by 5 minutes following two consecutive days with any self-injury attempts during that trial. For example, if self-injury occurred on two consecutive days during the 10 A.M. trial, the amount of time out of restraint was decreased by 5 minutes for the 10 A.M. trial only.

---

[15]The shift from the behavioral perspective to positive approaches can often be heard in the use of language. One wonders what function is served by the pseudoscientific jargon in which this narrative is written. Basically, this is about coercing a man who hits himself and disturbs the staff. But rather than talk about this in the language ordinary people use, the authors distance themselves from him so that he becomes a nameless subject (really an object) and what they do to help him becomes "a trial."

A more positive approach would begin by conceptualizing this man's difficulties somewhat differently. His primary problem is not just his behavior but his entire life. Where he lives and what is expected of him militates against his changing his behavior very much. Were he to be seen as a social equal and as a collaborator and instructor in planning services for himself, he might then have a life that would invite and help him to change his behavior himself. Rather than being the object of manipulations, he would be included with people he could trust and who liked and trusted him. None of these real-life needs are discussed because the focus of this endeavor is not to respond to this man personally but to control his behavior. Sadly, these helpers, in reacting to behaviors that were intrusive and difficult for *them*, ignored their own behaviors that were difficult and intrusive for this man.

During the time out of restraint, the subject was provided with a high density of preferred reinforcers including verbal praise, physical contact, edible reinforcers, and preferred activities. When out of restraint, any self-injury attempt produced three consequences. First, the subject was physically guided to perform a behavior incompatible with SIB. Specifically, he was guided to a standing position. Second, his leg was physically restrained by holding his ankle down until he stopped trying to raise his knee. Finally, access to all reinforcers was withheld until a 30-second period elapsed without any SIB attempts. Staff closely supervising the subject were able to prevent most knee-to-head contacts.

While in restraints, the subject was spoken to only when he was asked to eat or to go to the toilet. He was given physical contact only when his clothes needed to be changed, and he was denied access to preferred activities such as playing with magazines and ropes and going outside on walks. (p. 214)

This study is a good example of how clinicians have narrowed their focus at the expense of common courtesy and social justice.[16] The subject was functionally incarcerated strictly because of his having been labeled retarded, and yet he is the one who is made to be responsible for earning his freedom. Thinking of his behavior as an adaptation to living in an institution would lead us to recognize his skill in responding to his environment. This, in turn, would give us more confidence in trusting him to act in more typical ways in more typical places, particularly doing the things he most enjoyed.

Two objections to these suggestions are common. One fear is that engaging noncontingently in "preferred activities" will somehow reinforce the unwanted behavior. I think of doing enjoyable things as providing a positive context for people to develop relationships, and, in that context, for be-

---

[16]This treatment is not all that different, at the behavioral level, from the historical use of mechanical restraint as punishment where similar humiliation was implicit. Offenders placed in stocks were fair game for the spontaneous abuse of passersby. Not being considered except for toileting or eating is how a kenneled dog is treated, except that a dog would also be regularly walked. That this man's preferred activities for years involved magazines and ropes was seen as indicating the poverty of his intellectual capacity rather than as many people see it now: as the result of the barren environment and poverty of accommodation in which he was forced to live.

havior to change. If anything is being reinforced it is the relationship between the people helping and the person helped. For this reason, I encourage people to work with people they share interests with as well as some intangible but mutual sense of liking one another. The second objection is that there are insufficient staff to do all these "fun things." This objection is particularly odd when the people in this man's life spend so much time controlling his behavior with what seems to be anything but fun for him or them.

I would be curious to see what this man's behavior could have become had people spent their energy in cultivating a friendship with him. The way in which their time was used in this program would disincline most people from pursuing further association with this man. Obviously, this is not to encourage the use of relationships as a manipulable technology for behavior change, but to affirm that they are the context within which significant behavior change is possible.

Wouldn't it have made a great deal more sense to work with this man in a more ordinary place doing things he enjoyed? For example, if he liked to go on boat trips or to baseball games as well as walks outside, he could have tried doing these things without being shackled. For these activities to have any social value and avoid being a therapeutic ploy, he would have gone with people who basically liked him and who also liked doing these things: Friendships are built on some difficult-to-articulate "chemistry," and they are strengthened by shared interests. Of course, some people might like him but dislike walks outside. Perhaps through these relationships of shared regard he could discover new things to enjoy. Instead of these social possibilities, he was treated as if he were going to the hospital for a "behavior cure" and somehow had to demonstrate "behavioral health" before he could be discharged. Given what would help him change and what he was given, this seems very much like hearing someone say, "As soon as you choose to stop drowning, we will teach you to swim."

This kind of "readiness thinking" has serious implications for the lives of people who use services. By looking at behavior as symptomatic, many people who work in the field have been beguiled into thinking that reducing a person's difficult behavior to zero is a positive accomplishment. This is as mistaken as thinking that pleasure is an absence of pain. If we think of difficult behavior as a person's expression of pain, of negative experience, then simply removing the negative elements might make the person's life better, but not necessarily positive. Most of us have had plenty of experiences where nothing terribly bad was happening, but we still would not say we were happy. The nonaversive technologies make this same mistake. Simply because something is nonaversive does not make it positive. Besides, our best work calls us to ask and to listen to what makes people's lives richer and more exciting. This is not the same thing as asking what makes our own services to them not hurtful.

In this example, time out of restraint could easily have been used to teach him that his self-injury was unnecessary because he had better things to do with his time. Similarly, by not speaking to him while he was in restraint, his staff lost an opportunity to develop a relationship with him. A relationship could have provided a context of concern for him as a person rather than, as he is presented here, an emitter of self-injurious behavior.

Of course, to have attempted a personal and caring relationship would have made it emotionally difficult, if not impossible, to put him into restraint. People would soon have to abandon their restraints or their empathy. This failure to take ordinary social consideration into account is one of the most hurtful shortcomings of much behavioral practice. Gunnar Dybwad noted that behavioral procedures were not developed by the people working on the wards but rather by psychologists writing programs in their offices. This impersonality is supposed to provide the professional virtue of objectivity, but it is hard to overlook the psychologist's implicit assumptions about power and control in the "assignment of 15-minute restraint release times . . . on an arbitrary basis." Psychologists writing behavior programs chronically complain about the lack of staff cooperation in implementing their work even though cooperation obviously implies a two-way street rather than a one-way cul-de-sac. Even in community services, many behavior programs are written by someone who may barely know the person for whom the program is developed. This lack of relationship can be dangerous when remoteness is implicitly desired in most ideologies of technological control.

Even when controlling and artificial interventions are time limited and actually result in the extinction of a dangerous behavior, they often pursue what is socially desirable in socially undesirable ways. Saying that the end justifies the means is a comfort professionals typically extend to one another, but it fundamentally evades a hard truth: Making the ends and means of services congruent is more the responsibility of those providing services than it is the work of those they are provided to. This plan seems to have arrived in this man's life without his asking for it or having any way of stopping it.

Ultimately, this program of restraint compelled him to submit to the will of people who had no personal connection to him or hopes for him. Nothing in this plan would help him choose more freely the kind of life he himself might want to live. Instead, he was compelled to become more clearly the passive recipient of services.

By focusing on only one small part of this man's life, the authors failed to achieve their initial goal of his physical safety. By forcing him to fit in better with the institution, they left him at risk for being hurt, not by himself but by others. Institutions that began as safe havens for vulnerable people very quickly became as dangerous a place for vulnerable people as our society could provide. Although most people recognize the clear disadvantages of congregate settings, some people have made the opposite error of assuming that all can be remedied in people's lives simply by forcing them into ordinary settings.

In another example, a study (Duran, 1984) reporting on the use of mechanical restraint presented training for a 15-year-old boy with autism whose work performance was compromised by his laughing loudly for no apparent reason, running from the worksite, and hitting other workers. The response to these disruptions was to tie the boy's arms to his workstation with pieces of sheets leaving him only enough freedom of movement to complete his work. Tying this boy up, in effect, says that getting him to work in the "nonsheltered vocational setting" was more important than his happiness about it. It seems absurd to consider a job where workers can be tied up with bed sheets as ordinary. This intervention was published as a success story rather than as what it really was—a cautionary tale about putting people to work they neither like nor choose.

Rather than discussing at length why this boy needed to be tied up, it might have been more to the point to discuss why the people working for him could not find him more congenial employment. Because difficulties emerged when he was expected to do some kind of table-top task, it might be reasonable for him to work where he could walk around rather than sit all day. His laughing loudly and hitting others could most logically be seen as his expression of frustration with a job (or a workplace) he did not like. Indeed, given that he seemed not to have had any way of communicating verbally, it would be hard *not* to see that his only means of communication was his behavior.

Taking their lead from Freud, psychoanalysts plunged into the depths of the mind to discern motive. In their equal and opposite reaction to this, behavioral technicians took great pride in not caring about motives at all but only caring about the consequences of behavior. This seems to be an unnecessary error in the opposite direction. One does not necessarily have to inquire deeply and psychoanalytically into his past to see that this boy's behavior could communicate his desires. To ignore the communicative aspect of his behavior and then to tie him literally to a job he apparently did not want undercuts any spirit of help.

Rita was a 21-year-old woman described as nonverbal and profoundly retarded. Her school program assessed her as functioning at the 18-month level of motor development and at less than 1 year for feeding, toileting, and cognitive and social development.

Rita had spent virtually all her life in mechanical restraint. Her mother had discovered that by removing the tops and bottoms from cans, she was left with a cheap set of elbow cuffs that prevented Rita from bending her arms. If Rita was allowed to move her arms freely, she put her hands or objects into her mouth. Similarly, if she was allowed to move freely around the house, she got into things, so her family contrived to tie her to a chair during her waking hours.

When Rita was 16 years old, an aunt living out of state became sick. Rita's mother went to take care of her, leaving Rita's sisters to look after her. For whatever reasons, Rita did not get anything to eat or drink for several days and ended up losing a third of her body weight, suffering from hyperna-tremic dehydration, and being admitted to an intensive care unit. Then, two of her married sisters moved back to their family home along with their husbands and children. This crowding and the change in demands left Rita's family feeling that they could no longer care for her and that she should move into a community residence.

When Rita made trial visits to the group home, the staff felt that she was everywhere at once, into everything, and well beyond their abilities to keep up with her. In spite of their convictions to support people in ordinary ways, these people were ready to make an exception for Rita. In the course of several visits she had gone into the kitchen and, in just a few seconds, succeeded in drinking liquid dish soap and eating a loaf of bread as well as the plastic bag it came in. She went through the refrigerator trying to put entire oranges into her mouth. When she was not trying to eat things, she kept her hands in her mouth until she had enough saliva collected to smear on the tops of tables or onto the windows. When people took Rita for a walk, she grabbed as much as she could to put into her mouth. Sometimes she threw herself to the ground and refused to move. At mealtimes, she lunged across the table to grab food from other people's plates. Rita's erratic diet also seemed to make her digestion unpredictable. She could be constipated for 2 days and then have diarrhea for 3. Rita had no independent toileting skills and relied on others to help her change her soiled clothes after her toileting accidents. People had decided that Rita posed a "management problem."

Seeing her this way, people put their energies into managing her intensely. One person shadowed her to keep her hands out of her mouth; another was assigned to sit at all times blocking the kitchen doorway. After 2 weeks of this,

Rita had not changed at all and virtually everyone working in this group home was ready to quit.

It was at this point that I was invited to meet with the people working with her, ostensibly to develop a program to control Rita. In thinking a little bit about Rita's life, people came to recognize that while she had been taught almost nothing, she had been highly controlled. As they talked about her life of being tied up, they realized that just about everything Rita had touched in the last 2 weeks had been a completely new experience for her. This made it easier to see they could spend time teaching her how to make sense of her environment rather than working to separate her from it.

So, instead of seeing Rita as uncontrollable, people began to think of her as virtually unlimited in what she could learn and they could teach. Rather than keep her out of the kitchen, people recognized her need to learn what kitchens were for and how she could get what she wanted from them. This put people into the role of assisting, teaching, and encouraging her—"Here's something to hold"—rather than in blocking and controlling her—"Put that down!"

When Rita leaned across the table to grab food from other people's plates, we thought she might be saying, "I don't know where food comes from. I have to grab what I need to get enough." We even wondered if she knew what enough meant. As William Blake wisely wrote: "In order to know enough, we need to know too much."

People decided that rather than restrain her when they went out for a walk, they could let her sit down and pick things up. We thought when she put things into her mouth it might be her way of learning what things were. Naturally, if she tried to swallow something like a pebble or if she picked up something sharp, people would tell her, "No." Because people were finding safe ways for her to try different foods, feel lots of different textures, smell all kinds of scents, and just explore the world around her, we thought "no" would have some power for her, standing as it did surrounded by yesses. People saw themselves as teaching Rita discrimination by demonstrating it.

This also changed the way people thought about their work. As teachers, their success was measured by what Rita safely experienced, rather than by what she had not done.

People had avoided public places with her for fear that she would become unmanageable. With their new set of expectations, people understood Rita's need to get out into ordinary places so she could learn how to function in them.

Almost immediately, two things came of this: People found Rita a lot easier to be with; and, seemingly out of nowhere, Rita became less frantic. Sometimes we can set up cycles that lead to strength both for ourselves and those for whom we work.

Aversives: The Use of Pain to Control Behavior

Much of what we do in life is either rewarding or punishing, so the idea of clinical applications of these real-life experiences seems reasonable in the abstract. The problem, as we have seen, is that in their clinical applications these principles are skewed strongly in the direction of punishment.

What are typically considered positive reinforcements for most people with developmental disabilities are things people should have access to as a matter of good service. Most Americans do not consider a weekly trip to the mall as a "privilege" they should prove themselves worthy of—or else their reinforcements are too trivial to matter. Few of us would consider it encouraging to be given a cup of coffee each morning and afternoon contingent on our work performance. Many of us are committed to our own good behavior not by the force of extrinsic motivators, such as bonuses or a special parking space for the employee of the month, but by the engagement of intrinsic satisfactions such as believing our work has meaning and purpose and that we have tried to do it the best we can. And some of these "positive" programs don't work because much of difficult behavior is beyond extrinsic control anyway.

When the seemingly common-sensical technology of giving rewards and incentives fails, service providers are given a choice: either to deepen their commitment to support the person personally and see what that leads them to or to deepen their commitment to the technology. Too often, we have begun with good ideas for someone we love, only to fall in love with the ideas and then forget the person.

In many ways, ignore and redirect; overcorrection; time-out; and physical, mechanical, and chemical restraints are secondary adaptations when reward schemes fail. Tying someone up to prevent her self-injury is often an attempt—however misguided—to get the person under behavioral control and prevent her getting hurt, not to hurt her intentionally. If someone gets hurt during a physical restraint procedure, that is typically seen as an unfortunate side effect, not a rationale for the intervention in the first place.

When we come to aversives, though, we have entered another realm of behavioral control. Here, pain is not the unfortunate side effect; it is the entire point.

To make the discussion of this difficult topic even more complicated, I should explain my own involvement with this issue. On the one hand, since the 1980s I have been part of an alliance of parents and professionals working to pass legislation against these practices both in my home state and nationally. I am a founding member of the Autism National Committee, which was formed to advocate for and collaborate with people at risk for being hurt in the name of therapy.

On the other hand, at the same time I have consulted with some institutions where strong aversives have been used. My role in those consultations has been to find ways of helping the people move from these aversive programs to get supports in community-based services. Some colleagues have taken a stand that working in or for any institution is immoral. My presumption is that institutional staff typically do the best they can in a very difficult situation and in most of the places where I have worked, I have indeed found people concerned about the welfare of their clients.

I have also worked over time with the clinical directors and authors of some very painful behavior plans. Again, the stereotype of such people is that they must be heartless. Instead, I have been consistently impressed by those people who have used aversives reluctantly and often from some emotionally charged mixture of desperation and hope. The people I have found helpful to work with in finding better ways of supporting people in distress are those who have actively looked for decent interventions. In other words, some people who have used aversives did not fall in love with the power of the concept but have held fast to their beliefs and concerns for people with disabilities.

What I have found alarming are those people who insist these painful interventions are the most effective (and in some cases, the only) interventions for people in distress. Despite the rapidly growing body of evidence that shows how people do not need to be hurt to be helped, some people have clung to an outdated and discredited technology. The following examples show just how desperate this desire to control can become:

> A young man who tried to run away from his group home "lost privileges" for 30 days. "Loss of privileges" meant that everyone in the program was to ignore him totally, his beard was shaved, he was made to wear a helmet for the full 30 days, he was given only 15 minutes to eat cold meals, he was required to sleep without a mattress, and although his clothes were cleaned, he had to wear the same clothes for the full 30 days. (Commonwealth of Massachusetts, 1985, pp. 7–8)

One agency used the following hierarchy of aversives:

1. Ignore
2. Firm "no"
3. Token fines
4. Water squirt to the face or back of the neck
5. Vapor spray (compressed air alone or mixed with water) to the back of the neck for approximately 3 seconds
6. A football helmet with an opaque screen to occlude vision and a masking or other unpleasant repetitive noise
7. Vinegar, vanilla extract, lemon juice, jalapeno pepper spray, or other unspecified taste aversives applied to lip or tongue
8. Standing barefoot on an uncomfortable rubber mat while wearing a football helmet with white noise or other unpleasant repetitive sound as a time-out
9. Ammonia fumes sprayed near the nose
10. Compressed air sprayed to the face or the back of the neck for approximately 15 seconds
11. Compressed air sprayed to the face or the back of the neck for approximately 2 minutes
12. Contingent physical exercise (unspecified number of situps or toe-touches)

13. Compressed air or water sprays attached to the football helmet that occludes vision with white noise or other unpleasant repetitive sound
14. Loosely tying a student who misbehaves to another student he or she finds aversive
15. Hand squeeze
16. Wrist squeeze
17. Rubber band snapped on the wrist or the inner arm
18. Spanking bare buttocks or thighs
19. Muscle squeeze applied to the shoulder, triceps, pectoral, or thigh
20. Rolling pinch applied to buttocks, inner arm, inner thigh, bottom of feet, the palms, or abdomen
21. Finger pinch applied to buttocks, inner arm, inner thigh, bottom of feet, the palms, or abdomen
22. Bucket of cold water poured over head
23. One minute shower at approximately 50 degrees
24. Wrists and ankles restrained in a booth with compressed air alone or mixed with water
25. Multiple consequences
26. Combined aversives (Commonwealth of Massachusetts, 1985, pp. 7–8)

A sampling of reports from this agency showed that in 3 consecutive days one individual received the following aversives for aggression and self-injurious behavior (neither behavior was operationally defined):

Day 1:   10:30 P.M.–2:30 A.M.
  37 finger pinches to the thighs
  62 finger pinches to the buttocks
  12 finger pinches to the foot
  68 finger pinches to the hand
  37 spanks to the thigh
  49 vapor sprays to the face

Day 2:   5:00 P.M.–6:15 P.M.
  85 finger pinches to the feet
  20 finger pinches to the hand
  75 muscle squeezes to the shoulders
  15 vapor sprays to the face

Day 3:   6:00 A.M.–9:30 P.M.
  173 spanks to the thighs

50 spanks to the buttocks
98 muscle squeezes to the thighs, shoulders, and triceps
88 finger pinches to the buttocks
47 finger pinches to the thighs
    approximately 527 finger pinches to the feet
78 finger pinches to the hands (Commonwealth of Massachu-
    setts, 1985, p. 9)

In 1989, a court approved the use of an electric shock helmet for a young man for the exhibition of the following behaviors: head shaking, breaking objects, applying pressure to his collarbone, getting out of his seat, walking or running away from the group, blinking his eyes rapidly, holding his head to his shoulder, leg shaking, and clicking his teeth (Weiss, 1990, p. 2).

Most people reading these examples live—or strive to live—in a world whose ideals are respect, cooperation, and equality with others. In such a context, these examples seem extreme, bizarre, and abhorrent. But in the world of people with developmental disabilities, compliance is often the chiefest of virtues. In this world, being controlled by others is the norm and to break with that standard exacts punishment from one's controllers. It has been a long journey from tokens and contingent verbal praise to these hurtful extremes, but this is where the journey too often, literally, ends. People die in these kinds of programs.

Article 1 of the United Nations Convention on Torture has three key points in its definition: 1) severe pain or suffering; 2) being intentionally inflicted by or at the instigation of a public official; and 3) for such purposes as to obtain information on confession, punishment, intimidation, coercion, *"or for any reason based on discrimination of any kind"* [my emphasis] (Staub, 1990, p. 63). Agencies using aversive programming 1) inflict severe pain and suffering, 2) are often licensed by state and federal authority and are funded by public money, and 3) do so on the basis of people's disabilities.

Aversive therapy is, by definition, torture. Aversive therapy is a result of a person's political status, of discrimination based on disability, and of the lack of protections far more often than because his behavior warrants such treatment. No convicted felon can legally be treated as cruelly as the young people pinched and slapped and hurt in the examples above.[17] Ironically, people who have been convicted of serious crimes have better protections than people whose only offense is having a disability and frightening those nearest them. If severe behavior really responded to the use of pain, then correctional facilities would be leaders in its use. Instead, pain is used to control only people who have virtually no political representation or protection.

Staub (1990) cited some of the cultural conditions that promote the possible use of torture:

---

[17]In discussing aversives as torture, I am following the behavioral tradition of discussing behaviors, not behavers. Still, the motives of someone using aversives 10 years ago are more comprehensible than the motives involved in advocating for them now. Because the people subjected to these painful experiments were sufficiently rare, there was some optimism in thinking that this kind of pain could be helpful. Those days, though, are gone.

At the time of publication, the *APA Monitor* had a brief report on the work of Carl Goldberg, a psychologist who has developed "a new theory to explain the psychological basis of malevolent behavior."

Goldberg defines malevolence as the *deliberate* infliction of cruel, painful suffering on another living being. These actions are taken by people who know exactly what they are doing and are capable of understanding the consequences.

Based on nearly 30 years of work with patients "who have committed murder, rape, and mayhem in malevolent ways," Goldberg has concluded that evil deeds are "no more a product of mental illness than they are compelled by Satan." People don't turn into Hitlers or Jeffrey Dahmers overnight, but rather "learn by doing," Goldberg said. "Opportunities to choose between good and bad occur continually in our daily lives, even in the smallest matters. How we have responded to earlier choices shapes our moral decisions now and in the future."

Goldberg says there are six crucial features that make up the malevolent personality: 1) shame, or self-contempt, is the simplest and most common; 2) contempt for others, or the projection of the defects sensed in oneself onto others, hoping to deflate them; 3) rationalization, or explaining away malevolent behavior, "Each decision to rationalize a contemptuous act makes it easier to perform subsequent contemptuous acts. Inevitably, the result is an addiction to rationalizing cruel, insensitive behavior," Goldberg said. 4) Justification, or feeling that they are superior to others. "Indeed, some [malevolent people] boast that they live by a higher morality than conventional people," Goldberg said. 5) Inability or unwillingness to examine one's dark side, being fearful of unknown aspects of oneself; and, 6) magical thinking such as believing that one already knows everything that is needed to be known. ("News Briefs," 1995, p. 13.)

1. A history of *devaluation of a subgroup* of society and discrimination against this subgroup that preselects the group as a victim of scapegoating or ideological persecution.
2. *Strong respect for authority,* which makes it unlikely that people question the definition of reality provided by those in authority or that they resist authorities who lead them to torture and killing. A strong respect for and reliance on authority also makes it difficult for people to stand on their own when as a collectivity they face difficulties (Fromm, 1965; Miller, 1983).
3. A *monolithic culture or social organization,* with certain dominant values and goals and limitations in the freedom to express conflicting values and goals. Together with strong respect for authority, this makes a uniformity of views within society more likely and counterreactions by members to early reactions against victims less likely.
4. *Cultural self-concepts* such as a belief in cultural superiority. . . .
5. An *ideology* that designates an enemy is another important characteristic, at times existing in the culture for a long time, but frequently speedily evolving in response to life problems. (pp. 62–63)

All of these cultural conditions[18] are found in the way that pain is used to control behavior. The general devaluation of people with disabilities, the role of professionals as powerful authorities in the lives of people with disabilities, the monolithic culture of institutional practices so prevalent in services that use pain, and the unquestioned cultural superiority of these professionals and their values over people with disabilities are all obvious. The ideology that difficult behaviors, and implicitly the people who exhibit them, are a type of enemy is revealed in the behavioral jargon. "Undesirable behaviors," like enemies, are "targeted," "extinguished," and "eliminated." These programs set out to battle difficult behavior.

"Psychological self-defense of a probably essential kind requires the torturer to separate the self from victims, to devalue victims, and regard them as deserving their fate" (Staub, 1990, p. 61). Hence, the subjects of the abuse are in-

---

[18]This respect is presumably for a *dominating* authority. There are authorities worthy of respect whose power is based on choice rather than coercion. For many people, though, real authority relies on this power over rather than on the more inviting power with.

evitably powerless to begin with and their behavior is used to rationalize how they deserve their fate. Seeing people as inferior is a prerequisite to hurting them, but it can also become essential to sustaining the professional's sense of superiority. One of the most unusual studies of deliberately hurting people in the name of therapy noted that

> The most significant finding was that direct care staff in facilities which permitted the use of strong aversives reported more intense feelings of personal accomplishment . . . than did subjects whose programs were limited to mild aversives. Furthermore, there was a significant relationship among the personal use of strong aversives, number of years in the field, and the intensity of Personal Accomplishment. These findings suggest that allowing staff to use a wide range of interventions including strong aversives may diminish job stress and enhance one's sense of personal efficacy. (Harris, Handleman, Gill, & Fong, 1991)

People who hurt others in order to control their behavior often have many authoritarian characteristics. One advocate for clinical torture made it clear that using pain is not something just anyone can do. Only a highly trained clinician can be trusted. Staub pointed out that

> A number of motives are secondary, that is, they are not the source of the policy of torture or killing—although they may be a primary motive for certain individual perpetrators. Material rewards are often provided by the system. . . . Prestige and status are often conferred on direct perpetrators. (p. 61)

While the use of these powerful technologies tends to corrupt the users, controlling behavior with pain completely overlooks what people subjected to it are taught. For example, no one should ever be taught that it is a privilege to eat at one's own pace, to wear a beard, to go about without a helmet (if the helmet is a punishment serving no protective function), to sleep on a decent mattress, or to choose one's own clothing for the day.

These examples show the truth to the axiom that, in human services, *the worse the behavior, the worse the intervention.* The disturbing examples of premeditated harm that begin this chapter are only extreme examples of what is systematically practiced in many programs. Many people are restricted in their choices and are given consequences that are arbitrarily punitive rather than natural. If a person refuses to eat a hot dinner, then a sandwich can be offered as a reasonable alternative. If a person refuses to wear anything but one set of clothes, then keeping them clean can help promote respect. If a person refuses to sleep on one kind of mattress, then we can offer some comfortable alternative. But to withhold ordinary food, clothing, and bedding as punishment is cruel and unusual and, as such, in direct contradiction to the Constitution of the United States and Canada's Charter of Human Rights. Somehow when abuse is called therapy, it is seen as beyond the law and merely controversial. We need to make certain that we are not so blinded by these impulses to control challenging behavior that we lose perspective on the fact that the people we work with are citizens guaranteed the same rights and protections as everyone else.

One might reasonably ask how such barbarism is permitted. Using pain as therapy has received a great deal of publicity and some of its opponents have been puzzled as to why it has been consistently recognized in the popular press as simultaneously gruesome and acceptable. Smail (1984) offered a relevant analysis:

> In our society, balanced judgment, knowledge of facts, scientific and technical expertise become the property of an elite class of professionals, who alone are seen as being in the position to judge the uses to which such knowledge should be put. Subjective, ethical judgment and conduct become inverted and out of sight. This then leaves the "ordinary person" with very little role at all, except as object and consumer, for he or she has neither the "training" nor the "expertise" to make balanced, objective judgments, and depends utterly upon the professionals—academics, scientists, medics, lawyers, technicians, etc.—for the exercise of these capacities. Thus a faith in objectivity which serves to preserve our security also comes to serve the interests of those who become its conceptual custodians. It is not that the experts maintain their monopoly with a conscious malice or greed—in fact most would feel as well as profess a pride in their reputation for probity and a genuine satisfaction in their service to others. It needs a painful effort of

"consciousness-raising" even to begin to see what, for example, Ivan Illich (1977) means when he writes about the "disabling professions." To take the most severe view, however, it is possible to see professional experts as being on the one hand like intellectual usurers who, as it were, hire out their concepts to the uninitiated, and on the other hand like a priesthood which mediates the mysteries of objective knowledge to the masses, but does not permit them entry to them. (pp. 105–106)

The examples cited at the beginning of this section offend because of their quality even more than the rudeness of their quantity. It really would not be any less appalling if "only" one muscle squeeze or finger pinch, "only" one squirt of vapor spray, or "only" one spank had been used. The fact remains: The people who needed help were given pain. The argument is not whether a little pain is worse than a lot—it is. The argument is whether we can justify the use of pain at all.

Punishment in the behaviorist tradition necessarily works to eliminate a behavior because anything that reduces a behavior is, by definition, a punisher. Even beyond this tautology, though, few would seriously question that physical pain and social ostracism can change a person's behavior. Instead of asking if punishment with electric shock, slaps, or time-outs controls behavior, we might better question what using these technologies communicates? What does the use of them say about the practitioners of these bizarre technologies? To people with disabilities, these painful practices say, "You are beyond ordinary understanding and regard. You don't deserve understanding. You deserve to be hurt for being different." When we inflict pain, we are persecuting people for their disabilities. When we inflict pain, we are irresponsibly ignoring that our services have become dysfunctional, that it is *our* behavior that has become extreme and out of control. Rather than recognize our collective failure to serve well, we blame the victims of our confusion.

Technologies always attempt to appear modern, but stripped of their jargon we recognize these as barbaric antiquities. Functionally, electric shock is no different from the willow switch to which it is compared.[19] Soap in the mouth—once an unthinking response to a child's using bad language—is now recognized as simple child abuse. The difference is mainly in the controlled and calculated ways these are administered. If parents treat their children in violent and painful ways, they are justifiably liable to investigation by social services as child abusers. What is so disappointing in the literature favoring aversives is that all of this academic research and graduate training has produced nothing qualitatively different from the practices of a backwoods elementary schoolteacher of the last century.

The political implications, as opposed to the traditional clinical perspectives, of these practices helps put them in a clearer light. Most published studies on aversive conditioning reported using pain in laboratory experiments to change the behavior of animals. This takes little imagination because animals in our society are routinely treated as commodities and killed. The electric shock stick was taken directly from the stockyards where it is used to manage livestock waiting to be slaughtered. Obedience training manuals for pets routinely recommend the use of pain.

The literature on the clinical use of pain (usually electric shock) on people reports studies on alcoholics, homosexuals, exhibitionists, voyeurs, pedophiles, frotteurs, transvestites, and gamblers. The target behaviors here are all subject to "undesirable" social judgment rather than to any definition of medical pathology. For therapists to aggressively pursue these behaviors reflects their willingness to be co-opted by a prevailing social norm rather than to adhere to an empirically based clinical one.

---

[19]Almost 3 decades ago, Risley (1968) described the "device for shocking livestock" that he used to control the "autistic behavior of a deviant child" as having an "average voltage output [that] was in the range of 300 to 400 V, with occasional spikes exceeding 1000 V. Subjectively, the shock produced a sharp, extremely painful sting, localized in the area of the body to which the contacts were touched, much like being struck with a vigorously applied willow switch" (1968, p. 25).

Lovaas and Simmons (1969) described the effects of their device Hot Shot (by Hot-Shot Products Company, Inc., Savage, Minnesota), which was capable of delivering up to 1,400 volts at 50,000 ohms per "hot shot," as a strong shock that was "definitely painful (smarted like a whip, or a dentist drilling on an unanesthetized tooth)" (pp. 149, 156).

If the objective were seen for what it is—controlling social behavior—the use of pain as therapy would naturally raise ethical barriers. Ethical professionals are properly reluctant to act as surrogates for the judicial system and punish people or to act out the hostility of society at large toward devalued minorities. The use of pain as therapy, however, makes sense if people with difficult behavior are seen as "behaviorally disordered." This becomes the equivalent of mentally ill or sick, and these labels imply the need for treatment. All this forgets that mental retardation is fundamentally a social construct, not a medical diagnosis.

All of the groups represented in these studies are at risk, in varying degrees, of being the victims of simple prejudice both from the general public and professionals. Although alcoholics and gamblers have wide and deep recovery networks, and homosexuals and transvestites often have communities of acceptance, individual members of these groups can easily internalize society's general rejection or ridicule as self-hatred.

Some people have submitted to extreme measures—even choosing pain—to change themselves into something more acceptable to society rather than work to make who they are more acceptable to themselves. Exhibitionists, voyeurs, pedophiles, and frotteurs might privately seek desperate intervention, not out of any hope for personal growth but from the simple despair of self-loathing. More likely, people come to professional notice by way of the legal system. In all of these cases, people are protected from what the United Nations Convention on Torture considered torture and, if they found themselves in an abusive treatment setting, most people would have at least the awareness that they could get help. The one group that has a history rich in discrimination but with little experience of self-help, no strong legal protection, or community acceptance is people with developmental disabilities and disturbing behavior. In this vacuum of ordinary social norms, the use of pain has been made to appear as a reasonable alternative.[20]

_____

[20]The use of aversives with addictions strikes me as of particular interest. The point of addiction is losing control and this holds a natural attraction for behavioral technologies that traffic in control. However, the clinical practice of escalating behavioral interventions is very much like an addic-

Another group with poor social protections is children. Because children are not generally seen as competent to make decisions about their lives, their parents are asked to give consent.[21] This situation can put the parents of children with developmental disabilities in an untenable position, and they are often put there by well-intentioned professionals. Rather than acknowledge that their services have, in fact, failed to provide a child with ordinary opportunities or that the particular people involved do not know how to teach the individual child, the mental health industry displaces its responsibility and labels children it doesn't know how to serve as having "maladaptive behaviors." Our professional history is rich in examples of blaming the parents of such people as well. As parents become desperate to get the best for their daughters and sons, they come to doubt their own intuitions and abilities. If they are told that the use of pain is the best hope for behavioral change, parents are given little room for dissent. Historically, our society has overruled the wishes and beliefs of parents who fail to provide adequately for their children's safety, schooling, or medical care. So if parents fail to agree to aversive therapy, they find themselves in a no-win bind. They can be seen as negligent if they withhold professionally encouraged treatment, but if they consent to this form of child abuse, they fail to guard their children's safety.

The earliest study on the use of electric shock (Lovaas, Schaeffer, & Simmons, 1965) involved increasing the social behavior of twin 5-year-olds with autism.

The authors explained that these children had been "treated intensively in a residential setting" and that

---

tion itself: Addicts use something to make things better and when matters get worse, rather than try something else, addicts use even more. As we have seen, what begins benignly as positive reinforcement can too easily escalate to the all-out war that use of pain resembles.

[21]This subject warrants a longer discussion than is pertinent here. Suffice it to say that as long as children are as powerless and vulnerable as they are in our culture, they require protection. At the same time, protectors themselves have the potential to wreak the most harm. The most difficult to confront of all oppressors are those with the power to hurt you for your own good. As with most issues involving children with developmental disabilities, this one has serious implications for *all* children irrespective of their perceived abilities.

it was considered appropriate to investigate the usefulness of pain in modifying the behaviors of autistic children. Autistic children were selected for two reasons: (1) because they show no improvement with *conventional* [emphasis added] psychiatric treatment; and (2) because they are largely unresponsive to everyday interpersonal events. (p. 100)

Because autism is a neurobehavioral disability affecting communication and perception, we need to be sensitive to the fact that people with autism may *appear* "largely unresponsive" when, in fact, their responses are more likely to be different than absent. When we get to know them better, we are more able to discern their thoughts and feelings. Parents often know what their children are trying to express because they respond to body language. Professionals—especially during a brief assessment interview—can easily miss these subtleties. This would be acceptable if we simply acknowledged that we testers cannot reasonably be expected to know these finer points of communication. The danger comes when we act as if what we cannot see is not there.

One wonders how "everyday" the "interpersonal events" were that these 5-year-old children experienced as they were treated intensively in a residential setting. It is impossible to imagine they were spending their days with ordinary 5-year-olds—who would likely be both the best assessors and teachers of the ordinary social behavior of 5-year-olds. How did the people who were providing services understand these children? That children with autism might not respond to "conventional psychiatric treatment" says as much about the treatment and its practitioners as it does about the twins. It would seem more practical to recognize the mutual lack of connection and work to build that more respectfully. It hardly warrants the leap to conclude that pain was the only alternative left.

Interestingly, Lovaas et al. (1965) did not report looking for socially ordinary reinforcements, much less ordinary pleasures and encouragements, for the twins. Did these children like the loud noises of children's games, the excitement of roller coasters, or did they prefer the quiet of playing in a pool of water? Most 5-year-olds have had these experiences as well as discernible opinions about them. How did these two children react to such experiences? Since this study was published, neurology and neuropsychology have gained a much more sophisticated understanding of people with autism. Today it would be reasonable to ask what kinds of medical—especially neurological and neuropsychological—examinations these children had. This kind of information could show how the twins best understood the world and how we might work more empathically with them.

This study inadvertently demonstrated the authors' need to achieve rapid behavioral change far more than to provide anything the children themselves might actually need. These early studies failed to ask why we would willingly inflict pain to change other people's behavior when we are so poor at understanding them? Why do *we* need to hurt and abuse others to stop them from hurting and abusing themselves? Ordinarily we think hurting people intentionally reveals more about the abuser than the abused. When the abused person has far less power and the abuse is called therapy, we apparently lose our ordinary confidence to make a moral response.

The earliest behavioral strategies optimistically relied on the power of positive reinforcement. And yet the earliest clinical applications of behavioral theory had hardly begun when the literature (Lovaas et al., 1965; Risley, 1968) reported the use of cattle prods. This was not a case of early idealism yielding to grim reality. Rather it shows how quickly psychologists encountered, though did not learn, what it can take to exact behavioral control.

> Sometimes seemingly innocent ideas evolve into a source of maltreating and destroying people. In Soviet psychiatry, the evolution of certain theories of schizophrenia probably contributed to, and was used to justify, the incarceration of political dissidents in mental hospitals (Block & Reddaway, 1977). In Germany, the evolution in medical thinking of killing as a form of healing, the view that killing certain individuals affirmed life and strengthened the community, contributed to the involvement of German doctors in the euthanasia program and possibly to the very existence and extent of the euthanasia program (Lifton, 1986). This, in turn, represented a step in the progres-

sion toward genocide. The freedom of expression of ideas is essential to counteract early steps along a continuum of destruction. This freedom also places responsibility on bystanders to combat ideas and world views that dehumanize and carry a destructive potential." (Staub, 1990, p. 69)

The people at risk for being hurt by clinicians have lives governed not by themselves but by others, usually their families or clinicians. Given how routinely our culture submits to the judgment of experts, this leaves people with disabilities, for the most part, without any protections whatever. For many people with disabilities, there are no "bystanders" other than the very professionals who are hurting them. Even when a clinician of good will perceives a person to be in danger, confidentiality sometimes makes it difficult to publicize the person's plight. The closer people stand with and for people with disabilities, the more likely they themselves are to be ostracized. The same mechanisms used to oppress people with disabilities are used to discount the opinions of advocates: ignoring, segregation, impoverishment, denial, and active abuse. People with disabilities have clearly shown that they resent that the people who work for them too often have to choose between being loyal to them and keeping their jobs.

Lovaas et al. (1965) further justified aversive treatment because pain is essentially ordinary and even necessary for ordinary life:[22]

Psychological or physical pain is perhaps as characteristic in human relationships as is pleasure. The extensive presence of pain in everyday life may suggest that it is necessary for the establishment and maintenance of normal human interactions.

Despite the pervasiveness of pain in daily functioning, and its possible necessity for maintaining some behaviors, psychology and related professions have shied away from, and often condemned the use of pain for therapeutic purposes. We agree with Solomon (1964) that such objections to the use of pain have a moral rather than a scientific basis. (Lovaas et al., 1965, p. 99)

[22]For "the people of any given age and country . . . the rules which obtain among themselves appear to them self-evident and self-justifying. This all but universal illusion is one of the examples of the magical influence of custom, which is not only, as the proverb says, a second nature, but is continually mistaken for the first" (John Stuart Mill, 1859, p. 64).

This argument is a common one among those who advocate using pain to control people with severe behavior problems: These therapies parallel ordinary life. People with disabilities do not need *parallel* lives. They need lives that are directly involved with ordinary living. Although punishments and pain may resemble some aspects of society, the fact remains they are not identical. The only place we find systematic punishment is through the courts as a result of an adjudicated offense and with the rights to representation and appeal. People who are treated with these therapies are subjected to them on the basis of clinical judgment and often without any real advocates to argue on their behalf. Using clinical judgment as the determining criterion makes the process seem more like a medical treatment, which the use of aversives simply is not.

> Involvement with the system and the resulting psychological evolution may explain why some doctors and other professionals cooperate with torture. Some may have an ideological affinity as a starting point. . . . Although their participation may be seemingly humane, it usually serves the perpetrators not the victims. . . . As they participate in these ways . . . rather than protest and resist, doctors must employ psychological processes—such as justification of the torture, moral equilibration, and just-world thinking—to make their participation bearable to themselves. (Staub, 1990, p. 68)

Some behavior therapists, true to the implicit value of efficacy in the behaviorist model, use ends–means arguments to justify their choices. In 1976, Lichstein and Schreibman presented the behavior therapist as the aggrieved party:

> Despite the undeniable effectiveness of electric shock with autistic children, and the absence of major undesirable side effects, there exists a very strong spirit in this country which abhors punishment with this or any other patient population (e.g., Maurer, 1974; Shea & Shea, 1976). In the end, the force of community opinion will prevail over research evidence whenever the two are incompatible. Despite the extremely encouraging clinical research employing electric shock with autistic children in the mid and late 60s, the demise of one effective intervention may occur. Throughout the country, some state legislatures are concretizing this trend. The behavior therapist

who advocates the judicious use of electric shock with autistic children under highly specified, restricted circumstances (e.g., Oppenheim, 1976) is acting in accordance with an ethical imperative: to provide the best treatment for his client. Given the restrictions imposed upon us by some of our colleagues and portions of society at large, the thoughtful behavior therapist is confronted with a serious ethical dilemma. All of us would prefer the development of comparably effective, nonaversive treatments. But what are we to do till then? (p. 165)

The issue is not "effective treatment." The issue is how can a society that values all its citizens best respond to those in distress? Using punishment for undesirable behaviors is one way to control those behaviors, but we in the United States, since passage of the Eighth Amendment, have consciously renounced cruel and unusual punishment. No matter how heinous the crime, no one in America expects to be flogged or interrogated on the rack. But people with developmental disabilities, who are already handicapped by many undesirable clinical and social prejudices, find themselves left out of this basic consideration. Using clinical punishers only confirms and exaggerates the handicappist attitudes already prevalent in ordinary society.

The powerful urge among professionals to achieve results generally ignores any real understanding of the people from which the results are expected. The twins in the study using electric shock were hurt because they were "unresponsive to everyday interpersonal events," and then the abuse was further justified because of "the absence of major undesirable side effects." In both cases, all that mattered was their observable behavior. Beyond being "autistic twins," these children had no identity. It is hard to imagine two 5-year-olds with personalities so devoid of character that nothing about them could be said. What is telling is that the authors of that study chose not to discuss them as people in human terms. I know the conventions of research, especially those of 30 years ago, regarded personal details as extraneous and my criticism is not of this article in particular, but of that literary genre that accepts not talking about people in human terms.

Allodi and Cowgill (1982) assessed 41 people who had been the subjects of political torture and found that these people suffered from *psychosomatic complaints* (pains, headaches, nervousness, insomnia, nightmares, panic, tremors, weakness, fainting, sweating, diarrhea), *behavioral and personality changes* (withdrawal, irritability, aggressiveness, suicide attempts, severe sexual dysfunction), *affective difficulties* (depression, crying, fear, anxiety), and *changes in their abilities to think* (confusion, disorientation, memory disturbance, loss of concentration, attention, blocking). Some of these conditions are observable behaviorally (withdrawal, suicide attempts), but many are assessed only by self-report (loss of concentration, fear). If people with autism show their feelings differently, then "the absence of major undesirable side effects" may have less to do with absence and more to do with the inability of the researchers to recognize them.

If the use of pain is so effective, then one wonders why it is not vigorously advocated for the general public who also exhibit intractable, self-injurious, and aggressive behaviors. Tobacco use, for example, is well documented as dangerous and life-threatening. Many of the people who have tried and failed to break this habit are quite sincere in their efforts to control their behavior. Should we assume that the thoughtful behavior therapists who work with this maladaptive behavior and do not apply pain to these addicts have shirked their ethical responsibilities?

Actually, there is a mildly aversive technique for people who bite their nails or smoke and want to stop these habits: One wears a rubber band on the wrist and snaps it hard with every urge to bite or smoke. Behaviorists occasionally have cited this as an example of how socially acceptable the use of pain is. The parallel, however, is so inexact as to be useless if not insulting. What people do voluntarily to themselves with a rubber band bears no meaningful comparison to services systematically hurting people against their will. This is like saying that the hunger of affluent people on reducing diets is comparable to the starvation of the poor. Self-imposed discomfort is not torture. Self-imposed hunger is a choice and not a necessity imposed by a society too numb or incompetent to respond.

The use of pain as treatment is—incredibly—still debated. The arguments in its favor have been that it is effective

and that to stop its use would limit the options of psychological practice.[23] There is no denying that pain sometimes can
do what is claimed for it: reduce undesired behavior. The argument against it, however, lies not just in its explicit effects
but in its implicit effects as well. The use of pain on people
who cannot consent to its use disregards the function of their
behavior as communication. Systematically inflicting pain, as
a behavior in itself, communicates defeating messages: "We
don't care why you do what you do. And we don't care
enough to find out. Don't try to change us: We are more
powerful and will change you." These may be ordinary social
messages in a competitive world in which might makes right,
but are these the messages those of us in the helping professions in any way want to endorse?

When they first appeared, behavioral technologies were met
with a great deal of opposition by the then-prevailing practice of psychoanalysis. Primarily medically based and relying
on the patient's abilities to talk and gain insight, psychoanalysis was unsuited to help people with expressive disabilities
and had no particular success with people with cognitive disabilities.

Behavioral technologies, though, were seemingly ideal
for just such people. Behavioral interventions required no insight and did not rely on the verbal ability of either client or,
just as significantly, the therapist. All that was needed was the

---

[23]This argument is about 20 years old now and it would be pleasant to
note how times have changed and clinicians have changed with them.
Such, alas, is not the case. The American Psychological Association Division
33, a subgroup of psychologists working in the field of developmental disabilities, has spent many of the last 10 years worrying this same vexed
point—that banning the use of aversives is unnecessarily burdensome for
psychologists.

The only conclusion that I can infer from their dropping this odd
complaint has been that the use of aversives has either been forbidden by
state regulation or the general public has found it sufficiently abhorrent
that psychologists have less opportunity to use these painful interventions.
When a profession cannot regulate itself, then government has an obligation to intervene.

Lately, Division 33 *Newsletters* have discerned facilitated communication as a menace. *Mutatis mutandis*.

manipulation and control of environmental contingencies. Institutions provided the optimal setting for this level of experimental and political control. If the validity of behavioral techniques could be proven, then institutionalized people with disabilities were the perfect population on which to demonstrate clinical effectiveness.

Defending the use of pain as a last hope for the otherwise hopeless maintains that extreme behaviors warrant extreme interventions and that it is better to inflict pain to control a behavior than to permit a person to cause uncontrolled serious and permanent injury. Essentially, this bad bargain begins with the premise that control belongs with the behavioral technician alone and further presumes that the reasons for the behavior lie within the person causing concern.

One of the important lessons of behavioral thinking is the power of environments to teach. Hurting people to control their behavior necessarily takes place in highly authoritarian settings.[24] How often do our human services ask the simple human question: How can we help this person live where she is loved and have access to the people and things she herself loves? Instead, we generally demand that people demonstrate ordinary behavior as a prerequisite, not for a life that looks to their satisfaction and happiness, but for the simple absence of pain.

This irrationally defies all logic, and an error of logic and rationality is fatal to the practice of behaviorism, which has been aggressively anti-emotional and overly dependent on empiricism. The use of pain betrays its own bedrock perception: If environment is the great teacher and people are given violent environments, how in the world can they be expected not to be aggressive and self-injurious? The use of pain to control people has become both morally and intellectually bankrupt.

---

[24]Some of these programs take place in what appear to be ordinary homes, but architecture is a poor guide for defining ordinary in human services. One program uses pain in suburban ranch houses that look fairly unremarkable until one notices the surveillance cameras in all the rooms. This regime of surveillance and the punishments that follow in such a bland suburban setting would have deeply satisfied, if no one else, Orwell's definitive authoritarian, Big Brother.

In the 19th century, physicians conscientiously imitated the hard sciences to make medicine more empirical than the less reliable practical art it had been. Psychiatry first appeared as the medical community was becoming more concerned with controlled experimental study, and it was challenged to produce the same results as experimentation. Instead psychiatry relied on the case study as its chief research methodology. This gave psychiatry the reputation of being not quite scientific. Behavioral clinicians, however, were in a much better position to collect data, run controls, and achieve a statistical, empirical respect. The main alternatives to the less scientific talking therapies were lobotomy as a psychiatric intervention and the use of pain as psychological interventions. Both of these therapies used the most hopeless and desperate as subjects, hence, the most vulnerable, people: Those with social challenges.

Not surprisingly, in order to increase their professional status, the more empirically minded psychologists and psychiatrists intuitively found their model practice in the most technological of medical practices, surgery. Surgery has a low requirement for personal investment. Typically, surgeons do not rely on a "bedside manner" and avoid operating on those patients with whom they have emotional attachments. The success of their interventions depends on technical expertise in the radical elimination of something necessarily visible that can hurt the patient. Most people find surgery unpleasant to contemplate and even less pleasant to experience, but many people choose it as a treatment of last choice.

The clinical use of pain has typically been justified as an urgent last resort as well. The proponents for this have always, in my experience, failed to consider that the person has been developing these behaviors over time and did not just wake up one morning as mysteriously dangerous. Rather than take responsibility for the fact that earlier services to help this person were, however well-intended, ultimately incompetent, some clinicians abruptly seek out a "quick fix."[25]

---

[25]It's important here to make clear, once again, that this is not a matter of personal blame. Some of the proponents of pain to control behavior seem to have come to this position as an intellectual premise as behavioral

As with many of the parallels that some behaviorists have drawn with their work, the comparisons of aversive therapy to surgery ultimately backfire. Surgery made a major advance with the introduction of anesthetics that allowed surgeons the leisure of using more careful and more time-consuming procedures without inflicting pain. In contrast, aversives depend on the intensity, frequency, or duration of pain for their effectiveness. Surgery and recovery are relatively brief but aversive therapy can go on for years. Surgery acts upon observable and pathological tissue (e.g., a tumor) or corrects a pathological function (with pacemakers for heart disease or shunts for hydrocephalus). Aversives act upon observable behaviors as if they were pathological and independent of the person's history and environment. Surgery has gained social acceptance as a treatment of last choice because it can generalize to health and well-being. The use of pain, both in theory and in practice, shows that punishment does not generalize to greater autonomy. Instead, punishment only enforces compliance and control. Having to rely exclusively on others to guess and provide one's needs and wishes can be an intensely frustrating experience. Aversives fail to teach ordinary expressions for the frustrations and anger that are inherent in all our lives, irrespective of social skills.

Following the medical model for the use of pain, increasing the "dosage" is the response to people whose behavior does not respond to lower levels of pain. Just as physical pain is immeasurable, no measure exists (or has been sought) to assess how the person comprehends the contradiction of someone who says, "I am here to help," and then proceeds to inflict pain repeatedly. It may well be that this psychological torture has some effect in demoralizing the person on whom it is inflicted. Because people who use pain place a high premium on compliance, their success may well rest on the fact

---

practitioners. Others, though, have come to this as a simple expedient. I have met a number of people, usually working in public institutions, who have had admissions of people in crisis. Since they did not know these people and had no time to develop a history, they resorted to "quick fixes" that were intrusive but arrived at from desperation more than conviction. Most of us have done things in the heat of a crisis that we would have avoided had we been given the chance to consider them more carefully.

that the person is too disorganized and disoriented to respond to anything except to what he or she has just been told.

There is, however, a surgical procedure that the use of pain actually does parallel quite closely.

Behavioral Surgery and Mutilation

Bizarre illnesses may require bizarre treatment, and in psychiatry they often get it. They show so often a stubbornness and resistiveness to treatment, they expose so clearly the ignorance of their pathology and aetiology that they arouse aggressive reactions in the baffled and frustrated therapist. (Partridge, 1950, quoted in Valenstein, 1986, p. 23)

The impulse to medicalize—and thereby control and treat—difficult social behavior is apparently hard to avoid and has been for some time. Behavioral technologies are only the most recent attempts to find "great and desperate cures" for unusual behavior. Valenstein's (1986) elegant history of "radical treatments" cites the earlier uses of therapy we still have with us today. Electric current, used now as punishment, was used in the 19th century as electrotherapy to treat "rheumatism, nervous exhaustion, neuralgia, and paralysis," as well as "neurasthenia and depression."

As late as 1929, Richard Hutchings in New York recommended that every physical therapy department in mental hospitals should have a "low frequency generator, galvanic-sinusoidal machine," a static machine with at least 16 plates and an insulating stool or wicker chair. (Valenstein, 1986, p. 26)

Valenstein cataloged the somatic treatments physicians have used for psychological problems: faradization, galvanization, rest cures, hydrotherapy (including "baths, douches, wet packs, steam, spritzers, and hoses"), malarial fever therapy (which led to hot baths, hot air, radiothermy, diathermy, infrared-lightbulb cabinets, and "special electric 'mummy-bags'"), sleep therapy or "prolonged narcosis," "electronarcosis therapy," "carbon dioxide therapy," hyperbolic chambers to increase oxygen intake, injections of "inactivated horse serum" to produce "aseptic meningitis," hypothermia (cooling the body), and the "Therm-O-Rite blanket—a 'mummy bag' through which a refrigerant was circulated."

These presumably abandoned forms of treatment can still be found, although in the new, newer, and newest! guises technologies have always needed. Water spray; physical, chemical, and mechanical restraints; and interventions using electricity are still around. The older forms of these therapies were intended to fall within the Hippocratic oath of comforting the ill, but the more modern versions are clearly designed to inflict pain.[26]

Valenstein's (1986) exploration of the somatic cures led him to the work of Henry Cotton, who declared that "psychotic patients, without exception, 'all have infected teeth'" (p. 38). Cotton further discovered (and surgically "corrected") infected tonsils, stomachs, colons, cervixes, fallopian tubes, ovaries, and seminal vesicles.[27] At one conference when he presented this information, half of the discussants were supportive even though he reported: "In 250 operations, 62 have been recovered, or 25 percent; the death rate has been 30 percent; improved cases, 15 percent; and 30 percent unimproved" (Valenstein, 1986, pp. 38–40).

All of this sets the stage for the advent of prefrontal leucotomy (lobotomy), which was vigorously championed by the Portuguese surgeon Egas Moniz. Predictably, Moniz declared this mutilation of the brain to be a revolutionary and modern development in the treatment of mental illness.[28]

---

[26]Electroconvulsive therapy (ECT) is often confused with the behavioral use of electric shock. ECT is usually used on people with deep and unresponsive depression and is done under an anesthetic to make it as painless as possible. Why ECT should work (when it does) is not clear. The more recent use of applied electric shock is done without anesthesia precisely because of the pain it does induce.

[27]Valenstein implied that the surgery on the male reproductive system occurred less frequently than did assaults on the female. This certainly fits with the experience of women in operating rooms generally.

[28]Modern and revolutionary developments in medicine are a very old tradition. Valenstein cites the work of Rogerius Frugardi ("Roger of Salerno"), an eminent 12th-century surgeon: "For mania and melancholy, the skin at the top of the head should be excised in a cruciate fashion and the skull perforated to allow matter to escape."

In discussing the rapid and, as it turned out, premature acceptance of lobotomy, Critchley (1986) noted several factors that are remarkably parallel to the early acceptance of aversives:

1. In many cases an unexpected, even dramatic, change for the better came about in patients with chronic psychoses, hospitalized for years, who had resisted not only conservative lines of treatment but also courses of insulin coma as well as electroshock. To speak of "cure" would not be appropriate. But often a docile state of passivity would replace active symptoms of aggression, anxiety, hypomania, antisocial conduct, obsessional ideas or behavior. In other words, such patients were rendered more easily nursed, and quite often it became possible for them to be discharged home after years of incarceration within a mental asylum.

The use of aversives is also justified as a last hope. Although these painful interventions do not teach independence, they can make subjects more easily nursed.

2. There was, in such cases, an easing of the financial burden imposed upon the families of the patient, or, in the case of long-staying institutionalized sufferers, the tax-payers.

When aversive therapies achieve their typical goal of compliance, people require less attention and time from those who provide direct services.

3. The operation itself was rapidly performed, being relatively simple, entailing little surgical skill. The mortality was low.

With aversives, inflicting pain does not require any special skill and, as a result, can be done relatively cheaply—and usually is—by those in low-paying direct service positions.

4. Psychiatrists had in the past been either inactive in the face of these long-staying patients, or they had not been successful with their nonsurgical somatic therapy.

For people who appear to be unresponsive to typical reinforcements used in behavior programs, pain provides psychologists with something to do rather than explore more exciting reinforcements or concede uncertainty about their theoretical model.

5. Psychosurgery commended itself to the psychiatrists and others who were hostile toward (or disillusioned with) Freudian theories of causation and treatment.

For those psychologists who consider inappropriate behavior as essentially pathological or inexplicable, the use of pain permits another way of trying to exert control over the behavior.

6. Psychosurgery was also welcomed with varying degrees of warmth by those who held that most forms of insanity were the product of organic, that is, structural, brain pathology of an obscure nature.

The idea that destructive behavior is somehow intrinsic in the person rather than taught and maintained by destructive environments is unchallenged by the systematic use of pain.

7. Psychosurgery as a news item was a boon to the press. The publicity attendant upon the employment of lobotomy for the considerable population of the mentally deranged was enormous . . . (Critchley, p. 8).

Just as was the case with lobotomy, the use of pain as a "therapy" has been given an enormous amount of press.

As the use of aversives inadvertently reveals, the issue is not about responding and helping but about dominating and controlling. When people hurt themselves, they are at risk for being further mutilated as a treatment. In the institution, a person who kills himself intentionally is seen as more of a professional lapse than a person who is unintentionally killed in the course of ordinary treatment. The domination of oppressed peoples extends to their bodies and the right to control them. One person whose life indelibly taught me this is David Lewis.

David Lewis

"For many physicians, risking any therapeutic possibility was preferable to confessing helplessness." (Valenstein, 1986, p. 44)

David's birth had been difficult. Both his grandmother and mother had once been institutionalized (each had been labeled mentally defective). They were given no information about the new baby except that he was O.K. and that the state would take care of him. They accepted this, perhaps as a function of their intellectual limitations, but, having both been institutionalized, they might well have learned that questioning health professionals was unnecessary, useless, or even dangerous. David spent his first 3 years in a foster home with a nurse who kept him in a locked iron crib. During this time, his mother wanted to know why she could not see her son. When the state closed his foster home, David was seen at the most prestigious medical school in the state by a pediatrician who recommended that David be returned to his family. Instead, state social services placed him in an institution where he lived for the next 14 years in the infirmary.

During this time, he was seen as not only "sick," but also as "behaviorally disordered." He hurt himself regularly, either by banging his head or throwing himself from his bed or chair with such force that he broke his legs.

In February 1980, while still a teenager, David had an orthopedic consultation that ascertained:

He is very strong and on occasion quite destructive. He also seems to have a very strong type personality and tends to participate in violent acts on occasion.

1) The boy is quite active and at times quite violent and it is the opinion of Staff that he actually fractures his limbs deliberately by getting them caught in the bed rails, the sides of the wheelchair and throwing himself about until a fracture occurs. This brings up one solution and there is that he can be heavily sedated and kept out of positions where he can catch the leg. For instance, he could be put in a bed with wooden sides so that he could not catch the leg in the side rails. He could be put in a box-like wheelchair when up and probably restrained at times.

2) The patient has never walked and never will and frankly, he really cannot go on refracturing his legs at a steady pace without getting into major problems.

3) He was sent for Consultation down to [a major city] and at the Orthopedists [sic] suggestion, plastic splints were made for both legs at considerable expense.[29] The last fracture disloca-

---

[29]Money is often used as a rationale for hurting people with disabilities. Medical practitioners cite money as a reason for denying people life

tion of the leg occurred while the splint was in place and it should be noted that he has an ulcer of the left heel at the present time of rather major consequence. I think these splints can never be made completely comfortable and I think he will continue to develop pressure sores but that is the treatment at the present time. Because he was able to throw his leg about sufficiently with the splint on to produce the last fracture, it was thought that perhaps the legs could be tied together which is not really practical because of their natural bends and perhaps a pelvic band type of thing to attach both legs, the splints on both legs to the pelvis so that abnormal motion can be restricted, be tried. . . . Frankly, I do not think this will work for any particular length of time because of the great strength of the patient in the upper extremities and his determination to do as he wishes.

In summary, I would suggest that the patient be rather heavily sedated and restrained on occasion so that these episodes cannot occur. . . .

Given the political power experts have in our systems, they are literally a public menace when they stray from their areas of expertise. What had begun for David as an orthopedic consultation became a behavioral consultation. I have no interest in more arguments about the roles or relative importance of psychologists and physicians. However, if David had been referred to me for his behavior, and I had proceeded to make recommendations about his orthopedic options, most physicians and licensing agencies would forceably discourage me from practicing medicine. Institutions are particularly vulnerable to the overtures of medical practitioners. Their history is essentially the history of the hospital, their administrators are usually physicians, and, if nothing else, they see their mandate as essentially medical: promoting the health and safety of their inmates. The limits of the medical model are, by now, obvious. Nonetheless, in David's life, as in the lives of many people with disabilities, "Physicians set the agenda. The person . . . who has the ability to set the agenda has to a large degree the ability to control the outcome"

supports, and some psychologists employ it as a rationale for the use of aversives. Cutting expenses was a stated motive in David's record. As we keep discovering, the amount of money available is important but what is critical is *how* that money is spent.

(Turnbull, 1989, p. 28). This pursuit to control David's behavior by the medical community goes even further.

In April, three social workers, two pediatricians, and three nurses met to discuss David's "medical condition and recommendations for treatment." This group was concerned because David's continuing to break his legs had resulted in "internal bleeding" and "recurrent urinary tract infections."

> These considerations led those present . . . to recommend that the following alternatives be explored: aversive therapy, i.e., "cattle prod" shocks, with consultation from [a consultant known for using aversives]; total restraint on a 24 hour basis (chemical/physical); amputation if all else fails; or lastly, take no active medical intervention. [The psychiatrist][30] recommended that David be tried on Lithium which was reviewed and felt to be inappropriate.

The logic of this is clear: People saw David's medical conditions as the result of his behavior, but they did not think to refer him to anyone about his behavior; instead, they used their medical mandates to recommend interventions. It is unlikely that most people with internal bleeding, recurrent urinary tract infections, or even recurring fractures would be recommended for treatment with electric shock. Inexplicably, the most benign—relatively—of the recommendations, the use of lithium, was rejected as inappropriate.

Just as no one paid the slightest attention (at least not in writing) to the reasons David might have for breaking his legs, no one considered the effects these recommendations might have on David. Instead, they focused on the effects their recommendations would have on their own work.

> Complications from projected surgery included possible continued self abuse to stumps and difficulty healing. It was stated that programming/aversive therapy may still be needed post surgery for management. It was agreed David's mother would be contacted to discuss the alternatives. A two week time frame was set to explore options. Immediately following the meeting,

---

[30]This is one of the most difficult examples I have had of respecting confidentiality. My ethical obligation to maintain strict confidentiality protects professionals and their practices from peer review and litigation. At the same time, it leaves David himself hidden, vulnerable, and mutilated.

I contacted David's grandmother, as his mother has no telephone, and briefly explained the situation and asked [his mother] to return my phone call. On April 16th [his mother] called and I discussed the recommendations with her in detail to enable her to make a decision as David's legal guardian. She was quite concerned and responsive. [His mother] had spoken with family members the previous evening, as well as her minister, and had arrived at the decision to allow surgery. I suggested we meet with [the orthopedic surgeon] further . . . to once again review alternatives. The risks from surgery were defined and mother had the opportunity to ask questions. Upon our return to the State School, [David's mother] signed a permission form authorizing surgery. She and her husband also visited with David. It was difficult to ascertain if he recognized his mother but [she] felt he did know her. Family have been unable to visit regularly due to their financial situation and transportation problems, as well as family difficulties.

[David's mother] does appear to be a concerned parent, who despite numerous odds, made the effort to meet with [the psychiatrist] and I [sic] in person, even though it meant asking her minister for gas money just to get to the State School.

At his birth, David's mother had been determined by physicians to be an unfit mother. Now, physicians (and later the county probate court) determined that she was capable to make major life decisions for a child who had never lived with her. This flexible assessment of her abilities apparently provided the justification at each turn for using her to hurt her son. One wonders where else a person's mother could be deemed intellectually incompetent—hence unfit—to love him but, at the same time, intellectually competent to agree to such a drastic surgical procedure for someone she hardly knew. In other words, the professional and legal community were willing to deny this woman her natural human rights and powers to be a parent, but not her subordinating professional and legal role as David's guardian.

The infirmary pediatrican and orthopedic surgeons exchanged letters formally acknowledging David's case, and the psychiatrist who had unsuccessfully recommended lithium joined in the team assessment that amputation was best.

On June 10, the psychiatrist, an attendant, and the entire teaching staff met to report:

David's reaction to the loss of his legs was discussed and [the psychiatrist] stated that David might have a real bad reaction to losing his legs and he felt there will probably be some emotional reaction with either withdrawal or anger. [The psychiatrist] feels the scheduled programming is good because it takes David's mind off his legs.

[The psychiatrist] asked how David reacts to music and since he likes it, possibly this would be good for him. Therapeutic Recreation Department will be purchasing some decorations for David's room. It was stated that David's motivators are music, going outside, after shave and constructing things. It was stated that possibly some classroom items, now that school is out, could be put in the Infirmary for him. David is very curious.

On June 23, David Lewis's legs—first his right, then his left—were amputated. The Operative Report concluded: "Patient seemed to withstand the procedures well and left the Operating Room in reasonable condition."

—

When I first heard this story, I literally could not believe I had heard it right. There *had* to be some rational explanation for what happened. I have read the documentation; nothing in it helps me make sense of this story. What I found especially troubling was that everyone I spoke with agreed how appalling this was, but everyone felt that there was no point in pursuing it legally. The people in David's life told me, "That was a long time ago. It would be expensive to launch a suit. We're not sure that doctor is still around. And, besides, it wouldn't bring back David his legs, would it?"

Nowhere in this story is there a single sentence suggesting that David's life of profound rejection, isolation, sterility, and boredom might have contributed to his finding a strategy that forced people, however painfully and briefly, to engage with him on a personal human level. When he threw himself down or fractured his legs, people literally had to hold him. One wonders when in his life he had been held. An infant who grows up in a locked iron crib probably did not get the same amount of love, affection, and simple body contact most of us reading this did. The sound of his legs breaking was his one cry for help. Instead of being heard, his voice was taken away.

His reputation had disabled the people hired to serve him so much that they could not know who he was or might become other than as a problem to be managed. Apparently, we never outgrow our need and desire for some of the earliest and simplest things: to be held, to be wanted, and to have an effect on those we love. But none of those things had ever been present in David's life, and the tragedy is that their absence was never considered significant.

> He appears alert and aware of his surroundings. His bed is out in the corridor so that staff can keep an eye on him and he on they. David likes to lie in bed with the sheet and/or pillow over his head. He will occasionally play hide n' seek and peek out when his name is called.

Something has gone terribly wrong when people are able to see a 16-year-old as adequately amused by having his bed kept in a hallway so passersby can call his name. The environment of the institution completely overwhelmed his identity as a person so that he was an institutional client/behavior problem. I wonder what David's behavior would have been if he had been in a regular school with other kids his age. Who would have been his friends? Who would have hung out with him after school? What would his life have been like? His hometown has to this day a reputation for sending kids with disabilities out of town—anywhere—rather than educate them with their neighbors.

In every aspect of his life, David's being hurt made him worse. He was also known as a hepatitis B carrier, which caused concern among those working for him. But where did he get this and how? Hepatitis B is not transmitted through casual contact so how could he have been infected with the virus in an infirmary designed to provide him with medical care and in an institution whose entire reason to exist was to protect him from harm? His environment had abused him, but, as often happens to victims, he himself was seen as a perpetrator.

Similarly, when the psychiatrist speculated on "David's reaction to the loss of his legs," he might have been more proactively concerned about David's reaction to the loss of a life. David's projected response—"David might have a real bad reaction to losing his legs and . . . there will probably be some emotional reaction with either withdrawal or anger"— shows reasonable attention to how a person might feel having had his legs amputated without his consent. But the real point was missed: David's self-injury might well have been his expression of anger at having been deprived of every ordinary human experience. It is far simpler for people in services to make people fit the service than it is to change the service to fit the person. The literally procrustean solution of amputating David's legs to make him fit institutional life was simpler than the more daunting prospect of making a life where David would be loved and not need to hurt himself.

It is easy to second-guess a colleague, especially someone I have never met. As a person, though, I wonder what the psychiatrist's emotional reaction was. It could not have been easy, however forcible the logic of the moment had been, to agree to a double amputation like this. I wonder, too, if the people making these decisions have recognized how they themselves were perpetuating society's discomfort with and, at times, outright hatred of people with disabilities. There is a world of difference in judging malice aforethought from people doing the best they can in dysfunctional services. The psychiatrist's suggestion that "scheduled programming is good because it takes David's mind off his legs" seems more likely to be applicable to him than to David. I doubt David has ever had a day when he has been "distracted" from the fact that he was literally cut in half. Yet, it is easy to see how the work and overwork in professional schedules can successfully distract from some of the incompetence and unnamed malice done in the name of therapy.

It is beyond accident that the culture in which most medical practitioners work is authoritarian, utilitarian, and technological. In order to function in such a culture, something human has to be suppressed—or cut off. In many medical service cultures, error and imperfection are connected with shame rather than seen as intrinsic to the human condition. Rather than confront our own imperfections and embrace them, some of us need to project our self-hatred onto others and hurt them. Rather than confront our mistakes and learn from and mourn them, we can bury the annoying fact of their existence in a blizzard of overwork.

Control is the death of optimism and possibility. The tragic line in the report of the last team meeting before David's mutilation was the concluding note, "David is very curious." What would his life have been had he lived in a world where his curiosity was seen as a virtue, an open door, a way forward, and not just something to be exploited with decorations from the therapeutic recreation department and some items from a classroom.

Some people reading this will think that David's story is extreme and sensational and that this sort of barbarism cannot happen today. It can. This happened not all that long ago, and the attitudes that took David Lewis's legs are far from gone. I still hear stories of people having tooth extractions or other painful procedures without anesthetic because "those people don't feel pain the way you or I do."

Unnecessary pain for routine medical and dental procedures reflects the still unrecognized rights of people with disabilities.

People still do not have control of their bodies. Although more difficult to obtain, it is still possible for women to have radical hysterectomies or tubal ligations without ever giving consent. Involuntary sterilization is considered a direct assault on one's civil liberties unless she has a low IQ, and then public tolerance is easier to come by. I have known people labeled as "biters" who subsequently had all their teeth removed. That these biters might be legitimately angry about where they lived, about how their lives were being wasted, about how no one ever reached out to them and that their only way of touching—biting—was ignored and not even considered.

Chapter 5

People Who
Hurt Themselves

Agnes

I was asked to spend a day with the support team of a community-based residential agency thinking about some people they had found difficult to serve. One of the people of most concern was Agnes, a woman in her mid-30s, who had been supported in living in her own apartment in a fairly large city. She had been periodically breaking windows and slicing her wrists. When people asked her about this, she denied having done it. One strategy was for agency staff to explain to her the dangers of this behavior. At other times, she had behavior plans to reinforce "good social behavior" and the loss of privileges as punishment when she was "bad," psychotherapy to deal with mourning her mother's death, as well as stress and anger management instruction.

Agnes was seen primarily as manipulative and attention seeking. She had been direct in talking about her crush on Eugene, a staff supervisor, and people thought that she used these episodes of self-injury as a way of forcing him to comfort her. The staff felt that they were in a bind because they wanted to ignore these dramatic bids for attention but obviously could not because they were so life threatening.

When someone using a service is described as attention seeking or manipulative, the service system itself is likely to be in need of significant behavioral change. I say this without any malice or judgment: Just as people who use services adapt their behaviors to cope with a difficult world, so do the people providing services. And just as people who use services need acceptance, warmth, and understanding to change, so do the people providing that help.

People had earlier told me that there had been suspicion that Agnes's brother had been party to her being gang raped (perhaps often) and that her father had chronically abused her sexually and physically as well. Even though people knew these rumors, they did not inquire about them. When she began therapy, her therapist chose to start working on Agnes's mourning her mother's death 15 years ago rather than address her abuse. This is not a matter of an "either/or" so much as an "and." It would seem that Agnes might want help to mourn the loss of her mother *and* to begin to address the pain of her abuse. The way people were treating Agnes—with their silence and denial—replicated the silence and denial of her family. It would be simple to point out how incompetent the services around her were in overlooking such a painful part of her past, but it might be more informing to ask why people would avoid this. This particular agency is hardly unique. I know a number of people who use services—women and men—who have been sexually and physically abused and whose extreme behavior is never considered as significant to understanding their histories or what they might need in the present.

Part of the problem is the dominance of behavioral technologies that tend to discount the importance of emotional history—hence Agnes's finding herself on a system of rewards and punishments for her target behaviors of self-injuriousness. Another part of the problem, I suspect, is that we who provide services have our own unresolved histories. Many of us are survivors of child abuse ourselves. Some of us are aware of it but given the power of dissociation, we may have no immediate memory. Many behavior specialists have never been trained to help abuse survivors so this is yet another reason not to look for abuse among people labeled "intellectually impaired" or to minimize it when it is found. The remedy for this, I hope, is obvious: We need to provide more information for behavior specialists about abuse, and we need more people who are themselves survivors, especially survivors in recovery, to help.

Generally, I like to meet people—especially for the first time—casually over a meal rather than in a formal meeting, because I do not want people to think I am there to assess and "fix" them so much as simply to get a sense of who they are as people. Besides, it is simpler to have lunch with an out-of-towner and see that as a pleasantly engaging social event; a consultation has a completely different set of cultural references. Although keeping things relatively informal is a preference, sometimes the only practical way to meet people is in formal settings, which is why Agnes and I were introduced at a local mental health center. Agnes was nervous and wanted a cigarette, so we stood outside in the cold and chatted. She was someone I liked at once. Somehow, that alone can be enough to help people feel more comfortable.

I asked her if she understood why her service team had thought we should meet and she said, "Because I break windows and cut myself." She told me about her most recent difficulties in which she had broken a store window and then ended up, drunk and angry, in a police station. I found out later that she was well known at this precinct so they had her strip-searched before putting her in a holding cell. Even so, she had managed to conceal a razor in the hem of her dress and slashed her wrists. As if I might have doubted her, she pulled back the bandage on her right wrist to show me the deep fresh cuts and the thick criss-cross of dark sutures.

"What do you call yourself when you do that?" I asked.

She gave me a surprised look and said without a moment's hesitation, "Katrina. I told them the last time. . . . I called them up and they asked me, 'Is that you, Agnes?' and I said, 'I'm not fuckin' Agnes. My name's Katrina.' But they didn't pay no attention to that."

"And how would I get to meet Katrina?"

"Oh, I'd have to get drunk. I get really low and I just go

out to a bar and drink anything I can get . . . I don't care what it is and then when I get drunk, I slam the door on my way out and start breaking things," she said.

"Is Katrina stronger than you are?"

"Only when I'm drunk."

I think both of us were surprised that she had said so much, having known one another for all of 6 minutes. I asked Agnes if it would be O.K. to tell her service team about this. She thought it would help.

This bit of news took the group aback. They had been expecting a plan to control her behavior problem and what Agnes and I were suggesting was that she might be better understood as a survivor of sexual assault with multiple personalities. We talked about how she had, after all, emerged from her painful past as a strong, courageous, and insightful woman. I thought she would be a real asset to any group of people working to move from pain to healing. Perhaps rather than mourn her mother's death, she could begin working with her multiple personalities. People who have been seriously abused often dissociate with more than one personality, so Katrina was likely to be only the first of Agnes's other personalities.

The idea of Agnes as a survivor shifted her from *being* a behavior problem that needed expert management to a woman who could actively collaborate in her own recovery. The group was not unanimously comfortable with this new role. They were willing to abdicate their own judgment to my expertise, but as soon as I left, they decided Agnes had cleverly manipulated me—perhaps in the same way they felt I had somehow manipulated them. How she knew enough about multiple personalities and dissociative states to deceive me when they had not thought of this themselves was not clear to me. Later, someone pointed out that when I asked her what she called herself when she was hurting herself, she could just as easily have said "stupid" as "Katrina."

For some time, I have thought of people with difficult behaviors as our teachers if we are willing to be taught; they can help us create new ways of helping if we ourselves are open to being creative. This general principle has been a source of real education for me in many parts of my life. In this sense, Agnes also shows a new perspective in the ways we might work as professionals with one another. Using the medical model to understand Agnes's behavior would, naturally, lead to consultation so that a specialist in self-injury would come and give the team some additional technical skills to cure her. Of course, people did not think of my working with them in such extreme terms, but that was the underlying structure of my visit. Instead, I had suggested that their best service might be to connect her not with more professionals but with other survivors.

In retrospect, I wish I could have worked differently. Although I had worked with this team before, we really did not have enough experience in common for them to trust my faith and respect in their own abilities both as people and as colleagues. My casually having introduced something completely foreign to them caused confusion. I could have labeled them as resistant clients and dismissed their irritation; but, to be honest, I also have to admit that interpreting Agnes's situation in a surprising and, for them, novel way made me feel useful and expert. My ideal was to feel "power-with" them, but in fact the structure of consultation promoted my information as "power-over" them. So I learned (once again) that having some helpful ideas can be of use, but sharing them in the right way is more helpful still.

My interest in showing off was based, probably, on my only recently coming to recognize self-injury as secondary to serious child abuse. In *Cognitive Counseling and Persons with Special Needs* (1985), I wrote about a man who made superficial cuts to hurt himself and developed what I took to be a responsive approach to that behavior. What I wrote then was not so much wrong as simply not sufficient to the depth of what I suspect his deeper needs were.

Now I would have a very different set of concerns for him, and I would not, as I did then, focus on this behavior as merely a bid for social connection but as a cry for some acknowledgment of and help for past isolation and pain as well. It would not have occurred to me then to ask about his being a survivor of abuse and to connect that with his self-injury. The general perception is that psychologists make discoveries about human behavior and these are then taken up by the general public. We psychologists tend to forget that in the field of developmental disabilities, the leaders have largely been the parents of children with disabilities and, more recently, people with disabilities themselves. None of the great changes in developmental disabilities social policy began with the professional community. Similarly, in the treatment of addictions, clinicians have come to recognize 12-step or self-help programs as the single most competent resource for recovery. Much of the current information on recovery from childhood victimizations has come from survivors or from therapists actively collaborating with survivors as opposed to academic, research-based, and theoretical models of helping.

While I respect professional expertise (it would be curiously self-defeating for me not to), I also think the most powerful first step toward recovery is for survivors to join in working with others who have lived through the experience, either in self-help groups or with a therapist who is also a survivor. The great strength of groups is evidenced in overcoming the shame many victims unfairly feel. By their very existence, groups demonstrate to individual survivors that their hurt is not unique and that growing in strength is possible. Once people have some collective experience of one another's strengths and hurts, then individual work in therapy can be helpful because the person has some context for understanding the abuse.

Following our conversation, the behavior specialist on Agnes's team decided to re-read her history in order to establish how much of her story was fact. People feared that Agnes perhaps had manipulated them with her references to abuse, but at the age of 13 she had been sent to the local "developmental center" because she was in "moral danger," a euphemism for being sexually victimized. During this time, apparently, she was still going home for visits, and in her mid-teens she started hurling bricks through the windows of the police station and a couple of years later began to slice her arms with razors and glass. All along, she had been talking about having been abused by her father and brother to staff both in the institution and at the hospital, but nothing was ever done about it. When she was still a teenager, Agnes said she had even told her father's sister about her abuse.

Her aunt—Katrina—responded by trying to strangle her, screaming, "You're an evil, lying bitch!"[1]

The fact that she would try to attract the notice of the police came to make sense in this context. Since being deinstitutionalized, she sometimes called the police hundreds of times a day and either said, "I'm going to kill myself," or just hung up. At times the police threatened her with arrest, but usually they took her to the emergency ward of the local hospital where she had been diagnosed either as having "antisocial personality disorder with mild mental retardation" or as "psychopathic."

One psychiatrist said, "She's a cutter. There's nothing you can do. She just does it to get back into the hospital. The only thing you can do is contain her and hope she mellows out over the years." Agnes apparently found the institution a relatively safe place and typically hurt herself on visits away from it. Agnes had been prescribed medication that was thought to be helping, but she was discovered to be hoarding the medication rather than taking it so the prescriptions were discontinued. This pattern of behavior is typical of people diagnosed with "borderline personality disorder." I have come to suspect that the characteristics of borderline personality in conjunction with self-injury are more properly seen as the direct result of serious child sex abuse. For Agnes, as for many others, this "antisocial" behavior was seen in terms of a diagnosis rather than understanding it as an adaptation to her environment or a communication worthy of response.[1]

Agnes must have grown used to not being heard. In 22 years, she had been transferred from one institution to another and had lived on a total of 13 wards—not counting numerous hospitalizations for self-injury. Not surprisingly, given all of this rejection, she had a hard time with relationships and made it difficult even to be her neighbor. When Agnes first moved into the apartment complex where she

---

[1] I am unaware of any comprehensive explanation for the "personality" of the multiples. Agnes seems to have internalized her aunt's aggression while other people seem to have split into versions of themselves safe enough to retreat into. I would be curious how these personalities develop because the concept of "chance" strikes me as shorthand for "we don't know yet."

lived, she put lighted paper into her neighbors' mailboxes. This and the frequent visits from the police made the neighbors sufficiently fed up with her that the apartment management gave her notice that if she acted out again she would be evicted, and the agency told her she would then be homeless. This threat worked insofar as she then cut herself without disturbing the neighbors.

The agency staff who helped Agnes directly with her apartment clearly did not believe anything she said. "She's a liar. She talks about all this abuse and then has a funny smile on her face. It's obvious she's lying." Men were afraid to work with her for fear she would accuse them of inappropriate sexual behavior. Some months after Agnes left one institution, she talked about a relationship she had with a staff member. Even though she was quite specific about the sexual nature of their relationship, no one took her story seriously. She said he had promised to come visit and to continue the relationship after she moved to her apartment, but he did not and she felt used. The institution's "human rights committee" investigated and nothing happened. For Agnes, "It was just swept under the carpet."

Two critical points suggest themselves here: the issues of motivation and credibility. I have been interested in "motivation assessment" surveys that are widely available in the field. Essentially, these measures ask questions and then yield a motivation for a person's behavior. These would be harmless and amusing parlor games if they did not have such significant political impact on people's lives. Of course, they are not used as parlor games because the general public would find them too ridiculous. The motivations that these questionnaires reveal are both overly narrow and insulting. Typically, people with disabilities are thought to be doing things for attention, avoidance, or noncompliance. I don't know where or on whom these questionnaires have been normed, but they probably have not been tested on ordinary people. Most people in my experience typically feel demeaned when their behavior is summarized as attention seeking. When I think of the variety of reasons I do things (or do not), I feel oddly restricted trying to account for my behavior in terms of only three or four basic motives.

These kinds of analyses strike me as a sad failure of imagination. Psychologists in the field of developmental disabilities have no very deep or impressive record in this work from the perspective of social justice. Instead, we have often allowed ourselves to serve as a substitute for justice. We have more often been attentive to the needs of our theoretical models than to the needs of people who might benefit from them. Tests that appear to standardize and categorize motivations inadvertently lend credence to the dismissal of people's actions. Had Agnes been a senior manager who complained about a staff person's sexual misconduct, it is less likely—though by no means certain—that her complaints would have been trivialized as attention seeking.

Of course the larger issue here—of being taken seriously—is one that people without status have to contend with constantly. In that context, Agnes has the double disadvantage of being a woman and of having a perceivable disability. In today's Western culture, generally, women have less credibility in making claims of sexual exploitation than men do in defending themselves against such claims. It seems curiously naive for psychologists to add to this situation with scales that lend the aura of scientific validity to an unacceptable prejudice.

The behavioral specialist and Agnes's social worker invited Agnes to work with them in individual sessions on these "new" issues of her childhood abuse. Not surprisingly, she missed most appointments. They tried to talk about her father and Aunt Katrina but she would only say, "I hate them and don't want to talk about them." She preferred to talk about the nice things that happened with her mother and sisters. These counselors located a self-help group for survivors, but the group's facilitator said that because Agnes had a history of assaulting people she doubted members would welcome her. At the same time, the facilitator did not ask the group members what they wanted to do. Agnes said she liked her individual sessions, but she often lost patience with the counselors for saying the wrong thing. Agnes would be quick to tell them, "Don't be patronizing."

Ironically, Agnes's life has been filled with helpers. More than most of the people served by this agency, she had had specialized counselors and therapists for each of several issues in her life: for anger, for assertiveness, to match her with a citizen advocate, and to help her go on a vacation she said she wanted. The agency staff felt they had made a good faith effort in community integration, and yet they felt that there was little to show for the effort.

Recently Agnes sliced her arms to the bone. She was found by the police, who took her to the hospital. When she quieted down, the emergency room staff removed the restraints, but she then began throwing equipment around and pulling out her stitches. She was again forcibly restrained and moved to the psychiatric unit where she finally calmed down the next morning. She talked about how she began to feel depressed and angry on Saturday night, had something to drink, and then hurt herself. "I cut mostly on weekends because that was when my dad came home drunk and left me tied up naked on the floor without covers." This episode was similar to others in that it started late in the evening, around 10 P.M., and lasted until early the next morning. It would make sense that after her father tied her up, someone would come and release her the next morning. These episodes of self-injury seemed exact reenactments of her abuse.

People further described that when Agnes cut herself she was angry, but after the blood started to flow she would look "triumphant" and "relieved," with a "placid, sort of dopey" expression and curl up on the floor. Sometimes, when she was still angry, she used some of her clothing in an attempt to strangle herself (angrily calling herself Katrina), but she could switch to being "nice" in a second. People saw this as proof of her being manipulative. They might just as easily (and less punitively) have seen her behavior as a demonstration of the powerful adaptation that dissociative personalities have.

When she was asked what thoughts led her to cut herself, she described, "I am on my own, I get bored. There's nothing on TV, and I get feeling really lonely. I start thinking badly. Then I get angry and start cutting to get rid of the pain."

"What kinds of pain do you feel?"

"Emotional pain. The pain of living. I drink because it helps kill the pain. Just a few sips and it all gets started . . . but I'm so revolting, I want to rip my insides out. I just want to kill those people, but they're dead. And sometimes I cut and the release just isn't there . . ."

Agnes also found that particularly pleasant experiences could precipitate her hurting herself as well. It may be that the precipitating event was somatic. Her response to autonomic arousal might well be to control and regulate extreme somatic experience through self-harm. One idea that had not been pursued was that she might have been hurting herself in response to premenstrual tension, that the discomfort, pain, and change of mood precipitated self-harm. (This hypothesis was followed up with no apparent positive correlation.)

Agnes's pattern of self-injury has many features that fit into our understanding of addictions. People who act addictively often self-medicate to blunt real feelings, to control, to achieve perfection, to avoid feelings of shame, and to isolate themselves and, as a function of all these, fail to achieve psychological intimacy. Agnes's reasons for her self-harm ("I am on my own, I get bored. There's nothing on TV, and I get feeling really lonely. I start thinking badly. Then I get angry and start. . . .") are three of the four classic conditions for substance abuse (hungry, angry, lonely, and tired). Her reactions to her cutting (she would look "triumphant" and "relieved" with a "placid, sort of dopey" expression and curl up after the blood started to flow) sound very much like a substance-induced "high."

If this parallel holds true for treatment, the obvious implication is that some form of self-help recovery effort would be a more logical first step than the "moral therapy" she was getting from the staff lectures on the dangers of self-harm or the largely irrelevant system of rewards and punishments the staff had subjected her to. Although behavioral management of addictions has obvious appeals to logic, more people choose self-help recovery programs than behavior therapy. I know of some people with intellectual disabilities who have joined self-help groups, but the almost reflexive therapy advised for all their psychological problems is behavior modification.

As I write this, Agnes has been transferred to the state psychiatric forensic unit where she is being held for assessment. As one person predicted, "She'll be there for 3 months. They will find she has a personality disorder and can't be treated. Or they'll say she's retarded as well and absolutely can't be treated. She could be in there indefinitely and what can we do?"[2]

I'm not sure what they can do, but it strikes me that this has become more a matter of social justice than a matter of clinical expertise. Simply labeling Agnes—yet again—makes her a victim of the irresponsible use of power and authority. For someone in Agnes's precarious position, the dangers and opportunities are clear. The lack of professional confidence and experience might be used to "patientize" her further. However, this presents all of us with the chance to include her as a guide, collaborator, and teacher.

The latter possibility seems so much more attractive to me that it hardly seems a contest, but I know people who are frightened to let go of their supposed authority. Just as we need to learn to listen to the fears of people with disabilities, so too we need to listen to our co-workers and respect their anxieties. Many of our co-workers have been hurt, too. Patience and respect are the only ways I know to keep everyone involved human. Otherwise, the very systems we design to help end up replicating the original abusive family or repeating other old hurts where people are not individuals but players in a game whose rules they do not write.

Abuse, Trauma, and Self-Injury

By its nature, abuse degrades a person into an object. People who have survived physical and sexual assault find themselves thrown from the subjects of appropriate love and desires (I am loved and wanted by my parents) into objects to be

---

[2]"What can we do?" really is an apt question. Agnes's professional team were decent, intelligent, and caring people. Their involvement with her went beyond simply managing her as a case. But once Agnes had been taken from their community mental health service to the state psychiatric forensic unit, they lost all formal connection with her. In human terms, they still cared, and, plausibly, they could have continued to visit her as friends. Practically, though, they all had demanding caseloads and Agnes was quickly replaced by someone else just as deserving and perhaps even as needy as Agnes had been. Just as Agnes had been taken from her mother (who, for whatever reasons had been unable to prevent the abuse or protect her daughter from it), Agnes had once again been taken from people who knew her and cared about her and, for various good reasons, could no longer do so.

subjugated (You exist to serve me). This can kill their own capacities to love or to trust the love of others.[3] Services unthinkingly repeat the same process. Especially when people with developmental disabilities need help, they are at risk for finding themselves made into "objects" when their subjective reality ("I need help," "I am the survivor of sexual assault and child abuse") becomes objectified and essentially ignored by clinical labels ("a manipulative and self-injurious mentally retarded/emotionally disturbed client"). People who have been objectified by services predictably treat themselves as objects. Not surprisingly, Favazza and Conterio (1988) found that "habitual self-mutilators feel little or no pain (two thirds of our sample [of child abuse survivors]); only 10% feel great pain, and 23% feel moderate pain" (p.26).[4]

Repeatedly, we have seen that professionals have responded to emotional issues intellectually and behaviorally with control technologies. One of the serious dangers in our service culture is the widely unquestioned assumption that every aspect of life for people with disabilities can be determined by a group of people who do not have to live with the consequences of their decisions. If a young child with autism is banging her head, the behavior is probably communicating more than her emotions. Yet her behavior is often responded to as if it were an intellectual conundrum that could be solved

---

[3]"Cutting, burning, and poking needles in my arm is a security for me because I know if all else fails and leaves me feeling emotionless and empty, the pain and blood will always still be there for me. I am cutting myself more frequently now and I'm losing friends. I am starting to feel desperate. I feel like I am unable to love anybody and that I am incapable of being loved by anyone. Please help me. Hope is fading fast" (18-year-old waitress) (as quoted in Favazza & Conterio, 1988, p. 28).

[4]As one woman said, "When will I stop self-mutilating? I think it is related to the phenomenon of depersonalization and feeling 'not me' and feeling invisible and feeling that nobody can hear or understand my words describing my inner emptiness, its acute pain, and the 'tapes' I recall from childhood which depicted me as a monster who could hurt herself or die or never be born. Certainly understanding that it is within my control to stop it has not been productive—it merely makes me more frustrated (along with my therapist) when I do it again. In the past year or two, though, I have switched from quantity to 'quality' in what I do—now using a razor to do infrequent deep cuts that need stitches, rather than shallow cuts with blunter objects. This scares me a lot" (Favazza & Conterio, 1988, p. 26).

like the *New York Times* crossword puzzle. For some psychologists, their work often consists of 1- or 2-hour bursts. For the objects of this work—the people hurting themselves—these "behavior programs" can go on all their lives.

———

People who write behavior programs are particularly at risk for fitting neatly into the paradigm of abuse as abusers. The control most behavior plans require is usually presented as needed by the person with the disability when, in fact, a sense of control is something both that person and the people around her need. Making the person with the difficult behavior solely responsible for that behavior is precisely how the abused child interprets her abuse: If she were "better," it would stop. Again, I emphasize that this explanation is not an indictment. I doubt that most people writing behavior plans have ever thought they could be perceived as abusive, nor would they want to be. Because this dynamic is unseen—and therefore not consciously considered—it is vitally important that it be talked about. If we do not want to be abusive, then we need to be aware of when we are abusive so we can stop.

As more people break the suffocating silence in which their childhood abuse has been hidden, a greater awareness of dissociation emerges. Confronted with something too horrific to bear directly, the child escapes into different personalities that can be unaware of one another's existence. The elegance of this process is that it allows the child to "forget" the abuse. Some people with ordinary socialization may hide their experiences of abuse out of fear (many children are threatened not to tell) or shame, or they may conceal their multiple personalities for fear of being thought of as crazy. Some people with disabilities, such as Agnes, can be quite frank on these topics. Unfortunately, having multiple personalities is often still seen as a sign of mental illness rather than as the personality's adaptation for survival.

The ways people respond to those who hurt themselves range from providing comfort and support to the use of extremely painful management technologies. Some people have compared the management technologies to professionalized child abuse and this in turn has been criticized as making this issue ideological rather than scientific.[5] Personally, I am curious about the motives of people who consistently use pain as a control technology. The most commonly stated reason for helping people gain self-control is not at all persuasive either emotionally or intellectually. But absent any real accounts of how people become persuaded to hurt others in the name of therapy, I am willing to restrict my concern to their actual behavior, which is, at the least, overtly controlling people and, at the worst, openly hurting them.

As more people discard their undeserved shame and guilt and speak up, we as a culture become more aware of how many of us were hurt as children and in how many ways. Being abused is a direct function of one's powerlessness. The less powerful (and, therefore, the less believable) a person is, the more abuse is liable to occur. With this awareness, it comes as no surprise that people with disabilities are at risk for physical and sexual assault.

> According to Kempton (1977) there are many reasons why people with mental handicaps may be more vulnerable to sexual abuse. These include such factors as: increased trust in strangers and those close to them; an inability to determine what is appropriate behaviour in those caring for them; a tendency to more passive, obedient, and affectionate behaviour

---

[5]Somehow the idea that science is too pure to be political persists with no visible supporting evidence. The danger comes when people deny the political implications and origins of their work and retreat instead into a fantasy science independent of emotion, prejudice, impulse, and irrational faith.

> Recent work in the philosophy and history of science . . . has undermined seriously the view of science on which behavior therapy's self-image is based. . . . The form and content of scientific knowledge are strongly influenced by socio-political factors as well as those related to the attitudes and sensibilities of the community of scientists (Feyerabend, 1975; Kuhn, 1970a, 1970b; Polanyi, 1966). Because their subject matter bears so directly on and is influenced by the human self-image, the social sciences and systems of psychotherapy are even more limited in their ability to remain independent of cultural influence (Buss, 1975; London, 1964; Lowe, 1976; Sampson, 1978, 1981). . . . No social science can ever truly stand outside or transcend the social practices and institutions that served to constitute it in the first place (Woolfolk & Richardson, 1984, p. 777).

than their peers of normal intelligence (Breen, 1987); and often, poor judgment.

On a cultural level Brown and Craft (1989) point out such factors as the low status of people with mental handicaps in our society can lead to a belief that sexually abusing them is less reprehensible or less serious than abusing other people, and may be more easily "got away with." Added to this, the stereotype of hyper-sexuality with which people with mental handicaps are sometimes associated[6] may make it easier for potential abusers to overcome their own internal inhibitions to abuse.

Vizard (1989) reports evidence from the literature that abusers are extremely skilled in identifying and selecting vulnerable individuals. (Dunne & Power, 1990, p. 112)

Comparatively few adults have natural and legitimate access to a typical child's body. But many adults are often involved with children with disabilities: physicians, therapists, and other caregivers in addition to their parents. It is just about impossible to predict which people hired will work out well and people providing direct services are almost always poorly paid, which works to create a high turnover rate in service workers and a high probability for abuse. Even when allegations of abuse are made, many workers are transferred rather than fired or are allowed to quit rather than prosecuted. Very few people have routine access to the bodies of typical children as they grow to adulthood. For people who need help with toileting or washing, the number of such people who have been in their lives reliably increases with every year.

All of the offenders were known to their victims, being either family members or people living or working within the locality. Thus, the fear which many parents express, about their son or daughter with a mental handicap being abused by strangers in public places, does not appear to be borne out by the data.

This result is in line with findings from other surveys of victims of sexual abuse, which show that offenders are very often people whom the young victims know and trust. It concurs, therefore, with the conception of sexual abuse as partly an

[6]This, of course, may be a result rather than a cause. Inappropriate sexuality and hyper-sexuality are signs child care workers look for in identifying an abused child. If people with intellectual disabilities are more likely to be abused, then these signs would also be more common in them.

abuse of power relationships and trust (Sgroi, 1982; Bentovim, 1987). (Dunne & Power, 1990, p. 123)

More than "partly an abuse of power relationships and trust," Blume (1986) calls this incest:

> *Incest*, in my definition, occurs when these acts take place at the hands or command of someone who has power over the child due to trust and/or authority: an on-going, close relationship such as parent, step-parent, aunt, baby-sitter, mother's boyfriend, or even dentist, piano teacher, or priest, when there is bonding or a surrogate-parent situation. A blood relationship is not necessary for incest.
>
> Incest occurs most commonly in the family context of male-dominance: perpetrators are almost exclusively male. The perpetrator sees the child as his possession, with whom sexual activity is his privilege. While traditional attitudes have held mothers in these families responsible for what fathers and step-fathers were doing, *incest is never the responsibility of anyone but the person who commits the abuse*, and, in fact, these families are often so skewed in terms of power in the direction of the patriarch that the wife is often not in a position to interrupt the cycle, even if she does know about it. This concept is validated, in one way, by the high rate of wife-abuse in these families. (p. 5)

This description sounds familiar in the context of service cultures as well as in the authoritarian political culture that tolerates or uses control in all forms. Even when staff know about episodes of abuse, they often feel helpless to intervene for fear of reprisals.

Are there differences between the psychological effects resulting from physical assault and sexual assault? My sense is that the context of the abuse is as significant as the type of abuse.

> Specifically, it has been the author's clinical experience that if a child is exposed to especially high levels of humiliation and disgust . . . the child may come to the conclusion that she or he must "deserve" such treatment, and therefore must be as disgusting and abhorrent as whatever was done to her or him. . . . Such cognitions may be especially prevalent when the former victim finds herself/himself in (even slightly) similar situations later in life . . . and may motivate self-destructive thoughts and feelings. (Briere, 1988, p. 332)

People who have been hurt in the name of therapy may not understand their plight any differently from survivors of cult abuse or sexual abuse.[7] A common feature of post-traumatic stress syndrome is the flashback in which a person acts as if a memory is present reality. For example, one "graduate" of a program that used aversives became extremely agitated while being helped in the bathroom and ripped his helper's thumb off. For some, this would have been a sign that he "needed" to be hurt more, but the people working for him knew his previous program well enough to recognize that the bathroom had been where most of his abusive "therapy" had taken place. It might have been any of a number of cues, small or large, that made him think that, far from being helped, he was about to be seriously hurt again and his "explosive violence" was not a symptom of a "behavior disorder" so much as his best attempt at self-defense. Some residential services that use pain to extreme levels are proud of the home-like atmosphere of their residences, but when the victims of hurtful procedures leave, they are at risk for having flashbacks triggered by the most ordinarily unremarkable places and things—wallpaper, a song on the radio, or a room. In addition, every time they recall their previous maltreatment, unless their panic and rage are recognized as a function of stress, they are likely to be further stigmatized as "impossible to serve."

In describing the effects of ritualized abuse Young, Sachs, Braun, and Watkins (1991) found:

---

[7]Finkelhor, Williams, and Burns (1988) define ritualistic abuse as "abuse that occurs in the context linked to some symbols or group activities that have a religious, magical, or supernatural connotation, and where the invocation of these symbols or activities are repeated over time and used to frighten and intimidate the children." They propose three subtypes . . . "[the third being] *psychopathological ritualism*, where mentally ill adults abuse children while employing idiosyncratic rituals." Kelly (1988) defines ritualistic abuse as "the repetitive and systematic sexual, physical, and psychological abuse of children by adults as part of cult or satanic worship" (Jones, D., 1991, p. 164).

Obviously, comparing satanic rituals with systematic aversive programming at the level of intention would be more provocative than informing. But using the child's perspective, can we see the difference in intent? Adults acting in concert to hurt children is the key variable and although their verbal behavior is to help, it does little to mitigate the pain.

A set of symptoms [that] . . . included unusual fears, survivor guilt, indoctrinated beliefs, substance abuse, severe post-traumatic stress disorder, bizarre self-abuse, sexualization of sadistic impulses, and dissociative states with satanic overtones. . . .

PTSD [Post Traumatic Stress Disorder] symptoms were prominent, with high levels of anxiety and panic, easy triggering by external stimuli, flashbacks, nightmares and intrusive images. These symptoms alternated with states of withdrawal, feelings of numbness, or shifts into dissociated functional states or altered personalities.

Other symptoms common to the study population included hearing internal voices or conversations, experiencing a sense of being controlled by inner forces, and periods of amnesia. These were related to underlying dissociative disorder and were not symptoms of psychosis. (pp. 183–184)

Having been hurt and abused, people are then at risk for being labeled "dually diagnosed" rather than understood by their real status as survivors.

Depression is the most common presenting complaint although anxiety and difficulty controlling outbursts of anger are also mentioned. Moodiness and a sense that "I just don't know who I am" are described. The individual may have a history of suicide attempts or self-injury. (Lindsley, 1989, p. 66)

Depression, or more accurately, a depressed *person*, can be labeled unmotivated or noncompliant. Outbursts of anger become the province of control programs. The sense of "I just don't know who I am" can easily be overlooked as a function of the person's "impaired intellectual ability." My experience has been that people with low "intelligence quotients" often have very keen "emotional quotients."[8] Again, we have an example that people can have powerful insights into their lives and be powerless to effect the changes necessary for their growth and happiness.

Gold (1986) found that

---

[8]Even though this idea is a fairly common observation among those who are on good terms with people labeled retarded, I have found only one reference in the published literature. Stokes (1987) referred to making a distinction between "cognitive intelligence" and "emotional intelligence."

Victimized individuals differ significantly from nonvictimized individuals. Of considerable significance are the coping effectiveness and social support systems available to the victims of child abuse. More specifically, where a social support system, including a parent, failed to respond to the victimized child, the likelihood of adjustment in adulthood was seriously compromised. (p. 472)

Many programs that routinely use control techniques have a tradition of forbidding family visits anywhere from 3 days to 3 months. This is, ostensibly, to allow the person time to adjust. This period of unfamiliarity and confusion for the individual allows the staff to exert control with a minimum of resistance. For the individual, however, this period can emphasize: *Abandon hope. No one you care about cares about you. No one you know is coming to speak up for you.* In this way, control programs abuse the person actively and coerce families and friends into the passive abuse of abandonment.

Self-injury claims power in a world where power means pain. For example, a woman thought Christ's imminent return required her to cut off her hand. She failed to do this but damaged herself sufficiently in the attempt that her hand had to be amputated anyway. Afterward, she decided she had been misled by Satan (Favazza, 1989). This seems irrational without seeing her point: "If pain is intrinsic and inevitable in my world, *who* inflicts the pain is critical. Hurting myself is a way of expressing my taking charge of my life." For people who look only at observable and measurable exterior realities, this self-injurious behavior would be explained by the interior and largely unmeasurable concept of psychosis. Such explanations occur when we focus on our dismay with the results rather than on the person's satisfaction with the act.

The long-term effects of child sexual abuse in adults suggest . . . (1) There tends to be clear evidence of self-destructive behaviors in victimized vs nonvictimized patients. . . . (2) Women who have been abused show, as adults, significant adjustment difficulties in problems related to both interpersonal and sexual relationships with males and females. More specifically, it appears that incest victims carry hostile feelings toward significant adults in their adulthood. . . . (3) Sexually abused female children as adults also seek adult relationships which involve

sexually abusing encounters. . . . (4) The most significant diagnostic profile for adults who are physically and sexually abused
as children includes the following symptomatology: depression, self-destructive behavior, anxiety and traumatic stress,
poor self-esteem, a tendency towards revictimization, substance
abuse, difficulties in trusting others, and sexual maladjustment
in adulthood. (Miller & Veltkamp, 1989, pp. 123–124)

Just as we would not assume from a discussion of incest
that all family members are sexually predatory, neither
should we assume that all people who provide services are
abusers. But silence on this topic collaborates with a system
that has, for too many people, been literally killing. Parents
have allowed their sons and daughters to live in "special"
places because they trust the professional community to
know best. These professionals, in turn, rely on people to
provide direct help, often around the clock. This division of
labor diminishes the sense of responsibility so that no one really owns what happens to the person who is supposed to be
at the center of it all. In this dangerous vacuum, people are
victimized and hurt.

> Self-mutilation is a source of great shame and humiliation. But
> it is important to talk about because, like child sexual abuse,
> self-abuse grows worse in a climate of secrecy.
>
> To stop self-abuse, you need to get help. A skilled counselor
> can provide essential support. It's no longer necessary to hurt
> yourself. You deserve kindness from others and from yourself.
>
> To keep from cutting myself, I write affirmations. I do it
> right on my wrist. I'll write things like "I love myself," "I will
> not hurt myself," "I am good," "It's okay to be in pain. It's okay
> to say it." There was a while I'd change it every day. And then I
> tell people about what I want to do. I tell my group members. I
> tell my therapist.
>
> One survivor went so far as to write loving messages all over
> her body. As a child she had carved "help" into her arm. Now,
> wanting to make peace with her body, she gently wrote love
> notes to all her body parts.
>
> Once you decide that hurting yourself is no longer an op-
> tion, you need to find healthier ways to gain that feeling of re-
> lease. Physical activity and emotional release work can both be
> effective alternatives.

> Stopping a pattern of self-mutilation requires that you ex-
> press feelings directly. If you are angry, refocus your anger
> where it belongs—at the person or people who abused you. If
> you hurt yourself when you get scared, practice responding
> to feelings of terror in a different way. (Bass & Davis, 1988,
> p. 220)

The supportive and helpful language of and for survivors contrasts sharply with the panic and confusion with
which specialists in developmental disability typically discuss
self-injury.

> How does an organism, apparently programmed for survival
> in so many ways, come to emit behavior that threatens survival?
> Withdrawal from pain and from the threat of pain is a paradig-
> matic sign of sentience, and the absence of such a sign signals a
> crisis of life systems. The apparent attraction to pain—indeed
> its voluntary enhancement—is the staggering contradiction we
> view here. . . . (Kedesdy, 1988, p. 224)

Self-injurious behavior is almost always described in terms of
extreme danger, and the drama is used as a rationale for extreme methods of control. "Chronic self-injurious behavior is
a dramatic form of psychopathology. . . . Failure of adequate
control of self-hitting may lead to permanent injury" (Tate &
Baroff, 1966, p. 281). Self-injurious behavior has been described as "perhaps the most dramatic and extreme form of
chronic human psychopathology" (Carr, 1977, p. 800), as "a
devastating and life-threatening behavior . . . to the point of
broken bones, massive flesh loss, and even loss of a limb . . ."
(Edelson, Taubman, & Lovaas, 1983, p. 299).

People with developmental disabilities who systematically hurt themselves are often portrayed as particularly baffling and dangerous. People who hurt themselves can indeed
be frightening so that those who would help often react
hastily to stop the behavior. This makes good sense in an
emergency. If David Lewis had suddenly wrenched his legs
and fractured them, or if Agnes intentionally but unexpect-
edly cut herself with a piece of glass, one would act with the
best combination of intelligence and speed to stop them. But
if they attempt this frequently, then we need to take some
time to consider both their lives and our responses more
carefully. We need to recognize that sudden and unpre-

dictable behavior can become, over time, a pattern. Similarly, just as people's self-injury can become chronic, so, too, can our impulsive and improvised responses to it. As our understanding of individuals deepens, we need to move from simple control and management techniques to understanding, teaching, and recovery. What works to resolve a sudden and isolated crisis—physical restraint or getting the person to a quiet and soothing place in which to calm down—can, over time, become unhelpful or even actively hurtful.

I find it typically does not take more than a day or 2 to develop some positive approaches, even for people who are famous at a state or regional level for behavior that has been puzzling for many years. By taking some time to talk and think about the person *as a person*, with those who know and love him, I find concerned groups often come up with refreshing ways of helping. My role is often helping people focus on who this person is, really, and how can we honor his history accurately?

When we do take the time to learn more about people's lives, the temptation is to pursue a history of the self-injurious behavior (SIB) and not a history of the person. I often find, predictably enough, that people with dangerous behavior have had dangerous lives of hurt and rejection. Instead of recognizing our past failures to take people into account personally, I find we have often labeled them "emergency cases" and use that as a license to achieve a quick fix at any cost. Instead of getting to know more about people and why they might have needed this behavior to survive, many of us were trained to "extinguish" the behavior outright, as if their hurting themselves had nothing to do with the rest of their lives. Instead of respecting that hurting themselves was their best solution to a problem, I was trained to presume the behavior was "maladaptive" and required me to eradicate it, branch and root, at almost any price.

In reviewing studies of self-injury, Johnson and Baumeister (1978) found:

> The emphasis upon treatment of SIB is hardly surprising in that these behaviors, when they come to the attention of therapists, are usually very severe and require prompt intervention. Indeed, the very nature of these behaviors is often such that

the intervention itself must be rather direct, precluding extended analyses of antecedent and maintaining conditions. It is important, therefore, that the therapist have available procedures that are designed to produce rapid and general deceleration of responding. (pp. 465–466)

Unfortunately, this article is still typical of the field in presuming that the people we work for can suddenly become persistently and irrationally self-abusive.[9] The people I have known developed these dangerous habits over a period of years. A service system that has lethargically tolerated or intentionally ignored a life of pain springs to action, rushing to help. In our haste, we often overlook the deeper causes of frightening behavior. Typically, behavior analysis focuses on the immediate and obvious behavioral antecedents, which assumes that people primarily respond to their environment. This is true, if we include our inner life as a powerful environment. As we have seen from the experiences of survivors, memories can be triggered by physical surroundings, but the connection between an apparently innocuous stimulus and a highly charged response can only be made, if at all, by self-report.

Of course, self-injurious behavior can be interpreted in terms of reinforcement theory. But the environment may have a more powerful cumulative effect than any one, immediate reinforcement. Globally intrusive behaviors often reflect the larger environment of a person's political status, and the broad accumulated experience of a person's individual history. Just as memory is an environment, so are class, role, expectation, and other people's opinions.

---

[9]In some circles, people who hurt themselves have been replaced by their behavior and that, in turn, has been transformed into the acronym SIB (self-injurious behavior), which is another way for people to use language as a way of distancing themselves from the fact that a person is hurting. This dubious practice has undergone rhetorical inflation and SIB has sometimes become the more dramatic SSIB for severe self-injurious behavior ("Aversive therapy," 1991, pp. 919–920). This increased emphasis may be a signal that technologies of control are no longer the primary response to people with difficult behavior. In contrast to this hysteria, people who work in relationships tend to use language in the opposite direction to include people with an attitude of evenness, accommodation, and compassion.

While despairing of uncovering the reasons for self-injury, the literature typically fails to discuss the effect of this behavior on therapists. The following is one interesting exception:

> Of all disturbing patient behaviors, self-mutilation is the most difficult for clinicians to understand and treat. . . . The typical clinician (myself included) treating a patient who self-mutilates is often left feeling a combination of helpless, horrified, guilty, furious, betrayed, disgusted, and sad. Many times an otherwise promising treatment reaches a stalemate or ends because of the inability of the patient and the clinician to manage the self-mutilation in a fashion that will reduce or eliminate it. (Frances, 1987, p. 316)

"Patients. . . . have learned that physicians and nurses confronted with self-mutilation may act in an angry and inappropriate manner. For example, sutures may be applied without an anesthetic" (Favazza, 1989, p. 137). This emotional context helps explain the desperate acts done in the name of helping. The bizarre technologies that hurt people who hurt themselves might also be understood as a type of professional revenge in the name of therapy. Because most professionals discussing self-injurious behavior begin with their own sense of frustration and lack of comprehension, it is not surprising that they proceed to act as ignorant and frightened people often do: They scapegoat.[10]

---

[10]Scapegoating seems a common response when helplessly frightened. Hate crimes are seen to increase whenever pervasive social change threatens predictability. The most commonly cited example is Germany after World War I and the Nazi program for purifying the nation through mass extermination. It also seems that using the Fascist policy of extermination has come to make the German nation something of a scapegoat for our collective anxiety about race relations. To cite an example: As the prosperity of the 1920s collapsed into the Depression, lynchings of black Americans increased sharply. However, not all scapegoating is spontaneous and violent. In India, only Untouchables can butcher animals or prepare a corpse for burial; this caste is thought to be an institutionalized scapegoat as a way to negotiate the anxiety around dying and death.

American culture might be thought of as using the professionals who surround people with disabilities as Untouchables who mediate between the society at large and the anxiety that people with disabilities seem to evoke. If so, this is another of many ways the movement toward community inclusion has significant implications for cultural change. The resistance to it might be a prejudice against people with disabilities, but it also might be about the more forgivable anxiety that real change provokes in most of us.

The role of behaviorism, perhaps inadvertently, has been to help us distance ourselves from the real suffering of people with difficult behavior, if, when we are confronted with pain, we retreat into baselines and data. In this sense, the use of behavioral techniques with people whose behavior troubles us is negatively reinforcing. By not having to deal with them, their pain, their lives, or the frustration of not understanding them very well, we can protect our own feelings in that calm realm where data are studied, having been gathered by others.

Severe levels of self-mutilation have been reported in psychiatric literature, as in the case of the man who chopped off his finger and ate it. And yet, none of the "treatment modalities" proposed for him included aversives (Favazza, 1989, p. 137). Even in these troubling and difficult examples, some psychiatric workers understand the importance of addressing the real reasons for the behavior rather than simply what is behaviorally obvious. This attempt to understand motive has not carried over into services for people with significant cognitive differences, as if they are somehow less than human.

> When I was first hospitalized I was asked why I was cutting myself . . . and I told the doctor it was like a "bright red scream." Before every episode of self-mutilation, I feel emotionally overwhelmed. The sight of my blood seems to release unbearable tension. At first a bruise or a scratch was effective, but later it took more blood to ease the explosive tension. Now I cut my veins to get results (39-year-old school teacher). (Favazza & Conterio, 1988, p. 26)

It would be simple to see this woman's explanation of her behavior as an example of negative reinforcement: By hurting herself, the unpleasant tension is reduced. The problem, as with behaviorism generally, is not that this interpretation is wrong—that's not the point—it's simply too reductionistic to comprehend significant facts.

Medical Aspects of Self-Injury

I was asked to visit a day program to talk with people about Norma, a woman who seriously hurt herself. When I saw that she had concentrated on hitting the middle of her forehead I asked, "How long has she had allergies?" One of the staff told me, "Since she was about 13."

"And how long has she been hitting her forehead?"

"Since she was about 13. What is your point?"

My point, simply, was that people often have painful sinus headaches as a result of allergies. Because Norma had so consistently focused on hitting the area around her sinuses, I suspected she might have untreated pain. Anyone who has ever had sinusitis, for example, knows how unpleasant it can be. Just as people sometimes manage psychological pain by hurting themselves, others manage uncontrolled and intractable physical pain and discomfort by self-injury.

Norma had also been hitting her jaws. Because she was on anticonvulsant medication, I suspected she might have puffy and inflamed gums as a side effect. Happily, people had already taken her to a dentist. But he was frightened of Norma's hitting herself so rather than examine her, he rescheduled her for an appointment 3 months later. People were content with this. "It's really hard to find a dentist who will look at our people," staff said. That might be true, but it would be just as hard for the dentist to look at a malpractice attorney, and neither of these difficulties can begin to compare with living with a toothache for 3 months.

It took me a while to notice, but more people by far hurt their heads than their ankles. My best guess is that our heads are a rich source of difficult-to-detect pain. Generally, if we have something causing pain in our ankles, it shows up either as inflammation or swelling or on X ray.

Most people are able to at least indicate—to point however approximately—the location of pain, but people who do not use words to communicate and who have no understandable way to signal their distress may need to manage the pain themselves. Especially when the source of pain is not obvious, even well-intended practitioners might decide that the pain is "imaginary" or that the person is a "hypochondriac." Of course, if an aching tooth or ear is untreated long enough, the inflammation eventually becomes visible, but this is not usually true of a headache, a stomachache, or mild chronic joint pain. Some people might honor a person's hurting her head as a symptom and treat, for example, what might be a headache with aspirin. If the person responds, then we might have guessed correctly. We are also confronted with the possibility that the person's pain is emotional. "Physical symptoms [for people with multiple personality disorder][11] notably severe headaches unresponsive to medication may present. Abdominal pain, dizziness, and difficulty breathing are often mentioned as well" (Lindsley, 1989, p. 66).

Just because people cannot articulate their conditions and just because their behaviors do not change with standard clinical treatment does not make these experiences any less painful or real. Incredibly, some physicians are liable to dismiss psychosomatic complaints as not real and accept that the person's difficulties are behavioral. I just cannot accept any report that says a person in distress is not in pain. The best that can be said is that no obvious cause for pain can be found. Having ruled out only the most general physiological possibilities, some physicians refer people to behavioral psychologists who then proceed as if the behavior's origins were of little or no interest and all that matters is its consequences.

Some people on finding that Agnes misses work when she cuts herself would focus on her job and how to change it or make her conform better to its demands. However, given our understanding of Agnes's life, her job is probably a small and not terribly critical part of why she hurts herself. If Norma hits her jaw just as we present her with a table-top sorting activity, some might take that as a sign she is noncompliant to the demand. It might just as easily be coincidence. When we look at all the demands made on Norma in a day, it is not surprising that an untreated tooth would give a painful twinge at about the same time someone asked her to do something. Not everything that happens in sequence is cause and effect however much it appears that way.

This is emphatically *not* to suggest that Norma's behavior cannot also be communicative. Of course it can. In fact, her behavior cannot *not* communicate. Nonetheless, she might have a toothache when she is offered something she gen-

[11]This could just as easily and less pejoratively be termed *strategy for personal integrity* (multiple personalities).

uinely enjoys. This is yet another reason for people to know how to read Norma's nonverbal communication well. A functional analysis of her behavior could very easily—and with apparently convincing data—mislead us entirely about what she means when she hurts herself.

When I first started training as a psychologist, I was struck by the analytical power of taking data. I liked the textbook examples of Antecedent–Behavior–Consequence analysis to lay bare the true function of a baffling behavior. I'm not sure I approve, but the opportunity to act like Sherlock Holmes, plucking startling but irrefutable conclusions from apparently thin air, has its appeal for me.

The reality, however, has been quite different. I can't think of a time where data analysis helped me discover anything I needed to know. At this point, data gathering would only serve me as a distraction.[12] Even in programs that take exhaustive data, the quickest and most reliable sources of information about difficult behavior are the people involved with it. Obviously, the person herself is a good place to begin, although people who are frightening because of their self-injuries often do not use words to communicate. In that case, the people who work the closest with or know the person best should be consulted. When people are invited to guess freely *and* ("and" is critical) have some open affection for the person, then insight and empathy begin to collaborate.

Sometimes where people hurt themselves shows the exact spot where they hurt, but I wonder if people have not learned on their own some of the strategies of behavioral medicine. People with intractable and phantom types of pain have learned to use a competing pain as a way to get some relief. For example, some people have found transcutaneous electrical nerve stimulation (TENS) helpful. This device ap-

---

[12]Although I don't find much useful in this for myself, people of good will and good practice do. I don't want to be misunderstood as attacking numbers as a tool for discovery. Rather than dismissing this more linear way of working, I hope this argument helps expand the realm of respectable possibility. So far, our work has not been burdened with too many ways of knowing.

plies a low electrical charge as a competing stimulus.[13] One technique to manage dull and chronic pain (e.g., lower back pain) is for the sufferer to put a couple of fingers into a cup of crushed ice and water. The dull pain this causes is thought somehow to halve the uncontrolled back pain. When people routinely hurt themselves, it is not hard to see how their controlled use of pain replicates these procedures.

Indeed, Ross and Ross (1988) recommended teaching children to use Hoku points as a simple pain management strategy.

> One point that has proven useful in treating lateral and bilateral tension musculoskeletal headaches is located in each hand in the web of skin between the thumb and first finger. To identify this Hoku point the child extends his hand as though to shake hands with someone; the web between the thumb and first finger then becomes clearly visible and is distinct from the fleshy part adjacent to it. [This procedure], which is not applicable to migraine headaches, is summarized as follows: For headaches on the right side, the right-hand Hoku point is used; for those on the left, the left-hand point is used; for bilateral headaches both Hoku points are used simultaneously. We will describe the procedure in terms of headaches on the left side of the head, but the general method is the same for all three locations. Using the thumb and the forefinger of the right hand, firmly grasp the web of the left hand and exert pressure around the web area until locating the spot where the pressure is definitely uncomfortable. This is the Hoku point for headaches. Apply continuous pressure to this point for 15 seconds, then slowly release the pressure, and decide whether the headache pain is relieved. If not, or if it returns, repeat the procedure. The headache Hoku point is also the pressure point for dental pain. (pp. 201–202)

Some people who routinely bite this area find themselves on reinforcement programs to stop the behavior when they

---

[13]I remember when this device was introduced it was seen as a technological innovation, but Sjölund and Eriksson (1985) reported the use of electrical stimulation from Fifth Dynasty tomb carvings in which Egyptian physicians used the electrical fish (*Malapterus electricus*). Scribonius Largus cited the treatment of gout with a "living electrical ray" (*Torpedo marmorata*). This older use of electricity in no way diminishes the efficacy of TENS, but it helps to hold perspective on the concept of novelty in treatment (p. 15).

might find more direct help from two aspirin or a dental check-up. Once again, we see how people's behavior that begins as a way to comfort themselves can get misinterpreted, interrupted, frustrated, and controlled.

Sadly, when we teach people to use these paramedical techniques, we are heroes of pain management; when people apply them spontaneously to themselves, they are liable to be programmed or punished.

The Association for the Advancement of Behavior Therapy published a report on the treatment of self-injurious behavior (1982) that was largely dismissive of medical and psychodynamic approaches and noted the following:

> The primary focus of research in the behavioral field has not been on the etiology of self-injury, but on its treatment. Behavioral treatment techniques operate either on rearranging consequences for the behavior (e.g., removing reinforcement or punishing self-injury; reinforcing more desirable behavior); or rearranging antecedent stimuli which control differential occurrences of the behavior. (p. 535)

This analysis shows the great weakness of behavioral thinking. Just as analyzing behavior in isolation can give insight, the loss of context destroys meaning. These guesses can be useful because knowing why a person does something obviously helps us respond better. If a person really does self-injurious acts for attention, then we can easily provide attention in a way that makes the behavior unnecessary. If, however, a person is responding to an organic process, then our best response could be medical as well as social.

People with self-injurious behavior often have undiagnosed health problems and once their conditions are accurately diagnosed and treated, they act in much less distressed—and distressing—ways. This, however, is very different from the way self-injurious behavior is often treated: as if it were itself an illness. The dangers of medicalizing behavior are fairly obvious: If self-injurious behavior is an illness (even of obscure etiology), then it warrants treatment. If an illness becomes difficult to treat, then it is generally given more aggressive treatment. This inappropriate use of the medical model has led to the rationale of using extreme pain as a "therapy" for self-injury. Just as physicians may get angry and try to avoid patients whose illnesses do not respond to their treatments, some therapists come to feel that they are the aggrieved party when their good ideas fail to work.

Conclusion

The danger of thinking behaviorally about people is that we focus on the behavior of others and not our own. Even when we ask why a person acts in a certain way we are led to trivial and demeaning reasons—attention and noncompliance, for example. Behavior modification never asks, "How does this behavior make the therapist feel?" Because unacknowledged feelings are often more powerful than the ones we name, failing to take these unmeasurable, nonempirical, and largely "unprofessional" emotions into account directly threatens the clarity of our purpose and indirectly jeopardizes the well-being of the very people we would help. The responses to people whose behavior frightens us have been misperceived as a clinical problem, as if the history of the clinic were divorced from society and its values. Clinicians cannot act apolitically. No matter what our professional response is (or is not), it reflects or sets in motion a system of political values. To paraphrase Gloria Steinem's original adage, the clinical is political and, as she revised it (1992), the political is personal. We are all in a constant dialogue with the present and the past, our inner selves and outer selves, and the needs both of the individual and the group. It seems strangely limited—and limiting—to focus on only one person among many and on only one aspect of that person among her many aspects.

The most influential model most of us have for helping is of our own parents taking care of us. Our childhood experiences with adult authority and control are highly relevant to the way we work, although services often act as if what we most need is a graduate degree or an in-service training. Given the disparate power between helpers and those helped, our formative experiences and resulting biases are crucial to our own awareness in working. Too often we use programming as a substitute for actual human connection with the people who are programmed. Too often we use clinical neutrality or cold professionalism to mask our fears or even our loathing. How could our own stories be irrelevant to our understanding of how helpers help? How could we believe that, for people with as much power as we behavioral specialists, behavioral psychologists, and consultants have, our own histories and biases are irrelevant or unscientific? For survivors of abuse the helping professions can just as easily accelerate our work of recovery or push us into denial or into replicating the original hurts.

> Contempt is the weapon of the weak and a defense against one's own despised and unwanted feelings. And the fountainhead of all contempt, of all discrimination, is the more or less conscious, uncontrolled, and secret exercise of power over the child by the adult, which is tolerated by society (except in the case of murder or serious bodily harm). What adults do to their child's spirit is entirely their own affair. For the child is regarded as the parents' property, in the same way as citizens of a totalitarian state are the property of its government. Until we become sensitized to the small child's suffering, this wielding of power by adults will continue to be a normal aspect of the human condition, for no one pays attention to or takes seriously what is regarded as trivial, since the victims are "only children." But in twenty years' time these children will be adults who will have to pay it all back to their own children. They may then fight vigorously against cruelty "in the world"—and yet they will carry within themselves an experience of cruelty to which they have no access and which remains hidden behind the idealized picture of a happy childhood. (Miller, 1981, p. 69)

Unfortunately, in the behavioral paradigm there is no language—much less the occasion for such language—for our personal experience and feelings when confronting the difficult behavior of others. In actual practice, behavioral technologies have never really escaped their early experimental history with lab rats and pigeons. In its earliest stages, behaviorism embraced an extraordinarily narrow range of science, which further hindered developing an ideology that could include much of what we consider human—feelings and emotions, the nonverbal and the intuitive, and the irrational. The early proponents of behavior modification had experimental rather than clinical training and actively dismissed emotions.

It cannot be possible that behaviorally oriented psychologists have all had so little personal and potentially informing history of hurt, abuse, diminished self-esteem, or self-harm. They cannot all have completely hidden such hurt "behind the idealized picture of a happy childhood" or failed to encounter it in their own, nonprofessional lives. What emerges is a portrait of a profession that has divorced its collective, public identity from the individual truths of its practitioners.

Where hurt has been, there is fear; fear and love cannot live in the same house; and where there is no love, there must be control. This powerful syllogism can help us understand the lives of people with disabilities and our own, as well. If we are to be of help to others, we need to understand our own lives.

Many people working in direct services have histories of hurt and neglect themselves as the children of alcoholics; as survivors of physical, emotional, or sexual abuse; or as people whose early lives left them with more confusion and pain than hope. Many people grew up in homes that denied closeness or failed to embrace it, denied equality, or denied the very basics of respect. All of these hurts are, ultimately, the triumph of a power that abuses over love that nurtures and sustains.

Real behavior change comes from a relationship; the more serious the need for change, the more serious this relationship needs to be. This need leads us from the realm of technology with its powers of predictability and orderliness into the uncertain and shifting territory of philosophers and poets. What does it mean to be honest? What does it mean to be present for another person and for ourselves? What are the balances, at any moment in a relationship, between acceptance and challenge, between listening and being heard? How do we invite others to accept our caring and concern and how do we all grow to feel we are part of one another in this world? These uncertainties and failures have often led to difficult behavior in the first place. How do we grow beyond it?

Chapter 6

Choices
—————and Challenges————

The Practical Struggles of Positive Approaches

People who are difficult to serve can show us where our efforts are not as good as our intentions. Historically, we have used the term "difficult behavior" to characterize the person, but often who is seen as difficult reveals the nature of the service. For example, when it first became clear that institutions were obsolete, the common concern was for the client with severe to profound disabilities. It turned out that personal care and assistance could just as easily be provided for people in their homes as in institutions. But as our services have shifted from institutional and hierarchical thinking, the people now labeled difficult are often at the other end of the labeling spectrum. They are people who are quite capable of making independent choices about their lives. The challenge they present is that their choices do not conform with agency values, and they themselves do not submit easily to professional guidance.

The idea that choice is a critical expression of power for people who use services sounds simple and just. The implications for taking this idea seriously, though, are radical. The

idea that we include the people we serve as equal and partici-
pating partners opens an unfamiliar world where clinical
judgment is just one guide among many.

The real issue is not so much choice as power. Most ordinary people are not "allowed" choices; they just make them.
Everyone can agree that people have a right to choose where
they live and with whom—until those choices conflict with
other positive values. Difficult ethical dilemmas often arise
when good ideas compete.

———

As is often the case with people with severe reputations,
Angela was not really the person I expected to meet. For a
woman with so much turmoil and violence attached to her
name, she herself was remarkably calm and pleasant. Angela
had grown up poor in a large city and had the habit of dis-
appearing for a few days at a time, returning with nothing
except the clothes she was wearing. Her explanations of her
absences were typically vague, but she often worked as a
prostitute and then gave the money away to the people she
had been living with on the street. She had a steady
boyfriend who was known to abuse alcohol, drugs, and
Angela.

At one point, the agency supporting Angela had staffed
an apartment for her with 24-hour supervision. This had not
worked out very well. When Angela wanted to leave, members of staff would tell her she could not and when she was irritated by this restriction she would become emphatic by
breaking furniture and hurting people until she had sufficiently made her point. Seeing that this kind of external
management was provocative, frustrating, and dangerous for
everyone involved, Angela's agency helped her find an apartment that she decided to share with a friend. Soon after, her
roommate's boyfriend moved in, but he and Angela didn't
get along. Her solution to this was simply to leave the apartment to them with all her belongings. For a while she lived in
an abandoned building that had neither electricity nor heat.

When the agency furnished a new apartment, almost
everything disappeared. Sometimes people took Angela's
furniture to sell on the street. (She had a habit of giving keys

to her apartment to anyone she thought would need a place to stay.) Sometimes she just gave whatever she had away to anyone who asked for it. If she herself needed something, she would steal, sell herself, or go to soup kitchens. Once she went to the emergency room of a local hospital and persuaded them she was psychotic in order to get a few days of shelter.

Because all the usual ways of providing help had failed, the agency asked Shirley (a friendly staff person Angela had met along the way) if Angela could live with her. Perhaps, they hoped, the two might enjoy being housemates. In doing this, though, Angela forced Shirley and the rest of the service team to face a difficult dilemma. Shirley was confused: What is our relationship? Am I Angela's mother? An older sister? Is she someone who boards in my home?

Staff members recognized they could not control Angela even if they wanted. However, if they subsidized her living dangerously and she were to contract AIDS or get killed on the street, were they responsible? Their concern was not so much about legal complications as to discern what their responsibilities were both as ethical human beings and as responsible service providers. People liked Angela as a person, and they struggled in the same ways many families struggle when one member acts dangerously. At what point does being loving and helpful become enabling for people to hurt themselves?

All of the options apparently open to them were unpleasant. They could work to get Angela arrested for prostitution or for drug-related offenses and then see her either imprisoned or court-ordered to a "secure program." This kind of "tough love" seemed more tough than loving. Given the places where she would be likely to end up, people worried that she would be just another difficult client, likely to be discharged as untreatable or noncompliant. However, if they supported her unconditionally, they felt that they would be contributing to her hurting herself, perhaps fatally. Setting limits on her behavior by threatening the loss of her funding would almost certainly result in her living on the streets. This group was clear about their intentions: First and foremost they wanted to respect Angela's choices and respect her autonomy as an adult. They were confused about what that meant in terms of practical action.

I first met Angela in the agency's conference room where her service coordinator had organized an interdisciplinary team meeting. The service coordinator began by explaining the meeting was for Angela. This was only approximately true. The meeting was really for me to get a sense of who she was so I could make some recommendations. When people asked her what she wanted from them, Angela said she wanted to manage her own money, have her own apartment, and go to school. These bland ambitions seemed at odds with Angela's apparent need for drama and excitement. I was later told that Angela generally repeated what she thought people wanted to hear and that they were frustrated in trying to learn from her what she really did want. (Actually, I think her behavior made it clear what she wanted; their difficulty was in getting her to want a less dangerous life.)

Service systems—large and small—almost invariably imitate the people they attempt to serve. People who are dangerously aggressive tend to attract services that act out violently. Similarly, if a person hurts himself by banging his head and causing serious injury, the team members often act as if they were the ones insensitive to pain. With no irony whatever, they may decide that the first thing they have to do is establish a baseline, which collectively and neatly matches the individual's apparent lack of response to pain. A group of ordinary people would be far more likely to decide that the first thing we need to do is to protect the person's head from injury.

So, like Angela herself, the team was saying what they thought they should say: It is dangerous to have unsafe sex; it is dangerous to spend your life the way Angela was spending hers. Angela's behavior made clear what she wanted, but they could not accept her choices. At the same time, their behavior clearly indicated what they wanted, and she could not accept that. Neither party in this struggle was speaking *about* or *to* their own realities. This situation reminded me of the inane slogan in the campaign against drugs—Just say no—as if people took drugs because they were otherwise at a loss for words. The intent of the solution was clear, but it had no connection with Angela's reality of what her problem was.

Several factors combined to make serving Angela difficult for this group. Most obviously, their usual practices were irrelevant to her. This community service was, as is so often the case, in the community rather than of it. Typically, this group developed behavior programs as a way of managing people's behavior. Fortunately, they recognized that Angela was unlikely to respond to their usual overtures of rewards and punishments. Other reasons this group was at a loss with her were so obvious as to be invisible. Everyone on Angela's team (except Angela and Shirley) was white. All of us had graduate degrees of some kind, but Angela was still learning to read, and Shirley was working on an associate's degree. Most of the power over Angela's life was held by men. The obvious elements of class, gender, education, and race—all the fault lines along which United States society cracks when our common social ground quakes—potentially divided us. I say potentially because these differences divide us artificially. We can choose not to give our prejudices such power.

I suspect that when most of us look for help with a major personal problem we choose someone who loves us, whom we respect and love, *and* whom we think might have had enough similar experience to speak from first-hand knowledge rather than from a sense of what they were supposed to say. I think we need all these ingredients to feel comfortable with someone's advice. In this sense, we had two more barriers between us and our helping Angela. First, none of us was someone Angela would ordinarily call up to say, "I need to talk." Second—and this is important in another way—none of us had the kind of relationship that would have allowed us to discuss freely what, if any, experience we ourselves had personally with Angela's "problem behavior."

This lack of a relationship real enough to invite and sustain change was part of our dilemma. For example, Angela's behavior could be considered self-injurious in a way that has been associated with child abuse and neglect. The usual hopes for therapy, self-help, or a combination of these would seem unreal to her without a context in which she could trust that someone cared for her in a way she could not yet care for herself.

Difficulties such as these strike me as opportunities to think not just about Angela but also about why serving her should be such a conundrum. I am surprised at how many opportunities I have to rediscover that handicap is mutual: If Angela has not found a way to live safely and with some self-respect in our society, our society has yet to completely support those values as well.

Interestingly enough, this kind of bafflement provokes an impulse to decide what the "rules" should be. Angela evoked different rules that expressed different values. The people who felt her independence and freedom of choice should be preserved as a part of individual liberties found themselves at odds with those who held that preservation of life is a duty of society and that she should not be allowed to take serious risks with her health.

Two problems of content and process present themselves in this situation. The first is the temptation to decide which system's response contains the "better" value system. People who need help in making choices have long been seen as pitiful and menacing. The first view invites charity and the second quarantine and control, and both create social roles for people who know better. Unfortunately, this is often seen as a forced choice so that people tend to fall into one or the other way of thinking. In fact, neither view necessarily applies so much to people with disabilities as it does to our way of thinking about any group that is "not us." These views are less about people with disabilities than they are about the people who see them as different. Taking seriously people's rights and powers to make individual choices radically challenges our tradition of those who know better making choices for those who have yet to learn. A struggle results when we look for new ways to collaborate rather than for new rules that allow us to govern benignly.

This means listening to voices that have not always been listened to attentively, learning to include those who have been traditionally excluded, and opening the ways we think about things rather than refining the existing hierarchies.

For example, having been trained almost exclusively to think in ways that are traditionally male, I have found women's strategies for solving moral dilemmas to be an exciting expansion. In just a few words, Belensky, Clinchy, Goldberger, and Tarule (1986) gave me a great deal to think about:

> When we asked these women what they "should" do in a moment of moral choice, they usually told us that it depended on the situation. Asked Kohlberg's classic hypothetical moral dilemma—"Should Heinz steal medicine from a druggist who is charging an outrageous price, in order to save his wife's life?"—they tended to respond with further questions: "What does Heinz wish?" "What is the condition of Mrs. Heinz's life?" "Why is the druggist behaving so?" "Does Heinz have children dependent on him for care?" "Who would care for the children if Heinz went to jail?" In contrast, the mature men whom Kohlberg describes invoke a general principle: The right to life must take precedence over the right to property. (1986, p. 149)

Looking for new ways to collaborate also requires that we listen to other voices not always listened to. One way to understand Angela's story is that she felt so little connection with the culture of the agency that she expected people to lie to her. Until she met someone with whom she could connect, she was mistrusting. This might be seen as a problem from the agency's point of view, but on the street this is simply an essential life skill. Where, then, would she get some advice and guidance in a way and from people she could trust? One idea was to connect her with other African American women in a local church, and perhaps she would come to see them as reliable friends. Through a string of someone-who-knew-someone, Angela started to spend time with people in this church. The point of this, of course, was not to deputize the churchgoers into becoming Angela's monitors so much as to give her ways to spend time with people whose behavior was more ordinary. At about this time, she became pregnant and decided to have the baby. The agency struggled with the ethics of what they should and should not do to help.

Real-life stories do not end, they just get interrupted. Angela had her baby but then decided after a while to give her up for adoption. She decided to cast her lot with her boyfriend, and she independently left the agency declining all its services. This was not a hostile move on anyone's part but a recognition that Angela and her support team had too little in common to continue. Depending on the way you look at it, Angela's life, given what she has to work with, is either a tragedy and an indictment of the agency or it is a slice of real life and to the agency's credit that it was able to help Angela—and stop helping her—mostly on her terms.

The issues of choice and power have been something of a rhetorical touchstone for many of us working for people with disabilities. We hardly question the justice of making sure service users have choice and power in their lives, nor, really, should we. But somehow choice is seen as an end, that having said service users should have choice, saying makes it so; or that when service users have greater self-determination in their services, the service system will be made whole. Recognizing these needs will rectify the wrongs our services have, almost always unintentionally, perpetuated, but greater self-determination will only bring us new moral dilemmas and these dilemmas will require of us new ways of thinking. We are still learning how institutional, paternalistic, and hierarchical traditions do not transplant in genuine community services. And just as we can steal a person's individuality with a label, so too can we steal the uniqueness of these ethical conflicts with rigid rules and policies more often designed for reacting to a hypothetical problem than for responding to a real person.

It is in listening to people with difficult behavior that positive approaches contrast most clearly with current traditions of service. In the world of positive approaches, we work in collaboration and in a spirit of openness, honesty, and equality. We make decisions by listening to all the people involved (not just the person, the family, or the professionals, but all of them); in the context of the personalities, needs, preferences, and strengths of those involved, we come to some decision. This contrasts with how many services are organized. We may say we are working for the good of people with disabilities, but what that is and how it is to be achieved is decided for them. In many services, we respond to whoever can force us to respond. Too often we make compromises that come from resignation rather than from negotiation. Many decisions are made because of policy rather than because they make sense to the people involved.

In some ways the sharpest contrast can be seen between nonaversive behavioral strategies and positive approaches. Nonaversive strategies are behavioral controls with a pleasant face—the theory behind them leaps from the abstract to the particular, from the textbook to the person. Positive approaches are about behavior changes through personal growth and mutual responsiveness. This work starts with each person and each group, and as experiences widen and deepen some principles emerge, but they emerge from the lives of the people involved, and are not imported mechanically. Nonaversive technologies are about control and behavior change; positive approaches are about cooperation and personal growth.

Positive approaches are about ways to think generally about people who have been difficult to serve, and it would be easy to get overly distracted in the contemplation of what they truly are or truly aren't. What they truly are intended to be is a way of keeping people present as individuals in our minds and hearts.

Agnes, Ann, Betty, Carol, Carolyn, David Lewis, Frank, Gordon, Helen, James, Jeanette, Jerry, Mary, Maureen, Michael, Michelle, Norma, Paul, Rita, Robert, Sandra, Steve, Steven, and Wendy—this book has been in large measure about you. Thank you. Please accept this as an homage to and meditation on what you have helped me to learn from listening to you.

References

Literature Cited

Abberley, P. (1992). The concept of oppression and the development of a social theory of disability. In T. Booth & W. Swann(Eds.), *Learning for all (2): Policies for diversity in education* (pp. 231–246). London: The Open University.

Allodi, F., & Cowgill, G. (1982). Ethical and psychiatric aspects of torture: A Canadian study. *Canadian Journal of Psychiatry, 27*, 98–102.

Armstrong, D. (1992, January 21). Abused by the system: A special report. *Boston Herald,* pp. 1, 18–19.

Aversive therapy. (1991, October). *Lancet, 338,* 919–920.

Barker, R.G. (1948). The social psychology of physical disability. *Journal of Social Issues, 4*(4), 28–42.

Bass, E., & Davis, L. (1988). *The courage to heal: A guide for women survivors of child sexual abuse.* New York: Harper & Row.

Belensky, M.F., Clinchy, B.M., Goldberger, N.R., & Tarule, J.M. (1986). *Women's ways of knowing: The development of self, voice, and mind.* New York: Basic Books.

Berger, P.L., Berger, B., & Kellner, H. (1973). *The homeless mind.* New York: Random House.

Bergman, I. (1988). *The magic lantern.* New York: Viking.

Blatt, B. (1970). *Escape from pandemonium.* Needham, MA: Allyn & Bacon.

Block, S., & Reddaway, P. (1977). *Psychiatric terror: How Soviet psychiatry is used to suppress dissent.* New York: Basic Books.

Blume, E.S. (1986). The walking wounded: Post-incest syndrome. *SIECUS (Sex Information and Education Council of the United States) Report, 25*(1), 5–7.

Briere, J. (1988). The long-term clinical correlates of childhood sexual victimization. Human sexual aggression: Current perspectives. *Annals of the New York Academy of Science, 528,* 327–338.

Buss, A.R. (1975). The emerging field of the sociology of physical knowledge. *American Psychologist, 30,* 988–1002.

Butler, D., & Geis, F. (1990). Nonverbal affect responses to male and female leaders: Implications for leadership evaluations. *Journal of Personality and Social Psychology, 58*(1), 48–59.

Campling, J. (Ed.). (1982). *Images of ourselves.* London: Routledge & Kegan Paul.

Carr, E.G. (1977). The motivation of self-injurious behavior: A review of some hypotheses. *Psychological Bulletin, 84,* 800–816.

Confederation of Indian Organizations. (1986). *Double bind—to be disabled and Asian.* London: Author.

Critchley, M. (1986, April 24). Unkind cuts. *The New York Review of Books, 33*(7), 7–12.

Dartington, T., Miller, E., & Gwynne, G. (1981). *A life together.* London: Tavistock.

DeAngelis, T. (1993, August). Trivializing disabilities gives immunity to fear. *American Psychological Association Monitor, 24,* 47.

Dunne, T., & Power, A. (1990). Sexual abuse and mental handicap: Preliminary findings of a community-based study. *Mental Handicap Research, 3*(3), 111–125.

Duran, E. (1984). Teaching nonsheltered vocational skills to autistic adolescents and young adults. *Psychology, A Quarterly Journal of Human Behavior, 21*(3–4), 49–54.

Dybwad, G. (1985, March). *Alternatives in the '80s: Community versus institutional living.* Speech presented at the 11th Annual Legislative Breakfast of the Greater Lynn Mental Health and Retardation Association, MA.

Edelson, S.M., Taubman, M.T., & Lovaas, O.I. (1983). Some social contexts of self-destructive behavior. *Journal of Abnormal Child Psychology, 11,* 299–312.

Ellul, J. (1964). *The technological society.* New York: Random House.

Elton, D., Stanley, G., & Burrows, G. (1983). *Psychological control of pain.* Sydney, Australia: Grune & Stratton.

Favazza, A. (1989). Why patients mutilate themselves. *Hospital and Community Psychiatry, 4*(2), 136–147.

Favazza, A., & Conterio, K. (1988). The plight of chronic self-mutilators. *Community Mental Health Journal, 24*(1), 22–30.

Favell, J., Azrin, N., Baumeister, A., Carr, E., Dorsey, M., Forehand, R., Foxx, R., Lovaas, I., Rincover, A., Romanczyk, R., Russo, D., Schoeder, S., & Solnik. (1982). The treatment of self-injurious behavior. *Journal of Behavior Therapy, 13,* 529–554.

Fee, E. (1979). Nineteenth-century craniology: The study of the female skull. *Bulletin of the History of Medicine, 53*(3), 430–431.

Feyerabend, P. (1975). *Against method.* London: NLB.

Finkelhor, D., Williams, L., & Burns, N. (1988). *Nursery crimes: Sexual abuse in daycare.* Beverly Hills: Sage Publications.

Foucalt, M. (1979). *Discipline and punish: The birth of the prison* (A. Sheridan, Trans.). New York: Vintage Books.

Foxx, R., & Azrin, N. (1972). Restitution: A method of eliminating aggressive-disruptive behavior of retarded and brain-damaged patients. *Behavior and Research Therapy, 10,* 15–27.

Frances, A. (1987). The borderline self-mutilator: Introduction. *Journal of Personality Disorders, 1,* 316.

Fromm, E. (1965). *Escape from freedom.* New York: Avon Books.

Gehlen, A. (1980). *Man in the age of technology.* New York: Columbia University Press.

Gold, E. (1986). Long-term effects of sexual victimization in childhood: An attributional approach. *Journal of Consulting and Clinical Psychology, 54*(4), 471–475.

Gostin, L. (1980, November/December). Institutions observed. *Mind Out,* 69–70.

Hamad, C.D., Isley, E., & Lowry, M. (1983). The use of mechanical restraint and response incompatibility to modify self-injurious behavior: A case study. *Mental Retardation, 21*(5), 213–217.

Handel, A.F. (1960). Community attitudes and adjustment to disability. *Outlook for the Blind, 54,* 363.

Harris, S.L., Handleman, J.S., Gill, M.J., & Fong, P.L. (1991). Does punishment hurt: The impact of aversives on the clinician. *Research in Developmental Disabilities, 12*(1), 17–24.

Hayek, F.A. (1952). *The counter-revolution of science.* Glencoe, IL: Free Press.

Howell, R.W., & Vetter, H.J. (1976). *Language in behavior.* New York: Human Services Press.

Illich, I., Zola, I.K., McKnight, J., Caplan, J., & Shaiken, H. (1977). Disabling professions. In D. Smail (Ed.), *Illusion and reality: The meaning of anxiety* (pp. 105–106). London: J.M. Dent & Sons.

Jay, R. (1986). *Learned pigs and fireproof women.* New York: Warner Books.

Johnson, D.L. (1989). Schizophrenia as a brain disease: Implications for psychologists and families. *American Psychologist, 44,* 553–555.

Johnson, W., & Baumeister, A. (1978). Self-injurious behavior: A review and analysis of methodological details of published studies. *Behavior Modification, 2*, 465–487.

Jones, D. (1991). Ritualism and child sexual abuse. *Child Abuse and Neglect, 15*(3), 163–170.

Kedesdy, J. (1988). Self-injurious behavior, its treatment, and normalization. *Mental Retardation, 26*(4), 223–229.

Kelly, S.J. (1988). Ritualistic abuse of children: Dynamics and impact. *Cultic Studies Journal, 5*, 228–236.

Kipnis, D. (1984a). Technology as a strategy of control. In S.B. Bachrach & E.J. Lawler (Eds.), *Sociology of organizations* (pp. 125–126). San Francisco: Jossey-Bass.

Kipnis, D. (1984b). The use of power in organizations and in interpersonal settings. In S. Oskamp (Ed.), *Applied social psychology annual 5* (pp. 179–210). Beverly Hills: Sage Publications.

Kipnis, D. (1987). Psychology and behavioral technology. *American Psychologist, 42*(1), 30–36.

Kuhn, T.S. (1970a). Reflections on my critics. In I. Lakatos & A. Musgrove (Eds.), *Criticism and the growth of knowledge* (pp. 231–278). Cambridge, England: Cambridge University Press.

Kuhn, T.S. (1970b). *The structure of scientific revolutions* (2nd ed.). Chicago: University of Chicago Press.

Lichstein, K., & Schreibman, L. (1976). Employing electric shock with autistic children. *Journal of Autism and Childhood Schizophrenia, 6*(2), 163–173.

Lifton, R.J. (1986). *The Nazi doctors: Medical killing and the psychology of genocide.* New York: Basic Books.

Lindsley, H. (1989). Multiple personality disorder in persons with developmental disabilities. *Psychiatric Aspects of Mental Retardation, 8*(10), 65–70.

London, P. (1964). *The modes and morals of psychotherapy.* New York: Holt, Rinehart, and Winston.

Lovaas, O.I., Schaeffer, B., & Simmons, J.Q. (1969). Manipulation of self-destruction in three retarded children. *Journal of Applied Behavior Analysis, 2*(3), 143–157.

Lovett, H. (1985). *Cognitive counseling and persons with special needs: Adapting behavioral approaches to the social context.* New York: Praeger.

Lowe, C.M. (1976). *Value orientations in counseling and psychotherapy: The meanings of mental health* (2nd ed.). Cranston, RI: Carroll Press.

Mails, T.E., & Crow, F. (1991). *Fools Crow: Wisdom and power.* Tulsa, OK: Council Oak Books.

Mason, M. (1992a). The integration alliance: Background and manifesto. In T. Booth & W. Swann (Eds.), *Learning for all (2): Policies for diversity in education.* London: The Open University.

Mason, M. (1992b, May 2). Remarks delivered at the 2nd Annual Bolton Institute for Integrated Education and Community, Manchester, England.

Mill, J.S. (1859). *On liberty.* London: Penguin Press.

Miller, A. (1981). *The drama of the gifted child.* New York: Basic Books.

Miller, A. (1983). *For your own good: Hidden cruelty in child-rearing and the roots of violence.* New York: Farrar, Straus, & Giroux, Inc.

Miller, T., & Veltkamp, L. (1989). The adult nonsurvivor of child abuse. *Journal of the Kentucky Medical Association, 87*(3), 120–124.

O'Brien, J. (1991). Against pain as a tool in professional work on people with severe disabilities. *Disability, Handicap, and Society, 6*(2), 81–90.

O'Brien, J., & Lovett, H. (1993). *Finding a way toward everyday lives: The contribution of person-centered planning.* Harrisburg: Pennsylvania Department of Public Welfare.

Orwell, G. (1950). Politics and the English language. In G. Orwell (Ed.), *Shooting an elephant and other essays* (pp. 84–101). London: Secker and Warburg.

Pinchbeck. W.F. (1805). *The expositor; or many mysteries unraveled.* Boston.

Polanyi, M. (1966). *The tacit dimension.* Garden City, NJ: Doubleday.

Risley, T.R. (1968). The effects and side-effects of punishing the autistic behaviors of a deviant child. *Journal of Applied Behavior Analysis, 1,* 21–35.

Ross, D., & Ross, S. (1988). *Childhood pain: Current issues, research, and management.* Baltimore: Urban & Schwarzenberg.

Sacks, O. (1993). An anthropologist from Mars. *The New Yorker, 69*(4), 106–125.

Sampson, E.E. (1978). Scientific paradigms and social values: Wanted—a scientific revolution. *Journal of Personality and Social Psychology, 35,* 767–782.

Sampson, E.E. (1981). Cognitive psychology as ideology. *American Psychologist, 36,* 730–743.

Schaef, A.W. (1985). *Women's reality: An emerging female system in a white male society.* San Francisco: Harper & Row.

Schaef, A.W., & Fasell, D. (1988). *The addictive organization.* New York: Harper & Row.

Second revised draft policy statement for mental health system survivors. (n.d.). Seattle, WA: Rational Island Press.

Shapiro, J. (1993). *No pity: People with disabilities forging a new civil rights movement.* New York: Times Books.

Shils, E.A. (1981). *Tradition.* Chicago: University of Chicago Press.

Sjölund, S., & Eriksson, M. (1985). *Relief of pain by TENS (transcutaneous electrical nerve stimulation).* London: John Wiley & Sons.

Smail, D. (1984). *Illusion and reality: The meaning of anxiety.* London: J.M. Dent & Sons.

Snow, J. (1992). Giftedness. In J. Pearpoint, M. Forest, & J. Snow (Eds.), *The inclusion papers: Strategies to make inclusion work* (pp. 47–68). Toronto, Canada: Inclusion Press.

Staub, E. (1990). The psychology and culture of torture and torturers. In P. Suedfeld (Ed.), *Psychology and torture* (pp. 61–87). New York: Hemisphere Publishing.

Stokes, J. (1987, February). *Insights from psychotherapy.* Paper presented at the International Symposium on Mental Handicap, Royal Society of Medicine, Manchester, England.

Tate, B.G., & DeBuroff, G. (1966). Aversive control of self-injurious behavior in a psychiatric boy. *Behavior Research and Therapy, 4,* 281–287.

Tognoli, C., Hamad, C., & Carpenter, T. (1978). Staff attitudes toward adult male residents' behavior as a function of two settings in an institution for mentally retarded people. *Mental Retardation, 16*(2), 142–146.

Tomacek, O. (1990). A personal commentary on schizophrenia as a brain disease. *American Psychologist, 45*(4), 550–551.

Turnbull, H.R. (1989). *Testimony.* In Medical Discrimination Against Children with Disabilities. A Report of the U.S. Commission on Civil Rights, Washington, DC.

Valenstein, E. (1986). *Great and desperate cures: The rise and decline of psychosurgery and other radical treatment for mental illness.* New York: Basic Books.

Van der Klift, E., & Kunc, N. (1994). Beyond benevolence: Friendship and the politics of help. In J.S. Thousand, R.A. Villa, & A.I. Nevin (Eds.), *Creativity and collaborative learning: A practical guide to empowering students and teachers* (pp. 391–401). Baltimore: Paul H. Brookes Publishing Co.

Weiss, N. (1990). *The application of aversive procedures to individuals with developmental disabilities: A call to action.* Baltimore: Kennedy Institute.

Winner, L. (1977). *Autonomous technology: Technics out of control as a theme in political thought.* Cambridge, MA: MIT Press.

Woolfolk, R.L., & Richardson, F.C. (1984). Behavior therapy and the idea of modernity. *American Psychologist, 39*(7), 777–786.

Yates, J. (1990). *On-the-road updates.* Stoughton, MA: Author.

Young, W., Sachs, R., Braun, B., & Watkins, R. (1991). Patients reporting ritual abuse in childhood: A clinical syndrome report of 37 cases. *Child Abuse and Neglect, 15*(3), 181–189.

The
Expositor; or
——Many Mysteries Unraveled——

Delineated

In a Series of Letters, between a Friend and
his Correspondent.

Comprising
The Learned Pig—Invisible Lady and
Acoustic Temple,—Philosophical Swan,—Penetrating Spy
Glasses,
Optical and Magnetic
and
Various other Curiosities on similar Principles.

Also,

a few of the most wonderful Feats as performed
by the Art of Legerdemain:
with
Some Reflections on Ventriloquism.

William Frederick Pinchbeck
Boston: Boston Public Library
Printed for the Author,
1805.

To the Public

The intention of this work was not only to amuse and instruct, but also to convince superstition of her many ridiculous errors, to show the disadvantages arising to society from a vague as well as irrational belief of man's intimacy with familiar spirits, to oppose the idea of supernatural agency in any production of man, and lastly, how dangerous such a belief is to society, how destructive to improvement of the human capacity, and how totally ruinous to the common interests of mankind. To effect this design, as well as thoroughly and pleasingly to expose those once-thought mysteries this book contains, it has ever appeared to me no form was so adequate to the purpose as a series of letters.

As a writer, I pretend to no particular merits, nor can I clothe my sentiments in the luxuriant robes of distinguished fancy, but only in unvarnished narrative unfold dexterities (merely the effects of human ingenuity), which have so long astonished the world.

The feats of which these letters give an account are facts, and the definition of them implicitly correct; and on this the Author has founded the value of his book. Surely what is given by the inventor of some, and who has had ocular demonstration of the other feats, comprising the contents of these sheets, must admit of some certainty; and I positively affirm, that whatever I profess to define is done with honesty, and as accurately as practice has determined to be just. On this principle, the estimation and success of the work is submitted to the candor of a liberal and enlightened public,

By their humble servant,
The Author

As the public curiosity may be excited at the suppression of the dates and places whence my friend wrote his letters, as also the concealment of his name,—I would only say that these omissions were considered as unessential to the work.

Letter I
From A.B. to W.F.P.

Sir,

. . . Whenever I stop on my tour, I am sure to hear of the fame of your celebrated Pig. . . . An evening or two since, stopping at an inn, your Pig being the topic of conversation, I could not but listen to a grave old gentleman, who, putting on a very affected, sage-like look, declared his performances were the effects of the Black Art; that the Pig ought to be burnt and the Man banished, as he had no doubt you familiarly corresponded with the devil. O monstrous! Will time and experience never remove such credulity from the earth? Must ingenuity, the parent of manufactories, the progressive pillar to wisdom and the arts, whose summit supports a mirror where superstition may see her own gorgon image, be thus broken and overturned by the rude hands of ignorance and pride? We rejoice that we live in an enlightened part of the world, where liberty extends her choicest blessings, and where the Presiding Magistrate is a philosopher, and under his patronage men of talents dare be such, and these absurd opinions are but the dogmas of devotees and folly.

This grave old gentleman, had you and he, been residents in Spain, would have summoned you before the Inquisition. Your efforts in demonstrating to the world, that the most stupid and stubborn of all animals, by patience and perseverance, might be made the most learned and docile, would no doubt have cost you your life.

As I very well know your liberality in defining all such matters to me as may tend either to my instruction or amusement, a sketch of the method by which this animal could be taught to perform such wonders will very much edify and oblige.

Your sincere friend,

A.B.

Letter II
From W.F.P. to A.B.

Sir,

. . . You request information relative to the teaching of
animals. As I have ever considered it an incumbent duty to
withhold nothing from my friend, that may tend to his information, the resolving of your question becomes an additional
pleasure. Those who style themselves friends, should regard
nothing as an exclusive privilege, that might tend either to
the instruction or happiness of each other. But alas! How universally is the sacred appellation of FRIEND prostituted!
Amongst mankind they currently palm the term upon each
other. I have known those who style themselves friends, and
have been well experienced in the art of shaking hands,
whose souls never knew the social tie, or felt the soft effusions
of a benevolent heart; on the contrary, I should as soon expect to see an automaton shed tears from the violent emotion
of an adamantine heart, at the fatal destruction of his fellow
automaton, as to see such men, willingly, and from no motive
whatever but absolute humanity, part with a single five dollar
bill, to relieve the distresses of a man, whom just before they
style friend, and from whom perhaps they had received unbounded favors. However, leaving this digression, I hasten to
comply with your request. And, as it respects the Pig of
Knowledge, you shall be acquainted with the mystery which I
shall exhibit in Lessons.

Lesson 1

Take a Pig, seven or eight weeks old, let him have free
access to the interior part of your house, until he shall
become in some measure domesticated. When familiar,
you may enter upon his instruction. Take him to an
apartment for the purpose of teaching, sequestered
from any interruption, and three times a day instruct
him as follows: Put a card into his mouth, and hold it
shut, giving him to understand that he is not to drop it
until you please to take it from him. At first, he will
throw it from his mouth every moment, which you must
immediately pick up and replace it, reprimanding him

in a loud tone of voice. In a short time, he will understand when you are displeased, and consequently will hold the same patiently. You must give him a small piece of white bread, or a piece of an apple, etc.—whatever he is most fond of. Be very observing not to suffer any person to feed him but yourself. Swill is a food most natural and healthy you can give him. You need not starve the Pig, as has been represented by a number of persons; for that would make him so eager to obtain the morsel you give him by way of encouragement, that in his natural cravings for food, he would not be willing to hold the card a moment, neither must you violently beat him, as that would confound his instinct, and make him afraid to perform that, which otherwise he would do with ease, and without fear. Having learnt [sic] him to stand still, and hold the card, he is master of the first Lesson.

A gentleman has just called on me in great haste. In my next I will relate the second Lesson necessary for his instruction. And while I clap my hand to my heart, I feel no inconvenience in styling myself

Your sincere friend,
And very humble servant,
W.F.P.

Letter III
From A.B. to W.F.P.

Sir,

Soon as I read your friendly letter, I felt very zealous to become a school-master; and, anxious to convince my acquaintances of the faculty I possessed, I have undertaken to teach a Pig. Immediately upon receipt of your's, I purchased a nice little Shoat: I have taught him to hold a card, and believe he will prove a very apt scholar, though a very noisy one: He squeals and makes such a terrible outcry, that strangers passing by suppose I am severely chastising him, when all I did, was holding him, and insisting on his taking the card.

I am anxious for information how to proceed; and although the task be arduous, I flatter myself I shall be able to prove to the world that all the witchcraft necessary is a regular method of which you were the projector, supported by patience and perseverance.

I need not importune other necessary directions by return of post; for as the pupil must fail without the instruction of the preceptor, so must I without your assistance; who style myself, without blushing,

Your sincere friend,
A.B.

Letter IV
From W.F.P. to A.B.

Sir,

Upon perusal of your letter, forgive me, for I was obliged to smile at your late novel undertaking, and the earnest desire you seem to express for its success: I say, *smile*; but, my friend, not that smile of envy and contempt, which, while it expands the muscles of the face, contracts the heart with self-conceit and malice; such grimaces I abhor; they are the smiles of ignorance, and want almost invariably the capacity they ridicule.

But . . . I proceed to the second Lesson, relative to the instruction of your four-footed scholar.

Lesson 2

If you have taught him to hold the card, as described in my last, you may lay it on the floor, with one corner bent upwards; then forcing his head down to the card, put it in his mouth, and hold it up with the card, not suffering him to drop it; and so repeatedly. Do not forget to encourage him for his good performances; and when he will pick the card off the floor without your assistance, he is master of the second Lesson. I should have told you at this time to accustom him to your snuffing the nose, for purposes that will appear as he progresses in his learning.

Lesson 3

You must now lay down three cards. He will naturally try to take the one the most convenient for him; and your business is to check him, not snuffing your nose; and, taking it from him in an angry tone of voice, replace the same, and force him to take the one next to him, or the third, snuffing your nose. By persevering in this manner a few days, he will soon understand he must not take hold, until you give him the signal, which is breathing from your nose. When you have learnt him this, you may continue increasing the cards; and that animal, who in his rude state appears the most stupid, with the least share of tractability amongst all other quadrupeds, will be found sapient, docile, and gentle.

I am, with usual respect, and unfeigned sincerity of heart,

Your well-wisher,
And very humble servant,
W.F.P.

Letter V
From A.B. to W.F.P.

Sir,

Your's came safe to hand. Early the next morning I proceeded to give the second Lesson, which I found him very unwilling to perform; [testing the program] and I confess, that had not the information come from a man, in whose veracity I could confide, and whose patience and practice had been the means of perfecting fix, I should have given up the business, concluding this was not the method, and that there was another more practicable. From such suspicions the brightest geniuses fail in many of their most valuable undertakings; and thus from want of patience and perseverance fail of the termination of a design, whose accomplishment might insure themselves profit and respect, and prove a benefit to the community at large. However, I persevered; and it is with satisfaction I inform you, he will now pick and fetch either of the three cards I choose.

In concluding this Letter, I would not forget to mention to you I intend to increase the cards to fix. In the meanwhile, further information relative to his introduction will greatly oblige, and ever meet acknowledgment, from

Your sincere friend,
And humble servant,
A.B.

Letter VI
From W.F.P. to A.B.

Sir,

I think your scholar makes astonishing progress. I almost feel afraid of your working him too hard, and fatiguing yourself. At this period you ought not to exceed three Lessons in a day: You must remember the old adage, "All work and no play, makes Jack a dull boy." Should you, in your anxiety to make him become a proficient, give him too many Lessons a day, [importance of keeping goals simple] and by these means proceed faster than instinct has faculty to retain, he will become tired and confused; and, in endeavoring to learn the last Lesson, he may entirely or in part forget the first: Such a mistake would be no credit to the instructor. As he has made so good progress, I would not urge the business too rapidly. Do not enlarge the number of cards oftener than once a day; and let him be well acquainted with the object of your intention, before you take the step I am about to advise in the next Lesson.

Lesson 4

Spread twelve cards on the floor, in a circular direction, four inches apart; within this circle keep the Pig, and stand yourself. We will suppose you before an Assembly for the purpose of an exhibition; therefore you must give up sitting, as that posture would be very singular as well as impolite. The Pig observing you in this unusual position will be much embarrassed; and not knowing the meaning, will seek to amuse himself by running in every direction about the room. You are not to beat him into the knowledge of your design, but coax him to it, if possible. If this will not keep him by your side, tie a string about his neck, and when he would exceed the bounds of the circle, check him, using a soft or a loud tone of voice as occasion may require; for every brute has instinct to decide betwixt approbation and displeasure. At the length of the string, he will learn to walk the circle with his nose to the cards; and when he hears the signal before mentioned, will snatch at the card he shall then be opposite: Immediately step back, and he will follow with the same. Give him a small piece of bread as his reward, and by your approbation let him know he has done right; for one misunderstanding at this critical juncture will be a great source of unnecessary trouble. He will soon readily run for the cards, making many mistakes, which you must have the patience to endure and correct with good nature. If he takes the wrong card, replace it immediately, and show him the one you wanted. Much is to be done by raising and falling the tone of voice. In four or five days, you may venture to take the restraint from his neck; and whenever he exceeds his limits, put it on. By practicing in this manner, he will so perfectly understand his business.

In my next, I will give you a few more hints, which will no doubt complete your wishes, and your pupil will soon merit the title of the *Pig of Knowledge*.

I am, in reality,
what men call a friend,
W.F.P.

P.S. You must not expect him to understand this Lesson in less than a fortnight.

Letter VII
From A.B. to W.F.P.

Sir,

The fortnight has expired, and the Pig is completed. I have already exhibited him to a number of persons, men of ingenuity and talents, in whose judgment I can confide: They are astonished beyond description. None can account for the knowledge he apparently possesses, or discover the secret communication betwixt myself and the Pig. In fact, amongst the learned, I am thought a man of talents, whilst others less informed accuse me of the Black Art, and condemn me as a wizard. Shall I remonstrate with bigots? Shall I patiently sit down, and earnestly detail to them the cause? They would not believe me. No: I leave them to their enjoyment of their different reflections, and for my security and reward look to men of knowledge, whose approbation is more congenial to my feelings than the unbounded éclat of a barren multitude.

With every sentiment of respect
I am, &c. A.B.

Letter VIII
From W.F.P. to A.B.

Sir,

You inform me that your Pig is complete, and that his performances have astonished numbers. I confess I am astonished myself at his so early completion. And has no discovery taken place? Hath none detected the secret communication by which he is actuated? What will you conclude, when I inform you that even that communication is unnecessary? You may relinquish it by degrees; for the animal is so sagacious, that he will appear to read your thoughts: The position you stand in, not meaning any stipulated place, or certain gesture, but what will naturally arise from your anxiety, will determine the card to your pupil. I will only add, that I have been as much amazed at the performance of this animal, as the spectators before whom I exhibited him. Of all other quadrupeds, the Pig in my opinion is the most sapient, though writers on natural History say to the contrary, giving preference to the Elephant. Pope has bequeathed to this animal half the reason of man: How far he merits his eulogium, I am not able to determine; but of this I am convinced that the race of Swine claim a greater share of instinct than belongs to the Dog or the Horse.

I am, with the greatest respect,
Yours sincerely,
W.F.P.

Letter IX
From A.B. to W.F.P.

Sir,

After perusing your letter several times, and attentively considering its contents, I have with care and observation taken the steps you advised.

I find the Pig really the animal you describe him. I have entirely omitted the signal by which he was taught; and his penetrating nature, notwithstanding this omission, readily conceives my meaning. How am I to account for this miracle? What you have already expressed upon the subject I shall not attempt to elucidate, but perfectly acquiesce with you in the estimation of his abilities.

But the Pig no longer excites admiration. There is a certain Philosophic Machine lately arrived from France, which engrosses universal attention. The admittance to view this curiosity is fifty cents; and people throng in crowds to view it.

Yours,
A.B.

Appendix B

_____Handicap Consciousness_____

I think it is important to go back a little before speaking about what it means to be handicap conscious.

In my case, I have lived in institutions for 32 years of my life.

First, I went to a school home, Hallagården. I was sent to school there because I was so weak, so I was told. But this was not the whole truth, because at the time I was sent to this school home, children were sent there. People thought that was the best thing to do for the child in question.

Hallagården was a home for mentally handicapped children. When I went, they were divided into two groups. There were the mentally handicapped who could be educated and the mentally handicapped who were not capable of being educated.

It's frightening, thinking back to those times, that not everybody was allowed to go to school.

For my part, I had the honor of going to school, if it can be considered an honor to go to school in Hallagården.

When I was 18 I was sent to a work home, Rönneholme Castle, which is in Skåne.

Now Rönneholme was an open institution. Hallagården on the other hand was a closed institution.

This appendix is printed with permission of the author, Åke Johansson.

But living in an institution for so many years makes it very easy for a person to become passive. It is something you become without noticing it yourself. In the long run, a person can be very hurt by living in institutions. It can be very difficult to break away from the passive life one leads.

You have to work very hard with yourself to make a recovery. Which brings me to the question of handicap consciousness.

I've thought a great deal about why nobody told us who were living in the institutions, why we were there and why we should be there. Little by little I came to the conclusion that they didn't believe we could understand what it was all about.

In the first place, nobody said the words "mentally handicapped" or told us why we should go to the place we were going to.

As a mentally handicapped person, as I see things today, when I was at the institution, there were very bad attitudes towards us who were mentally handicapped.

I feel today that there was a wall between the staff and us who were living there.

Then I ask myself, why it was so difficult to talk about the words "mentally handicapped."

Now I want to say how important it is that one talks about the words "mentally handicapped" and what sort of handicap it is. To be able to get a handicap consciousness it is important that one finds out about it as early as it is possible to speak about mental handicap.

If I think back to the time when I was at the institution, I would have liked to find out that I was mentally handicapped. But this is what we did not find out, and that is the big mistake that was made, that nobody told us what was wrong. This played a large part in making our situation difficult.

Should I have been able to become aware of my handicap much earlier than I did? It is not right that one should have to go and wonder why one is in an institution, why one is there.

It's the same for those living at home with their parents. They too go around wondering why they are where they are. And if one doesn't get an explanation at an early age, well, one goes around imagining what is wrong, and then one gets a totally wrong picture of what the matter is. It also makes it difficult to respect oneself as a mentally handicapped person in the future.

I can understand it in one way. It is so that there is a fear in everybody which stops us speaking with the handicapped person. But it must not be like that. The important thing is that we try, all together, to speak about the words "mentally handicapped."

Now, I am aware that this is difficult. But we must do it to get a handicap consciousness—everybody in society.

To get a handicap consciousness, that means that one goes through a series of crises with oneself.

It may be a very difficult time which one has to go through because there are so many crises and it is the same for a person who is not handicapped.

The first step one takes is that one talks about the sort of person one is and the situation one is in. After a very long time one comes to the point when one learns to say, "I am mentally handicapped."

But it is very difficult to say "I am mentally handicapped." In the first place, there is so much feeling in these words. In the second place, I cannot do it until I have respect for myself, that I am a mentally handicapped person.

Now, one cannot talk about oneself all at once. I know from my own experience that it takes a very long time. And today, I usually say that it is good if it takes times, talking about oneself, I mean.

Because there is so much one must learn about oneself, because handicap consciousness means knowing that it is a question of myself.

Now this cannot be done all at once. It is something that one must work on for a long time. It is a crisis which one must struggle with. Because it must come from inside, and by that I mean that one has to search for the handicap one has. This is the crisis which can be very difficult for some people. Because it is now one asks oneself, "Am I mentally handicapped?"

What one needs now is the help of somebody who is mentally handicapped. I said a moment ago that one must struggle with oneself. Well, this is true to a certain degree.

It is so that one cannot become handicap conscious by oneself.

When I had come to this point in tackling my situation, it was very easy for me to over-emphasize my handicap.

Now, you shouldn't think that you who are not mentally handicapped, do not over-emphasize our handicap, because you do. You can over-emphasize it in such a way that you find it difficult to accept a mentally handicapped person.

When we have come this far in working with our situation, then it may be difficult to accept that one is mentally handicapped. It is then very easy for us to do things which are too difficult for us. We do this only to prove that we are not mentally handicapped. One undertakes things which one knows "I can't do this really, but I will do it anyway."

This has a lot to do with the difficulty I have in seeing my limitations. I want to be as good as possible, and then think it will be easier for me to get understanding and respect from those who are not mentally handicapped. But this is not so.

Another reason may be that I have not consciously respected myself as a mentally handicapped person. This then, is when I make these mistakes, only to get understanding. It is now that I need help. Now it is not possible to struggle alone with myself any longer. For me to get a handicap consciousness, there must be two of us.

What makes it so difficult to get a positive handicap consciousness?

Well, I suppose it has a lot to do with the fact that we still have many prejudices and also we don't have the right attitudes towards the handicap. There are some walls which prevent us from speaking about the words "mentally handicapped." It is the wall of *respect* which must be pulled down. I know that it is the wall which is most difficult to pull down. One wall which we must break through is the wall which prevents us from getting understanding.

Now I come to the difficult part. That is, to get a positive handicap consciousness. This is when the big crises hit us.

Because the handicap itself is a part of my own picture, it can be both painful and difficult to accept help if one doesn't know what one is capable of. Then being helped can feel insulting for a person.

I must be able to feel secure, be able to take an initiative, be independent, and have a sexual identity.

But the difficult part of being able to get a positive handicap consciousness comes when I have to learn that my picture of myself is a part of it.

If I have come through these crises, I can discover other mentally handicapped people and can feel solidarity with them. One gets strength to deal with the sorrow caused by the handicap. Knowledge of my handicap makes it possible for me to accept responsibility for myself. This is when I can say I have a Positive Handicap Consciousness.

But then we have something called Negative Handicap Consciousness. I want to tell you that it is difficult to be negative to the handicap one has. I know that there are many more people who are negative than there are positive people.

When a mentally handicapped person comes and asks, "Am I mentally handicapped?"—the fact that a person asks a question like that is because he has been going around thinking, "What am I and what am I not?"

Now it is very important that one doesn't just answer "Yes, you are mentally handicapped," but one must try to get to the bottom of his question. It is now that the best time has come to speak about the words "mental handicap."

I will go so far as to say that a person cannot answer this question if he or she does not have a positive handicap consciousness.

If a person is negative, they will do anything not to be mentally handicapped. One cannot feel any solidarity with others who are mentally handicapped either, because one wants to be better than one is all the time.

Moving away from a negative handicap consciousness towards a positive consciousness is very difficult. One needs a lot of help because it is very difficult.

Permissions

Permission to reprint the following extracts is gratefully acknowledged:

Chapter 2
The Politics of Labeling Behavior
Page 34: Schaef, A.W. (1985). *Women's reality: An emerging female system in a white male society.* San Francisco: Harper & Row; reprinted by permission.

Pages 35–36: Van der Klift, E., & Kunc, N. (1994). Beyond benevolence: Friendship and the politics of help. In J.S. Thousand, R.A. Villa, & A.I. Nevin (Eds.), *Creativity and collaborative learning: A practical guide to empowering students and teachers* (pp. 391–401). Baltimore: Paul H. Brookes Publishing Co.; reprinted by permission.

Pages 48–49: *Second revised draft policy statement for mental health system survivors.* (n.d.).(pp. 4–16). Seattle, WA: Rational Island Press; reprinted by permission.

Chapter 3
The Politics of Behaviorism
Pages 60, 67: Woolfolk, R.L., & Richardson, F.C. (1984). Behavior therapy and the idea of modernity. *American Psychologist, 39*(7), 777–786; reprinted by permission.

Pages 61, 62–63: Jay, R. (1986). *Learned pigs and fireproof women.* New York: Human Services Press; reprinted by permission.

Pages 64, 66–67: Kipnis, D. (1987). Psychology and behavioral technology. *American Psychologist, 42*(1), 30–36; reprinted by permission.

Chapter 4
The Hierarchy of Control
Pages 82–84: Foxx, R., & Azrin, N. (1972). Restitution: A method of eliminating aggressive-disruptive behavior of retarded and brain-damaged patients. *Behavior and Research Therapy, 10*, 15–27; reprinted by permission.

Pages 146–148: Hamad, C.D., Isley, E., & Lowry, M. (1983). The use of the mechanical restraint and response incompatibility to modify self-injurious behavior: A case study. *Mental Retardation, 21*(5), 213–217; reprinted by permission.

Pages 161, 169–171: Staub, E. (1990). The psychology and culture of torture and torturers. In P. Suedfeld (Ed.), *Psychology and torture* (pp. 61–87). New York: Hemisphere Publishing; reprinted by permission.

Pages 163–164: Smail, D. (1984). *Illusion and reality: The meaning of anxiety.* London: J.M. Dent & Sons; reprinted by permission.

Chapter 5

People Who Hurt Themselves

Pages 211–212: Bass, E., & Davis, L. (1988). *The courage to heal: A guide for women survivors of child sexual abuse.* New York: Harper & Row; reprinted by permission.

Page 223: Miller, A. (1981). *The drama of the gifted child.* New York: Basic Books; reprinted by permission.

Index

Disabilities, people with—*continued*
 as ineducable, 8
 labeling, 2–7
 language describing, 31–38
 as members of society, 9
 mutual relationships with
  professionals, 42–43
 naturalizing, 36–37
 negative effects of community services
  on, 29–30
 pity toward, 37
 prejudice toward, 11n
 protector-oppressors of, 10–11, 67,
  125
 rights of, 17
 segregation of, 8–9, 40–42
 self-identity of, 37–40
 sense of feeling needed by, 28
 sexuality of, 14–15
 social needs of, 25
 specialized instruction for, 10
 terminology describing physical
  disabilities, 33
 time-out for, 99
 as victims, 37
 vulnerability for physical and sexual
  assault, 205–206
 work for, 50–51, 64
 see also Developmental disabilities,
  people with; Difficult behavior,
  people with; Intellectual
  disabilities, people with; Mental
  retardation, people with
Disabled people, use of term, 32n
 see also Disabilities, people with
Disciplinary society, 69
Discipline-blockade, 68–69
Diversity, response to, 36n
"Dually diagnosed" people
 labeling as, 209
 medication for, 131

ECT, *see* electroconvulsive therapy
Edible reinforcers, 74–76
Education
 behaviorism versus, 62–63
 monitoring and control in, 78–79
Efficiency, as goal, 79–80
Electric shock, 165, 178
Electroconvulsive therapy (ECT), 179n
Electrotherapy, 178
Emergency (p.r.n.) medication, 141–144
Emotional intelligence, 209
Emotional problems, in people with
 mental retardation, 131–133
Environment, work, 64

Escort, 141
Ethics, of aversives, 166
Excellence
 in education, 78–79
 *Expositor, The: or Many Mysteries Unrav-
  eled* (Pinchbeck), 61, 241–251
 motivation to achieve, 79

Family visits, prohibiting, 210
Flashbacks
 following abuse, 208
 following aversive therapy, 208–209
Former Mental Patients' Liberation
  Front, 145
"Four point" restraint, 120–121
Freedom, as goal of liberation
  movements, 10–11
Freud, Sigmund, 57
Friendships
 as alternative to mechanical restraint,
  150
 mutual support as, 27–28
 see also Mutual relationships; Social
  relationships; Support

G. Allan Roeher Institute, 33
Gayness, awareness of, 34
 see also Homosexuals
Good behavior, rewards for, 73–74
Group homes
 arbitrariness of, 18–19
 as institutions, 123
Group identity, in institutions, 15

Hallucinations, auditory, psychotropic
  medications for, 132
"Handicap," as a label, 6–7
Handicap consciousness, 253–257
Handicappism, 7n
Handicaps, *see* disabilities
Handiphobia, 37
Hate crimes, 215n
Hoku points, 220
Homosexuals
 awareness of, 34
 labeling of, 38
 terminology describing lesbians, 33

Ignore and redirect, 88–96
 cultural reference for, 93–94
 lack of social context for, 92
 negative effects of, 88–91
 power struggles initiated by, 92

WITHDRAWN